DYNAMIC LEADER, ADAPTIVE ORGANIZATION

DYNAMIC LEADER, ADAPTIVE ORGANIZATION

TEN ESSENTIAL TRAITS FOR MANAGERS

LARRAINE SEGIL

John Wiley & Sons, Inc.

ISBN 0-471-02830-4

Printed in the United States of America.

10 9 8 7 6 5 4 3 2 1

To my husband Clive,
who supports me in all I do

CONTENTS

INTRODUCTION

The world changed on September 11, 2001. Leaders and aspiring leaders reevaluated the meaning of their own lives and the purposes of their organizations. Although outwardly not much may have changed for many people, inwardly every person has been touched in some way. For many, this has brought about a crisis of meaning—how, what, when—why am I living this way? Out of the panic and fear, some new leaders arose; and some anointed leaders failed to live up to expectations. But consistently, in every organization, group, or community, heroes from all walks of life showed strength of character, versatility, flexibility, determination, and focus of purpose.

It is a time for reflection and reevaluation. Multiple generations have been touched by this challenge: baby boomers, Generations X and Y, and those who have been through this before, the generation of the first part of the twentieth century.

If you are one who wants to identify the issues that need to be changed, not only in your own organization but in the lives of those around you, and if you are willing to make change happen, the message in this book provides the tools to bring about transformation.

The real challenge will be your own willingness to change along with your organization. If your answers to the following questions are *yes,* this book is essential to your success:

- Are you focused only on results, or also on the way to get them? That is, does your organization have a heart?
- Could your organizational environment do more to support people—with out-of-the-box thinking, community outreach, flexible work rules?
- Do your employees need to be more open to change? Does your organization support and adapt to change?
- Would it benefit your organization to be the preferred place to work in your industry? Are you creating employee loyalty?
- Can you better align managers with organizational goals? And are those goals valued?
- Could your organization be more competitive?

Today's manager needs to exhibit a special kind of leadership; he or she cannot avoid or deny the issues that are the most difficult. This special kind of leadership must exist not just in the person at the top of the organization, but at all levels of management.

In this book I use a metaphor to describe the issues that are often the most difficult and therefore sometimes either ignored or denied: *The elephants in the room* are those things that no one wants to talk about but that represent *the* issues needing to be addressed. The way issues are identified and the change process used to move them out and bring value instead comprises a delivery system that I call the *Larraine Segil Matrix* of characteristics—*The Ten Essential Traits.* By applying the matrix to yourself, to those around you, and to your organization, you will become a premier elephant spotter and change agent. Your organization will have the potential to be the place to which good people gravitate and where they want to stay.

The concept for this book has evolved over the past eight years. When I began researching and writing my first nonfiction book (*Intelligent Business Alliances,* Times Business, Random House, 1996), it became clear that the personalities of managers and corporate cultures are essential in creating and managing effective alliances. The completion of my second nonfiction book (*FastAlliances: Power Your*

E-Business, Wiley, 2001) convinced me that many organizations tend to ignore the real issues that prevent them from profitable change while grasping onto the next new thing (e.g., the Internet or some other initiative).

Over the past ten years, my work in helping clients to develop strong alliances has identified the trickle-down effect of these challenging relationships, from CEOs and senior management to middle and evolving managers to supplier and purchasing groups to all functions of the organization (including sales and marketing, engineering, research) to a variety of service organizations and functions. Alliance failure rates are high. One of the contributing factors is lack of executive sponsorship or buy-in. This has led me to the following conclusion:

Nothing will ruin a good alliance faster than lack of leadership, no matter at what level it manifests in the organization.

I began to examine what kind of special leadership could be applied to both simple and complex tasks and relationships. Recently, I participated in the prestigious annual PC Forum created and hosted by Esther Dyson (seer of what's hot and what's not in the technology world). Approximately 700 of the world's leaders in technology fields join together annually to share insights and predictions, make deals and friends, and stimulate thought and discussion. With so many leaders present, this was a good laboratory for my research. I heard lots of ideas and also offered a few. One concept, extrapolated from a presentation by Steve Hayden, president of Worldwide Brand Strategies, Ogilvy & Mather Worldwide, was particularly germane to the thesis in this book.

"The most critical moment of truth for an organization lies between two states of consciousness—intelligent arrogance and arrogant stupidity."

The moment of *intelligent arrogance* is when you realize that you are so clever and good at what you do that you and your organization are, quite simply, the best. It is shortly after this moment that the elephant (i.e., the issue holding you back from the next step) quietly enters the room. The elephant stays around, gradually moving to the center of the room as the organization moves toward the point of *arrogant stupidity.* Even if your competition has eaten you for lunch, you are still prancing around as if you were king, ignoring your biggest issues.

Here is a conversation you might hear in a company as it transitions from intelligent arrogance to arrogant stupidity:

Intelligent Arrogance

"We are the best, we are cool, we can do it. Let's apply our brilliance to always being number one." *(Elephant enters on the sidelines.)*

"We may not have done that task brilliantly, so we lost a customer—but they were impossible to deal with. It's their loss. Don't sweat it. Focus on how great we are." *(Elephant moves center stage.)*

"Are we the best, or what? Look, the industry/economy/security problems are making for tough times. Good thing we are still the best. *(Elephant gains weight.)*

Arrogant Stupidity

"After all, we are a worldwide brand. Our way is *the* way—we created the industry, for heavens sakes!" *(The elephant now has a sign around its neck that says* ARROGANT STUPIDITY. *It digs in—the elephant is planning a* long *stay.)*

(In walk the The Ten Essential Traits.) "Time to move on," *they tell the elephant (which no one else can see).* "Move!"

The organization moves toward intelligence again, and the cycle begins anew—unless The Ten Essential Traits managers take up residence where the elephant once was and make the organization an elephant-free zone.

My research about this large migration of seemingly invisible elephants into the center stage of organizations in multiple industries began by interviewing executives in companies as varied as consumer products to missile manufacture and in countries from Singapore to Stuttgart. My task was to have them identify the organizational issues that bothered them but were not often discussed or dealt with. This led to discussions about what kinds of employees would be able to break through to make change happen in their organizations. Their responses provided many of the qualities that form the basis of the matrix in this book. The executives were participants in the seminars that I present on Alliances (Appendix C), which are held in conjunction with the following:

- Frost and Sullivan in Europe, including companies such as British Telecom, Royal Mail, Alcatel, Ericsson, and Uunet

- The Lared Group and Larraine Segil Productions in Los Angeles

- The California Institute of Technology in Pasadena

- The Institute of Management Studies (Europe, the United States, and Canada)

- Marcus Evans in Europe and the United States

- POD Ltd. in Singapore, including companies from Asian countries (Japan, China, Taiwan, Indonesia, Myanmar, Malaysia, Korea) such as DBS Bank, Singapore Civil Defense Force, DuPont Singapore.

- José Macaya in Buenos Aires, Argentina, and Santiago, Chile, and companies such as Exccel Conglomerate and Lan Chile Airlines

- Boards and advisory groups on which I serve—the Los Angeles Regional Technology Alliance (LARTA), consisting of over 5,000 small technology companies in Southern California; The Price Center for Entrepreneurship at the UCLA Anderson School of Management

Over a five-year period, from 1996 to 2001, I met with hundreds of these companies' executives, selecting randomly from all the regions mentioned, gathering data and anecdotal information.

From this initial research I expanded the interview process greatly. Beginning in 1997, I personally interviewed a variety of leaders, many of them as guests on my live satellite television program, *Larraine Segil, One on One* (Primedia Corporate University Network), and others through my consulting and speaking work with organizations worldwide.

This group included CEOs, company presidents, and senior managers, including the following:

- George Fisher, then chairman and CEO of Eastman Kodak

- Phil Carroll, then CEO of Shell Oil Company, and the company's CEO who followed him, Jack Little

- Lars Nyberg, CEO of NCR Corporation

- Dennis Gertmenian, CEO of Ready Pac Produce
- Fred Lukas, chairman and then CEO of Trident Data Systems
- The Right Honourable Kim Campbell, former prime minister of Canada
- Cathleen Black, president of Hearst Publications
- Valerie Salembier, publisher of *Esquire* magazine
- David Dickson, group vice president of Hormel Foods
- James Ramo when he was a senior executive at DirecTV
- Ron Johnson, former general manager of Target stores (a division of Dayton Hudson)
- Brian Farrell, CEO of THQ, the lead company in the electronic gaming industry
- CEOs of multiple emerging Internet companies

I was fortunate to interview other executives in many of those organizations: senior managers (CFOs and executive vice presidents), division presidents, and, in the case of Shell, a number of the presidents of its global companies (e.g., Shell Services and Shell Chemical). I also had the privilege of speaking to middle managers and individual contributors, and over the past 17 years I have given hundreds of presentations to hundreds of thousands of people. This book is reflective of that experience.

Through my interactive satellite television programs on Alliances and Global Management through Primedia, as well as through my speeches and programs worldwide, I had ongoing communication with middle-level and fast-track executives who participated in my live programs and shared what it means to be at the inner core of organizations such as the following:

Bell Helicopter

Dial

Glaxo Wellcome

Hughes

Lucent

MCI

Medtronics

Motorola

Niagara Power

Perkin Elmer

Texas Instruments

As a partner in and consultant for Strategic Alliances and Global Management in The Lared Group and as CEO of Larraine Segil Productions in Los Angeles, I have served, among many others, the following clients:

ASM Lithography

Compaq

Lockheed Grumman

McDonald's Corporation

Northern Telecom

Nynex

Oracle Corporation

The People's Republic of China, Science and Technology Commission

Pioneer Hybrid International

Praxair (formerly Union Carbide)

The Ritz Carlton Hotel Company

Rockwell

Sematech

TSI Connections

Finally, starting in 2000 and through the end of 2001, 150 companies answered a 55-question survey (reproduced in Appendix A). The results of that survey make it clear that this information can add great value to the business community, which is the reason for this book: to reach a broader audience than my present speaking and consulting activities will allow.

What You Will Learn from This Book

Ten key characteristics comprise the Larraine Segil Matrix (LSM), and they must have the proper organizational environment in which to excel. As this book explains, ten characteristics that are both personal and organizational, accompanied by the proper implementation strategy illustrated herein, will enable you to do the following:

- Understand and analyze your organizational environment
- Evaluate yourself
- Apply a gap analysis to yourself and your direct reports and use the framework as a development tool
- Diagnose the degree of fit between yourself and the organizational environment
- Swiftly execute the strategies that create the desired results
- Identify your elephants and eliminate them

While no one person or organization will excel in developing each and every characteristic, the combination/networking of all these traits in strong doses positions an organization to succeed.

The subtitle of this book specifically says "Ten Essential Traits for Managers." I have deliberately not distinguished between leaders and managers. It is true that some employees may profess little interest in improving their capabilities to become leaders and would rather remain simply managers. However, the distinction is a paradigm of the Industrial Age. It is less relevant today. Knowledge workers have to self-motivate, self-manage, and integrate their activities into teamwork and organizational processes. This requires showing a level of self-leadership. The Ten Essential Traits are desirable for good employees regardless of their position in the organization. Improving these traits will lead to promotion, recognition, and reward. Choosing to lead will become a choice for those who wish to take that route. But developing the traits can only add to employees' value to themselves, their work, and their organizations. In this book, I use the terms *leader* and *manager* interchangeably.

The Elephant in the Room: What No One Wants to Talk About

Create the environment, give people the tools, then get out of the way.
>—George Fisher, former chairman and CEO,
>Motorola and Eastman Kodak

hange is the buzzword of this decade. The problem is that most people don't want to recognize or accept it. Adapting to change is the hardest thing an individual can do. For an organization, it is agony.

That is, unless there is more pleasure than pain in making the change. If not, people will resist change with all their energy and wit. And organizations are clearly all about people.

Organizations resistant to change suffer from the syndrome I call *the elephant in the room.*

Do you remember a childhood fable called "The Emperor's New Clothes"? Everyone in the kingdom told the emperor how wonderful he looked because that's what he wanted to hear. Yet he had no clothes on. No one had the courage to tell him the truth. One day, as the emperor paraded down the road showing off the new suit of clothing that his courtiers had oohed and aahed over at the palace, a small child in the crowd said in a loud voice (as children sometimes do), "But he hasn't got any clothes on." Suddenly truth broke out all over the kingdom.

Let's take that fable, expand it, and look at it in a business context. Before the procession begins, there is a *large* elephant walking behind the emperor. The elephant walks into the palace and stands in the middle of the room. No one wants to be the first to say, "There is an elephant in the room." No one says anything. So the elephant stays around, and everyone tiptoes around him. Having an elephant in the room is a bit of a problem. First, elephants make a *huge* mess. Second, elephants don't fit in such an environment (unless you are running a circus, and some organizations feel like a circus). Finally, and most important, it will *not* leave until someone recognizes its presence (like the child in the crowd who was not afraid to tell the truth), deals with it firmly, and leads it out to elephant land.

Whether your elephant is a bureaucratic promotion system run by corporate politicians, or a weak leadership team, or a strategy that doesn't get implemented because the initiative of the day rules, or a so-called reorganization that simply moves the same people into different teams and titles, or great ideas at the top that lack the necessary communication to those responsible for implementing them—whatever your elephant is, in order to effect change and do better, someone, somewhere has to be the child in the crowd who says, "Doesn't anyone see the elephant in the room? Let's identify it, talk about it, deal with it, and move it *out* of here!"

The Internet is one of the many elephants that has moved into most corporate headquarters. Change has been redefined according to an Internet-savvy economy. For some time, organizations didn't want to deal with the fact that the Internet was changing the way business worked. Regardless of the success or failure of the dot-coms, most organizations now recognize the Internet as essential to doing business if their organizational structures and the individual qualities that comprise them are going to excel. The nature of work (when, where, how) has dramatically changed.[1] Proprietary knowledge is moving even more swiftly into the public domain—product life cycles are shortening, and organizations must leverage their employee resources more effectively. The time for denial is over, the elephant has been recognized, yet the qualities of leadership necessary to make multilevel ongoing adjustments to organizations are slow in coming.

Employees have to leverage off each other in teams and small work groups to remain agile, which is critical to success. To achieve this, organizations must interconnect in alliances internally (across divisions) as well as externally (with other organizations)—this means good communication and knowledge sharing. There are certain qualities and management processes that encourage (or discourage) effective results.

There is an urgent need to identify these qualities and manage them, to cut out the elephants, to improve what's useful, to do it right and *fast!*

This book offers clear vision for you and those with whom you work to be able to spot the elephants in the room. You identify them and get them out of there, while simultaneously introducing valuable activities in their place, by becoming the embodiment of The Ten Essential Traits that make up the Larraine Segil Matrix. The characteristics help you identify the elephants in the room, diagnose the reasons why people have difficulty seeing or dealing with them, recommend the new qualities that help replace the elephants and lead them out to pasture, and finally, measure the results of such action. The Ten Essential Traits are based on my research of more than 150 companies. I recommend ways (many of which already exist in the world of management science) to augment the good and cut out the bad.

The Ten Essential Traits approach requires cultural adaptation and cross-fertilization of perspectives to be successful in a multilingual, multicultural, and networked environment.

First, however, we need to examine the concept of a networked environment. (See Figure 1.1.)

Those who become good at spotting the elephants in the room take into account a networked approach in their intelligence gathering. They look in every nook and cranny of their lives, knowing that leaving an elephant where there is no room for one eventually causes a huge stink and allows for no growth. In doing this, elephant spotters establish the groundwork for becoming effective change leaders.

George Fisher (the ultimate Ten Essential Traits example), described the challenge for leaders of the future in an interview on my television program on leadership through Primedia:[2]

A leader's role is really to anticipate the future and envision where the organization can go and articulate that. Enable the people of the organization to do what is necessary to see that future and to

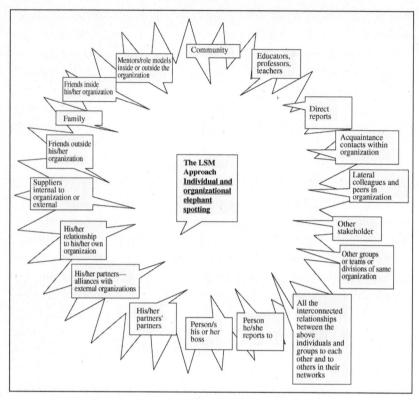

Figure 1.1   The Networked Environment

make sure it executes. A good leader is one that strengthens and creates the culture of the organization. To succeed in today's markets, leaders must give the people closest to the action more say and less bureaucracy, giving them the responsibility and authority to make timely decisions and to move quickly.

Present and future business and economic conditions lead to the inevitable conclusion that *one size does not fit all*. The Ten Essential Traits (see Figure 1.2) approach in a fast-changing environment offers a flexible management and leadership strategy that addresses not only the factors present today, but also the unforeseen changes of the future. And only The Ten Essential Traits managers will survive and thrive in that future. This has become even more pertinent as security considerations and crisis management require more from managers and leaders than ever before.

Personal Characteristic	Organizational Environment Needed	Example of a Management Process for Implementation
1. *Fearlessness*	Permits failure	Shared learning and shared power
2. *Completion:* Ability to complete; has patience and is flexible	Results-oriented with process freedom	Horizontal, project-oriented management processes with cross-functional and multi-locational teams
3. *Commitment:* Emotionally vested	Encourages individual contributions	Small work groups and flexible work behavior; fun
4. *Inspiration:* Inspires and communicates vision; motivates	Access to internal and external people networks	Constant visibility and accessibility
5. *Assuredness:* Knows what he or she wants	Opportunities for advancement and reward	Career progression process
6. *Penetration:* "Of the people" and builds personal equity; listens with respect; empowers with dignity; confident; good mediator	Flexible organizational structure	Free information exchange, communication, and benchmarking across groups and divisions
7. *Intelligence:* Talent to place right people in right place	Resource commitment to learning	Training and education
8. *Energy:* Opportunistic optimism and sense of urgency	A why-not (not why) culture; open to new ideas and resistant to bureaucracy	Continuous improvement and innovation processes and rewards and quick decision making
9. *Integrity:* Trust and credibility	Values honesty	360-degree feedback
10. *Perception:* Being in the customer's head	Customer-focused, both internal/external and domestic/international	Creates and values alliances

© 2002 by Larraine Segil

Figure 1.2   The Ten Essential Traits: The Larraine Segil Matrix

Over the next 10 chapters, we build the matrix and its rationale in tandem to enable you to adapt and change behavior.

Applying a new way of thinking is a lot easier when a need is identified. That is why gap analysis is so critical. It gives visual and mental clarity to the concepts described.

The Gap Analysis

The *gap* is the deep chasm that lies between the qualities that were valued yesterday and today and those that make sense for tomorrow. A few organizations are pulling the future toward themselves by applying energy and resources to building and nurturing certain organizational and individual characteristics in the present. These are the characteristics, individuals, and organizations featured in this book. It is useful to note how they, The Ten Essential Traits managers, fill the gap to bridge tomorrow into today. The chart shown in Figure 1.3 explains.

My research into 150 companies validates that The Ten Essential Traits in the Larraine Segil Matrix (LSM) and their accompanying organizational characteristics are keys to success in a fast-changing economy. The fact that each quality must reside in a networked environment (Figure 1.1) is one of the crucial differentiating insights. The research provided many other deliverables, listed on pages 7 and 8.

Yesterday	Gap Ten Essential Traits Managers	Tomorrow and Beyond
Local/regional	Bridging the gap between today and tomorrow:	Think Global/transnational but implement local
Employees more dependent	• 10 characteristics of organizations that create and encourage managers	Employees more self-dependent
Organizations loyal	• 10 characteristics of individuals who are or can become managers	Organizations not loyal
Information is power		Information is knowledge capital
Hierarchy and structure		Permanent change and flexibility
Community is peripheral		Community is key
Technology development		Technology integration
Shelf life of knowledge is long		Shelf life is short (public domain)
Security low priority		Security high priority

Figure 1.3 The Gap Analysis

1. The Ten Essential Traits (Larraine Segil Matrix) are those essential to prescribing the best profile for individuals or organizations (small, medium, or large, for profit or nonprofit) to succeed in an uncertain and precarious world.

2. The ten factors that characterize high-value-adding individuals are closely aligned with those that characterize the organization—that is, organizations without these critical attributes will have difficulty in attracting or retaining the key fast-track employees everyone wants. The Ten Essential Traits provide a way to find the gaps between the organization and desired employee capability and to fix the problem areas.

3. The alliance with internal customers is a critical success factor. It requires being able to spot the elephants in the room. Not being able to do so will hamper otherwise successful organizations from competing effectively. Organizations in the survey felt they were better at external alliances than internal ones.

4. Being a manager with The Ten Essential Traits is not enough— the network component of interrelating in internal and external relationships is the factor that differentiates successful from unsuccessful or mediocre leaders.

5. External alliances are essential for organizations of the future, and 91.6 percent of the organizations surveyed were involved in or establishing them. To make alliances work also requires effective leadership and a networked organization (failure rates hover around 60 percent according to earlier research I have done).[3] Hence, The Ten Essential Traits capability is key for present and future competitive advantage.

6. Despite the importance of internal and external alliances and networks and the belief that they are crucial to present and future competitive advantage and customer loyalty, over half the organizations expressed disappointment with their internal and external alliance results.

7. Existing employees provide a huge reservoir of potential that is not being tapped and that constitutes a massive resource for growth opportunities and profitability. After all, the costs of acquiring employees and maintaining them in the organization,

are sunk costs. The Ten Essential Traits enable this pool of existing talent to be enhanced.

8. Certain stages of the business life cycle connect the organization to the most-value-added employees better than other stages.

9. Certain industries appear to be better aligned with the most-desirable employees than other industries, and certain characteristics are more important to some industries than to others (e.g., telecommunications versus service sector industries).

10. Senior managers surveyed differed from middle managers in key perceptions about the organization that could affect its ultimate competitiveness. For example, they saw different (or no) elephants in the room!

These research results are referred to in the following chapters where appropriate.

Why Are the Ten Essential Traits Relevant?

The accelerated rate of change is accompanied by three major phenomena.

1. Every company is grabbing for the best, the brightest, and the most innovative employees. In good times or bad, every organization wants only the best.

2. All forward-thinking organizations are examining whether they have the right structure and cultures to compete in the future—to create profitable growth or competitive advantage through innovation and service, or the adaptability to weather all economic conditions.

3. Cultural acceptance of change has not caught up with the huge investments in IT infrastructure and technology. One reason is the challenge of managing at Internet speed, which is changing the way businesses must operate, as fear and resistance prevent knowledge from being shared and leveraged through networked internal and external alliances and collaboration.

The Internet revolution goes way beyond the dot-coms. It is all about supply chain and customer relationship management—the topic of my book *FastAlliances* (Wiley, 2001). It is changing organizational structures from hierarchical and centralized to decentralized and flat. Reengineering and mergers meant to save costs cause huge organizational disruption, management redesign, and employee turnover. Yet these restructurings have not necessarily prepared organizations for growth. Trends are pushing managers to change their cultures, but there is confusion about how to effect this change. The result is discontinuity. But it is also a time of opportunity. Those who are good at elephant spotting will be in high demand by organizations that understand that change is a continuous process.

For many in the Internet space, the elephant in the room was:

No profitable business model existed!

The new elephant in the room for traditional companies represents:

The Internet was only about dot-coms—we don't have to worry now!

Any methodology for change must take into account the following mandates:

- Serve alliance partners both within the company and external to it.
- Convert employees into knowledge workers who collaborate and build on each other's ideas in a global workforce.
- Nurture and reward elephant spotters who can lead change and add value.
- Grow the top line while growing the bottom line.
- Compete with new competitors appearing unexpectedly from other industries (e.g., telecommunications now has competitors from multiple sources, whereas ten years ago this sector had a near monopoly).
- Profile, attract, and retain the people you want.
- Reeducate the people you have.
- *Do it fast and do it now!*

Organizations need to ask themselves the following burning question:

**How do we determine the needs of tomorrow? And how do we edu-
cate those who need to implement them?**

A recent Conference Board study[4] of leadership practices of Fortune 500 companies uncovered the following:

- Nearly half the companies reported a shortage of leaders (only 8 percent reported that their leadership capacity is excellent).
- CEOs recognized a serious lack of leadership at lower levels, but only 8 percent of companies emphasized leadership development for frontline managers.
- About 64 percent of companies reported that leaders are graded based on how their teams perform.

This book creates the formula (The Ten Essential Traits) that will
enable your company to find the missing elements and bridge the gap
between yesterday's model and tomorrow's mandate.

Some Earlier Perspectives on Leadership

Management and leadership theory has gone through many phases
over the past century, but it is clear that business has changed enough
so that we need to rethink these approaches. Let's review some history.

- The Industrial Age: Leaders as robber barons.
- Post–World War II: Leaders as heroes
- Baby boomers: Leaders as change agents
- Generation X and the coming of Generation Y: Leaders as Everyman

The Industrial Age: Leaders as Robber Barons

As America began literally churning out products at the beginning of
the twentieth century, leading people was not a priority. Organizations were stringently hierarchical, and everyone was treated accordingly. The management of repetitive tasks (not people skills)
constituted leadership, and the measurement of a good leader was

output. This era epitomized what Douglas McGregor described in his 1960 book, *The Human Side of Enterprise,* as "Theory X," the idea that workers are mules who need prodding and domination in order to perform.

The workforce at this time was primarily uneducated, trained for only a few specific tasks. Individuals did not ask questions, and managers did not volunteer answers. Rigid structure and stern taskmasters were expected, and to some degree welcomed, by workers who had few if any other choices for employment.

Post-World War II: Leaders as Heroes

The 1950s and 1960s saw market demand for products explode. Volume was king, and the conveyer belt mentality of the Industrial Age continued, but at a much greater speed of production. Leaders were really managers of operational efficiency, and a whole new population of middle managers was born solely to manage people in their day-to-day tasks.

After the turmoil of two wars, employees wanted the safety and security of a paternalistic environment, of being told what to do. In keeping with their admiration of war heroes, workers found inspiration in larger-than-life business leaders, those who made these huge organizations work. The concept of "leaders are born, not made" became popular as these titans dominated the scene.

Baby Boomers: Leaders as Change Agents

Although an overall level of satisfaction permeated organizations in the postwar era, the infusion of large numbers of women into the workforce and the growing unrest of America's blacks who'd fought in the war cracked the comfortable veneer of the typical organization. With the education level of the general populace rising, all the old standards were questioned.

Because of a general distrust of authority, baby boomers found the old organizational models of hierarchy and paternity unacceptable. Leaders had to be different—they had to be noble, people-focused, and willing to break rules. With this demand for higher standards, managers were suddenly forced to deal with different people demanding individualized attention. This new focus on "me" completely negated Theory X; instead, it became fashionable to believe that every individual had a unique contribution to make to an organization.

During this time period, the distinction was made between managing tasks and leading people, and so began the wave of leadership "as science" and the search for quick-fix, cookie-cutter models for great leadership.

Generation X and the Coming of Generation Y: Leaders as Everyman

The seeds of change and diversity planted by the boomers have taken root in a mercurial business environment in which uncertainty is a daily reality. Gen Xers not only expect change, they like it, and the leaders they respect must feel the same way. Today's workforce is the most highly educated in the history of the world, and they have democratized the corporation—anyone can become a CEO; anyone can become a leader. As a result, the demand for leadership tools, theories, and techniques has grown exponentially as individuals strive to be admirable leaders—emulating the corporate magnates of the past, such as Jack Welch (GE) and George Fisher (Motorola and Kodak), leaders who care about people *and* create results.

In a brief amount of time, Generation X has made nonstandard practices standard—flexible work hours, telecommuting, cross-functional work teams, partnering with competitors. In fact, they would break all the organizational hierarchies into small domains run by individual leaders if only the postwar network would let them. And now, with the continued influence of the Internet, they're not waiting for permission.

As early as 1980, Alvin Toffler, in his groundbreaking book, *The Third Wave,* said,

> New ways of organization along less hierarchical and more ad-hocratic lines are springing up in the most advanced industries. Pressures for the decentralization of power intensify. And managers become more and more dependent on information from below. Elites themselves, therefore, are becoming less permanent and secure.[5]

The ad hoc description evolved into the concept of the virtual corporation. There, a constellation of alliances[6] between organizations is managed by an entity that pulls them together and creates an enterprise. This is an organizational model favored by those in entertainment, construction, electronic commerce, and software. The concept is also making inroads in traditional manufacturing industries through more integrated and complex outsourcing contracts. Resistance to this model still exists, but my research into The Ten Essential Traits indicates that this model of individual and organizational behavior enables flexibility to enter previously uncharted waters. Add to that the new awareness of the fragility of all things, the precious value of relationships, the concerns about security, and the challenge of terrorism, and the adaptive organization has become the preferred model for today's world.

Major Trends That Have Changed the Game

- Deeper awareness of meaningful work
- Facing change at Internet speed
- Globalization and transnationalism—of business and of terror
- Knowledge capital: its capture and use; knowledge workers
- Managing a multidimensional workforce
- Balancing growth with continuous restructuring and a path to profitability
- The adaptive organization

Deeper Awareness of Meaningful Work

It is ironic that the most recent trend in management style toward more meaningful work began even before the tragic events of September 11, 2001, occurred. Now and for the foreseeable future, there is a definite deepening of that trend, and organizations must now answer this challenge for themselves as well as their people: "What's the point of what we/you do every day? Does it have meaning for us and for others? I don't want to waste a moment of my precious life on nonsense, even though my reward is an economic benefit. I want meaningful work."

The trend toward meaningful work could benefit those organizations who have a clearly stated mission, who are committed to following that mission, and who incorporate many of the ten traits for versatile leaders into their value systems. However, it will quickly differentiate organizations that are deficient in these traits. Prioritizing what is important, becoming part of a broader picture of community, not wasting time—these are the elements impacting the adaptive organization and ensuring a meaningful connection between the entity, its leaders, and all who work there. Every communication of the organization to its members should include reference to these elements. It is what people really want to hear.

Facing Change at Internet Speed

Anyone, anywhere, anyhow—this is the mantra of the decade. Those who suffer change lightly will not survive. Although dot-com valuations may rise and fall, the Internet is here to stay as an integral part of our lives.

Individuals adapt to change much more quickly and nimbly than do organizations. Managers with the ten traits are empowered to act on their own instincts and intellect; they can absorb, interpret, and apply change in whatever form it takes. They harness change, treat it as an ally, and use it to advantage. It is their organizations that have difficulty adapting to a world that requires substance with speed and in which price commoditization rules and information slips easily into the public domain. The change created by the Internet is fundamental.

Globalization and Transnationalism—of Business and of Terror

Nondomestic and emerging markets comprise a growing percentage of overall economic growth. As corporations find or develop new businesses in other countries, strong, savvy, capable individuals who can devise, manage, and implement a global strategy will be critical to the success of such ventures. The Ten Essential Traits managers have the skill set and the vision to operate in a world of conflicting considerations. It is necessary that insights about The Ten Essential Traits managers be couched in the global environment. Throughout the following chapters, an effort is made to correlate the characteristics of managers who embody the ten essential traits with those who are effective globally. The definitive book on globalization in recent times is *The Lexus and the Olive Tree* by Thomas L. Friedman. Especially pertinent to my model are his comments about "The Electronic Herd" of investor capital that moves at lightning speed around the world as concerns increase or wane about economic and political issues and stability.[7] The qualities of The Ten Essential Traits predispose those who embody them to ready themselves and their organizations for the stampede—no matter what its direction.

The globalization of terror has given new meaning to corporate and individual security. Companies are thinking twice about whether to send executives to various parts of the world where kidnapping has become a normal activity, as personal safety could be in jeopardy. In addition, there's a new awareness that online security is the responsibility of every employee and a potential failure point for every organization. Developing new relationships with companies in emerging economies means doing a due diligence that is quite different from the past.

Veritect, a company that specializes in online security issues, told me in a recent interview about key issues of global terrorism in the private sector. A Moscow company called Itera, which has the world's fourth largest gas reserves, has a murky past and a credibility problem. According to rumor, most Russians thought that Itera's assets were stolen from the state, whereas U.S. law enforcement suspected Itera's activities involved money laundering. Western energy companies were afraid to do business with the Russian company, so Itera hired a security firm in the United States to convince the world that it was honest, had overcome any past indiscretions, and would be a good partner.

In another example, a Philadelphia company hired a security firm to look into rumors about its operations in Hungary. The Budapest arm apparently controlled "shell" companies,[8] which allegedly employed gangsters. The company was lavishing huge sales commissions on a man called Semion Mogilevich, the alleged godfather of a sophisticated and murderous crime syndicate. This ended up in court and became public knowledge. The company was also overpaying for the equipment purchased from mob-controlled firms and had money stashed in secret unauthorized bank accounts. The horrifying truth became clear. The company in Philadelphia had actually done an alliance with a company that was a front for organized crime. Executives had done due diligence from a business standpoint—visiting Hungary, looking at the manufacturing plant, checking the books— but that was not enough.

In times of global terrorism, global business has to be even more diligent, tapping into the resources of private firms, which often include investigators who are ex-CIA, ex-FBI, and ex-Secret Service agents, as well as former police and prosecutors, customs agents, federal marshals, military intelligence experts, veterans of Britain's M16, Europe's Interpol, the Canadian Mounties, and, of course, lawyers, accountants, forensic specialists, database specialists, and journalists, to name a few! As one security expert told me, "Pay now or pay later. Companies that go the extra mile on security now will reap the benefits when security is breached. Damage control is too expensive; damage prevention is key."

What price is human life or the building of a business over years? It seems trivial to be negotiating about such things as cost, yet the budget has to come from somewhere. Leaders are rarely dealing with unlimited resources. These are business and moral decisions that will determine the way your organization treats its people and adapts to changed circumstances.

Knowledge Capital: Its Capture and Use; Knowledge Workers

"In an economy where the only certainty is uncertainty, the one sure source of lasting competitive advantage is knowledge," says Dr. Ikujiro Nonaka, professor and director of the Institute of Business Research at Hitotsubashi University in Japan, as he describes the evolution of Yamaha's core competency with respect to motorcycles.[9]

Consider that in 1983, the percentage of U.S. GNP comprised of knowledge work (education, media, research and development, information systems) was just over 50 percent.[10] Today it is over 80 percent. Although there are no precise measures, all industries are increasingly being driven by knowledge. The workforce has been changing for decades—moving from industrial and agricultural jobs to services, from object-oriented industries to idea industries. Professional and technical workers now outnumber industrial workers 3 to 1.

In a knowledge economy, intellectual capital in forms such as patents, processes, and people are the most important assets of any company. The challenge for organizations to remain successful is to find, develop, and maintain these knowledge resources. As Chris A.

Barlett of Harvard Business School warns: "You cannot manage knowledge by measuring and controlling it through sophisticated systems because it resides deep within the organization. So the ongoing revolution in organizational models and management processes has been about top management getting closer to those with the knowledge through de-layering their organizations and empowering the front lines to develop their knowledge and diffuse it rapidly through the organization."[11] Knowledge workers, the real source of this tremendous economic advantage, will have endless opportunities, either with your competitors, in new ventures, or as individual contractors—opportunities they are taking in droves as organizations fail to create a place for them to flourish. By nurturing managers with The Ten Essential Traits, organizations can protect this incredibly valuable resource. Peter Drucker agrees, "One does not 'manage' people as previously assumed. One leads them. The way one maximizes their performance is by capitalizing on their strengths and their knowledge rather than trying to force them into molds."[12]

I would take it one step further. Knowledge workers don't want to be led as much as they want to be self-led—namely, to be given the vision and the tools, then connected to a network and left alone. In other words The Ten Essential Traits model is the paradigm of management that works for knowledge workers, the most important competitive advantage of developed and emerging economies.

Managing a Multidimensional Workforce

Recent studies show that our workforce will continue to diversify in age, ethnicity, and nationality. David Dickson, senior vice president at Hormel Foods, who classifies himself as a baby boomer, commented to me on the different management styles of boomers versus Generation Xers:

> I think we [boomers] were used to having more control and structure and authority. Everything that I observe about the younger people coming along says they are much more independent. "You tell me what needs to be done, set my goals or help me set my goals and turn me loose and get out of my way." We're finding some difficulties in managing some of our younger people because we don't understand that concept. We still want to overmanage them, and they're used to being a lot more independent.

Balancing Growth with Restructuring

Today's business chaos presents the challenge of creating growth while divisions and departments are downsized, right-sized, and reengineered. NCR Corporation faced this daunting task in 1996, accomplishing a massive turnaround from a negative $900 million business to a plus $99 million while being spun off from then parent AT&T. The restructuring-while-growing challenge continues today.

Per Olof Loof, senior vice president of NCR's Financial Solutions Group, explains in my recent interview with him why The Ten Essential Traits are critical for success in these types of situations:

> ... If we're in a business where we need to grow, we must have all our people find these new opportunities. Each one must feel empowered to be able to go out and do some of that. And I think in an old company like NCR, this is sometimes where our legacy kind of hits us and people feel a bit constrained at what they are "allowed to do." So I like the concept of the The Ten Essential Traits. It's a critical success factor.

The Ten Essential Traits will play a critical role in organizational growth by finding new opportunities, solving old problems in creative ways, and persevering through tough restructuring times.

All of these factors combine to paint a dramatic picture of a current and future business environment in need of underlying flexibility.

The early work of Abraham Maslow (1908–1970), an icon in the world of psychology, established this perspective, recently endorsed again by Peter Drucker in an article in *Forbes*.[13] The Ten Essential Traits provide the flexibility that the Age of Discontinuity requires.

The Revolution

The problem with most management and leadership theories is that to implement them, the entire organization needs to be completely reinvented. Some may argue that if this is so, then perhaps these organizations *need* complete reinvention. But is such a dramatic change realistic, especially considering that these revolutions must begin at the top and take time to overhaul an entire organization?

One reason The Ten Essential Traits approach is so powerful is because it can be implemented on as small or as large a scale as desired, from an individual to a team to a division to the entire organization. The Ten Essential Traits don't have to be driven from the top down; in fact, they will very quickly percolate from the middle up and down or from the bottom up. The Ten Essential Traits model can consist of one outstanding individual, and thus becomes a portable commodity independent of any organization. Or it can become a standard for all. Perhaps most important, it is more than leadership (which implies that someone is leading and another is following) or even management (which implies someone is being managed!)—it is a way of *doing* that works in the present environment.

The Malcolm Baldrige National Quality Award, in its scorebook criteria for participants, describes the leadership category as follows:

> The leadership category examines the company's leadership system and how senior leaders guide the company in setting direction and in developing and sustaining effective leadership throughout the organization. This describes the needs and expectations of all key stakeholders, including how the leadership system addresses values, performance expectations, focus on customers and other stakeholders, learning and innovation. It also addresses how senior leaders set and communicate company directions and seek future opportunities for the company, taking into account all key stakeholders and how they communicate and reinforce values, performance expectations and participate and use the results of performance reviews in evaluating and improving the leadership system. This includes how they use their reviews of the company's performance and the employee feedback on the evaluations.[14]

What the preceding Baldrige summary does *not* say is what this book is all about:

- What about the stuff that everyone knows but no one will speak about? The truth about what is really happening?
- And what would happen to the person who saw the truth and then not only spoke about it but made change happen?

The Ten Essential Traits matrix provides the environment for leaders who are willing to see the truth about what is really happening and do something about it.

Let's begin the exploration of The Ten Essential Traits (Larraine Segil Matrix) by examining the first quality—*fearlessness*.

2

Fearlessness: The Courage to Act

Unless you're prepared to take risks that may result in failure, you'll never really know what you're capable of. And you will always be afraid of something that is different.

—The Right Honourable Kim Campbell,
former prime minister of Canada

A leader with The Ten Essential Traits must be *fearless*. He or she is always moving in new directions, and those first steps take courage: the courage to be first, the courage to be different, the courage to speak out, the courage to act, and the courage to fail. (See Figure 2.1.) Without fearlessness, no significant progress, innovation or contribution is made. And The Ten Essential Traits manager cannot be afraid of elephants. In fact, elephant spotting has to become a favorite sport, and fearlessness will contribute toward that.

The Ten Essential Traits manager stands out, primarily because he or she is out on a limb. For example, in March 2001, Daimler-Chrysler was in a mess. Jürgen Schrempp, the company's outspoken

Personal Characteristic	Organizational Environment Needed	Example of a Management Process for Implementation
1. *Fearlessness*	Permits failure	Shared learning and shared power

Figure 2.1 The Ten Essential Traits: The Larraine Segil Matrix

CEO, had made some unfortunate statements about Daimler's acquisition of Chrysler that caused morale in the U.S. operations to go down fast. The new CEO of the U.S. division (Dieter Zetsche) came in to find a resentful, scared, and unhappy workforce. The elephant in the room was sitting with its trunk curled in a knot and its big legs crossed, loudly bellowing:

> You lied to us. You said it would be a merger of equals. You don't respect us. You want to control us. You have taken away our sense of competency, and, darn it, we are really good at some stuff— that's why you bought us. We have been saying this for the past year, ever since you showed up, so how come the CEO from your company couldn't hear us? And now what are you going to do about that?

Zetsche saw and heard the elephant in the room. He took immediate and aggressive action. He knew that the days of pretending this was a merger of equals were over. He bet on honesty and went forward with the takeover. He closed down a number of plants, changed the senior management, inserted some of his own key people, and started to change the culture. He also changed some of the habits people were accustomed to seeing in senior management before and after the acquisition. He was oblivious to the concept of large offices and felt no need to change the furniture. He ate in the cafeteria—not as a scheme to curry favor with employees, but because he does not consider himself better or worse than the other people who work in the company. He shared some of his own personal challenges in being away from his family and missing them and his country and culture. He was, in short, a man comfortable with his own convictions and with a belief in self that carried him through the tough decisions that would affect the lives of many. His willingness to be fearless was tempered by his ability to be "of the people" (Chapter 8) and his determination to complete the task he undertook (Chapter 3). The organization was in failure mode. He shared his thoughts, his plans, and his power. DaimlerChrysler has a good chance of making it out of its slump with such fearlessness. And The Ten Essential Traits managers in the organization will rise to join him.

Fearlessness is an essential element in the active pursuit of innovation. The Ten Essential Traits managers do not wait for opportunity to find them; they seek out new situations and do their own investigations. In order to fearlessly search for new opportunities, The Ten Essential Traits managers are not afraid to do new things, stretch and bend their minds, push their abilities further than they thought they could go.

One such stellar leader is Joerg Agin, former Kodak senior executive who ran the very important entertainment division, which is the world leader in supplying products (film and a variety of digital services) to the movie industry. A myriad of new ventures in this division requires different, more entrepreneurial skills and out-of-the-box thinking. Agin discusses why and how he returned to Kodak after his departure many years earlier.

> When he came to Kodak to turn it around, George Fisher convinced me to return to Kodak after many years at Universal. The way he did it was twofold. First, the chance to work with him was an opportunity I could not pass—he is a management icon of huge proportions, and his talent and style attracted me greatly. But the other side of it was that George had the ability to make me believe that I could do more than I had ever imagined I was capable of. He expected it of me, and so I did it. He did not set the goals or the limits. I did that. It's the environment that he created that made me and those who work in my division feel that even the very difficult things that we sometimes had to do were possible. It trickles up and down in the organization—sometimes, admittedly, not as fast as we'd all like, and sometimes actions we took didn't work and had to be changed. The challenges are never ending. But the freedom to set goals without fear was there.

Being out on that limb also means that you are risking a fall. The Ten Essential Traits manager is willing to fail because *new* and *different* are synonymous with *unknown*. This willingness to fail not only sets the example for others to take risks, but sets extraordinary leaders apart from the rest. Consider Lou Gerstner, who turned IBM around. His consumer-focused strategy—the need to offer customers solutions rather than just individual hardware and software products—was a risky approach. Now it has become the goal of the entire technology industry.

What if the manager with The Ten Essential Traits fails? He or she turns that negative into a positive through learning. In that way, failure becomes success. George Fisher tells the story of "perhaps one of the most notorious failures" during his time at Motorola, launching a factory in Fort Worth, Texas:

> . . . We messed up several dimensions and basically fell flat on our face, costing Motorola a ton of money. And, unfortunately, impacting a lot of people's careers. And I think from that you learn a lot. I've learned a lot from product development and how to bring new products in, how not to expect too much, how not to have a house of dominos, where if one goes down, everything goes down. I've learned trivial things—like, if you have a power backup system on a computer that is driven by diesel engines, then it is a good thing to have people check to see that there is diesel fuel!

The absence of fear requires self-confidence, a considerable belief in self. First, you must have conviction in your ideas in order to be willing to fail. Second, after a failure you must be able to stand up, brush off the dust, and try again. After just four months in office as the first female Canadian prime minister led to a devastating public election defeat, the Right Honourable Kim Campbell put an immediate stop to feelings of self-doubt. "I went off to do things that reinforced my sense of self-worth," she explained of her first activities after the election. "I surrounded myself with people who were interested in what I had to say to reconfirm my own sense that I was somebody who had done important things, done valuable things, and had valuable experience."

The fearless manager with The Ten Essential Traits speaks up, expressing his or her opinion or the truth when others don't want to hear it. That same manager is savvy enough to know when it is best to be diplomatic, when it is best to keep quiet. The leader or manager with The Ten Essential Traits is not afraid to debate and to listen to divergent opinions.

Daurdie Banister, president and CEO of Shell Services International, describes fearless meetings at Shell Oil: "We don't always reach consensus. It's not necessary to reach consensus on all issues. And in fact my take is that it's better not to reach consensus. If we're all thinking alike, then we are not being creative."

Do not think that fearlessness is a John Wayne–type approach of galloping down mountains in search of the bad guys, the damsel in distress, and the hope of glory. Nor is it taking foolish risks, endangering the careers or well-being of others, or digressing from ethical behavior in order to score the "big kill." Recklessness is *not* fearlessness. Recklessness has no thought, no methodology. The Ten Essential Traits model entails the assessment of risk taking—the best timing, conditions, and results.

Kim Campbell, former prime minister of Canada, believes in calculated fearlessness:

> You can take as many risks as you have the nerve and guts to take.
> I often say that I am a bungee jumper but I'm not a kamikaze pilot.
> I want to know that if I jump, that the cord is going to hold. And it's
> the calculation in the risk evaluation that is important.

The Fearful Leader

Fear is a damaging trait. It causes insecure behavior, which can run the gamut from defensiveness and negativity to paranoia and operational paralysis in the extreme. If an organization breeds fear, this behavior can take the company into business decline.

In these circumstances, which are seen often in the transition to flat or minimal growth, the organization slides into corporate sclerosis. Process is used as a barrier and creates a series of hurdles, not for the purpose of learning or quality or even validation of ideas and projects, but rather as opportunities for denial of innovation and the slowing of change.

See what happens to the innovation process in Figure 2.2 when fear enters. The figure summarizes the preceding points by showing how The Ten Essential Traits managers approach new opportunities without fear.

Executives who support a fearful organizational environment will generally be perpetrators of the not-invented-here (NIH) syndrome. For those who give up on trying to change the environment, the qualities of The Ten Essential Traits will fade and diminish in importance. They can be rejuvenated by a turnaround in some cases, but the scars will linger, and some people will quickly become disillusioned at the slightest hint of returning to the bureaucracy of yesterday.

NCR Corporation has struggled with this very dilemma. As part of AT&T, the company wrestled with an identity crisis. Never quite fit-

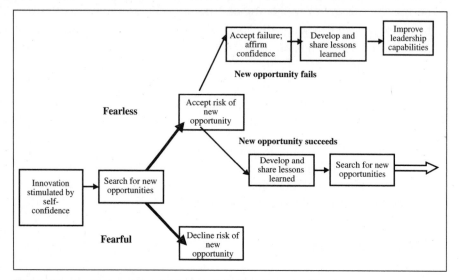

Figure 2.2   Fearless and Fearful Approach to New Opportunities

ting into the AT&T culture, NCR nevertheless vacillated between its prestige of being a 114-year-old company with a proud tradition housed within a mammoth giant and its yearning for the independence of a start-up.

Per Olof Loof, senior vice president of NCR's Financial Solutions Group, looked back at the first years after AT&T's divestiture of NCR.

> Our task as a leadership team was to turn the company from a loss to a profit. We did that. We cut out expenses and excess processes and people and even divisions. It was impossible to run the company as it was structured and be profitable. Cost cutting was the easy part. The real problem has been getting the company to grow again. And there you face the difficulty of creating an environment where people lower in the organization can actually get involved in the strategic process so that it isn't something that comes only from the top. So what we do is go a couple of levels down in the company and try to get buy-in, build morale, and convince people that this is not just corporate talk but that we really mean it.

NCR has to overcome the fact that many of its people have been burned, so the path to fearlessness has been slow, although some divisions have succeeded. The resistance to change in large and mature organizations is substantial.

When asked why some divisions seem better able to turn around than others, Loof answered:

> Well, I think it is better to ask for forgiveness than for permission, particularly if we are in a business where we need to grow. We must have all our people find these new opportunities, and then they must feel empowered to be able to go out and do some of that. You look for people who are willing to go and do things, not people who want to maintain the status quo.

In turnaround or restructuring situations, people with The Ten Essential Traits accelerate buy-in. They understand the new direction and changed driving forces of the organization. They work together and network to leverage their skills. As George Fisher said when I asked him what he does about people who can't get with it in a turnaround such as Kodak's, "You have to move them along, either to another position within the company or maybe out of the company altogether. The point is that some people may do better in another environment."

The question is, how long will it take to find the people who, as Fisher says "can't get with it," especially when time is of the essence and shareholders are impatient? By using The Ten Essential Traits as a guide, managers can more quickly identify those who have the capabilities to accept change and to be part of the new direction of an older enterprise. Unless The Ten Essential Traits managers are identified, the forward progress of the enterprise comes to a halt.

The first stages of turnaround will include creating senior management teams, such as those at Kodak and NCR, and identifying the kinds of people that can accelerate change: the existing or emerging Ten Essential Traits leaders. The first cut is generally the most obvious and the cleanest. The more difficult challenge is to find a way to drive the process deep down into the organization.

In truth, the term *fearful leader* is an oxymoron. A fearful leader becomes a micromanager and will not survive in a turnaround or any major change situation. There are degrees of fearlessness. None of the ten matrix characteristics are totally black and white, packed in neat little boxes, but rather, they vary along a continuum from high to low intensity. Moving people along to a higher level of qualification appropriate to the industry they are in is what counts. My research into over 150 companies (Appendix B) details the industries in which certain qualities are high or low and the life-cycle stages of the companies in which certain qualities are more prominent than others.

The Environment That Allows Fearlessness

This environment permits failure and recognizes that failure is a learning tool. The progress of The Ten Essential Traits from failure to learning enhances the leadership and knowledge capabilities of the individual. If the organization is supportive of failure, the learning can be shared. If not, The Ten Essential Traits manager may find an organization more in tune with his or her philosophy.

Even the most successful individuals will experience failure eventually. If they don't, it means they have not pushed the limits of their abilities. As Candy O'Bourn, a senior executive at Kodak, told me, "I know that we have stretched ourselves and the organization in new and exciting ways. We are learning at an increased pace."

To be a good home to the fearless leader, an organization must recognize the potential of new ideas and make a resource commitment to innovation. This means giving people rewards for thinking.

The 3M Corporation prides itself on its innovation competency: It is expected that people in research groups will spend 15 percent of their time thinking. The results of that activity are then shared with others in the form of brainstorming, new project development, and research for the sake of creating new and novel ideas. These ideas may go nowhere from an economic standpoint as stand-alones, but when that learning is shared, the synergy could create applications for another's innovation.

Thinking can also cause people to become willingly self-critical, as the keen eyes of The Ten Essential Traits manager often recognize what is right and wrong about the organization. These managers also listen well. Sometimes the very issues that create work for consultants who come in and do major evaluations (at exorbitant prices) of the state of the corporation are already clear to those in the middle of the organization—if someone would only ask them! And then, of course, listen to what they say.

One large Fortune 500 company for which we, at The Lared Group, have consulted on alliances, is a case in point. Here's what one middle manager (a leader with The Ten Essential Traits in the making) has to say:

> The folks from corporate came here to the divisions on a massive drive-through-type visit. They asked lots of questions, And we answered truthfully. What do you think they did with the information? Nothing. What a waste. We took days away from productive work to educate them and then they did nothing. They created a bureaucratic nightmare, and they could have saved everyone's time and stayed at headquarters to do that.

Another characteristic of risk takers is that they take risks even when senior management doesn't agree. Jack Welch gives an example: "We're [GE] in the cat-and-dog insurance business in England. I don't really want to be in that business, but the guy who brought me that idea wanted to be in it, and I trust him."

Shell Oil Company is another example of an organization that allows for fearlessness and permits risk taking and failure.

Jerome Adams, formerly head of the Business Transformation Team and the Learning Center at Shell and now a senior executive at the company, agrees:

> The idea is to be cutting-edge, not popular-edge. And if we keep that as a value proposition, then we're always exploring the next level of thinking and risk or insight or breakthrough. That would preclude people from being comfortable and then getting into a groupthink mode.

Volkswagen of America is a company with many cultural and management differences in its worldwide operations.[1] The German parent company holds for Theory X (see Chapter 1). However, the chief executive of the American division, Clive Warrilow, has been implementing Theory Y (see Chapter 1). Transferred from South Africa to North America to turn around the sluggish sales and demoralized workforce, Warrilow immediately undertook a number of actions.

He gave autonomy to VW area managers to spend their allocated budgets and to make decisions on options for budget applications as they saw fit. For example, if they wanted to use the money for bonuses, or maybe advertising, or even premiums, these were their decisions. Dealers who missed their targets were not censured, ridiculed, or terminated; instead, as became clear from the report-back process, they used the freedom as a learning tool to discover what they might do differently. As the experience was shared with others in the group, group expertise increased.

With this level of freedom, The Ten Essential Traits managers will succeed, even if it's through failure; the fearful will leave.

Management Processes for Fearlessness: Shared Learning and Shared Power

To create an environment of fearlessness (i.e., one that permits failure), one strategy is to establish shared learning mechanisms. An initiative such as the dealer feedback sessions and quarterly budget reviews of VW is one method. Processes like these are critical because failure becomes success only if learning is extracted and shared within and across the organization.

A more difficult manifestation of fearlessness is the process of sharing power. If there is a focus on creating learning opportunities for all, derived from experience within the company, there will be a tendency to share the power that knowledge creation gives. This will not happen in an atmosphere of distrust, intense personal rivalry, and territoriality. Organizations that permit failure and encourage learning from it will reward those who share the power of their positions as well as their accumulated knowledge.

Some of the most respected leaders are those who have learned this well. George Fisher states it best: "Power sharing requires maturity and self-confidence. It means valuing the contributions of individuals and giving credit and rewards that are for both the group and for those who emerge as stars."

Hierarchical companies do not share power well. They are structured to reserve power at the top and dilute it farther down in the company. At Kodak, Fisher promoted and encouraged layers of high-energy managers to move through the organization. It took time, longer than he would have preferred, and continues even now after his departure. The message has not been totally incorporated in every division nor throughout some of the bureaucracy that still remains. As cost cutting continues at Kodak, the present and future management will gain efficiencies by increasing levels of power sharing and shared learning, a significant change in company culture.

Shell Oil and Shared Power

Culture change in the arena of power sharing was the goal of Phil Carroll when, as CEO of the U.S. operation, he initiated the transformation strategy at Shell Oil Company.

Shell was formerly a hierarchical organization in the United States, with 14 vice presidents for an organization of 20,000 employees. The company was run with a strong control structure, so tight that those who excelled, though generally good corporate citizens, were very much part of the old boy network. The saying "once an oilman, always an oilman" was never truer than at Shell, and long-term employees were accustomed to the hierarchical structure of the company. The attitude was one of, "If it ain't broke, don't fix it," which meant "business as usual." Part of this comfort level was based on an assumption that had lasted for a long time: that oil reserves were the key factor affecting the market and that the price of oil would continue to increase. Generally, the feeling was that any fall in oil prices was a temporary upset and would pass in time. Indeed, Shell had operated on these assumptions very successfully in the past. After decades of good business performance, the late 1980s brought change to the industry, and senior executives at Shell were unwilling or unable to see that the whole value chain of suppliers, producers, and distributors was different. Some of Shell's competitors were beginning to see the shift.

As Phil Carroll rose through the ranks of the organization, he realized that many aspects of the organization had to change. The strong power structure was the antithesis of information and power sharing. Knowledge was seen as power and the fairly rigid structure of the organization meant that Shell was vulnerable to the market and to changes that were besetting the oil industry.

By the late 1980s, the independent oil companies were beginning to compete differently and fiercely. They were now becoming efficient in the upstream markets (i.e., the recovery of oil and gas), an area where the major oil companies had not traditionally been profitable. The strategy that Phil Carroll evolved was valid for the market environment not only at that time (1992 to 1993), but for the next 10 to 15 years.

The current manifestation of earlier upstream competition is now seen in the hypermarkets in oil products and in the downstream operations where the majors historically controlled the markets. Over the past few years, oil companies have been combining not only with each other in mergers, but also in their downstream operations (e.g., the joint venture between Shell and Texaco, called Equilon). The push for consolidation is accelerating. Texaco has agreed to sell its holdings in two large ventures as part of an agreement with the Federal Trade Commission staff for permission to merge with Chevron. This is a huge $38.9 billion stock swap acquisition of Texaco by Chevron. One of those joint ventures is Equilon Enterprises LLC (the other is Motiva Enterprises LLC), and the purchaser of both is Royal Dutch Shell (pending). If Royal Dutch Shell ends up not acquiring them, Texaco and Chevron will petition the FTC to put the ventures into a trust. Regardless of the outcome of this and other deals evolving before and after this book is published, the industry has consolidated once more—and challenges facing these companies as they integrate their employees are monumental. Ten Essential Traits leaders will be in great demand, and they will be pushed to their limits!

This is not new for Shell. The company has lived with an awareness and commitment to cost containment and consolidation for many years. At Shell USA, Phil Carroll lived and breathed the needs of the corporation as his career evolved. He was always a good corporate citizen. A long-time Shell employee, he was finally able to realize his dreams when he became CEO. The position gave him a chance to communicate and share his vision for transforming Shell, a vision that has applicability now in defining Shell's role in a vastly different industry environment.

Linda Pierce, executive director of Shell's Leadership Council, was part of the entire transformation process that began under Phil Carroll. "Phil knew that he had to significantly change Shell Oil Company. He realized it had something to do with command and control, and that he had to find a way that the organization could devolve power. There was inertia and also a fear of change."

The process began with the creation of the Leadership Council, a group created in the fall of 1993.

"The Leadership Council," Pierce continues, "was another name for what the group really did. Its true title could have been *learning council*. That's what it became. It was a place where leaders could come and learn from one another, from their own experiences, and from the challenges that they have."

The Leadership Council was the first step in the restructuring of Shell. It was a bold move in creating a new kind of governance. But the real start of change began in August of 1994 with a significant event. Pierce remembers it well:

> The Leadership Council went off for a two-day retreat to talk about the path ahead. It was in that meeting that Phil introduced his ideas about a governance structure that would actually create separate business units, which would operate under internal boards as internal corporate centers, or what we came to call *firms*. This was a new idea for us. It marked the beginning of the understanding that in order for us to compete, we needed to do so by dividing the business as well as the functions into smaller entities that would be required to compete in their business areas.

What was fascinating about this shift was the way Phil Carroll created the buy-in and stimulated the change. He appealed to The Ten Essential Traits in his team, encouraging fearlessness. In addition, he realized that the elephant in the room for many years at the company was the reluctance (or maybe just ignorance of each other's needs and issues) of the various divisions and groups to work collaboratively together. The structure of how they were working internally and externally did not support competitive advantage in their business arenas. He was determined to change that. Linda Pierce explains:

> Phil had some intuitive ideas about what this would be like. He had asked each council member prior to the meeting to think about how they would restructure the company. Of course, he had also done his homework about how he would do it. Each member of the council drew their suggestions on flipcharts. Phil was the last to present his model. And, while there were aspects of everyone's model in his, his was the one that was the most comprehensive and represented the most dramatic change. That was in August, and by January the following year (1995), that model became the new governance structure of the company.

What was the process by which Phil Carroll developed his ideas? The sharing of learning and power were key elements. One of the council members asked him in that meeting how he had come up with his ideas and how he had developed such a deep understanding of the transformation needed for the company. He answered as follows: "I learned from every single conversation."

Phil Carroll's conversations were with people at every level of the organization, those on the council, those outside the company. His intention was to devolve power in order to place accountability and flexibility within the entities that were being developed so that they might compete effectively.

The way the senior management team worked together at Shell was facilitated by the fact that they were all located in Houston. They committed to meet at least once a month. These executives had not shared personal relationships before that time. As Linda Pierce put it,

> They lived in their silos, and their business functions had not required meeting together in the past. So the journey for them, from the first meeting onward, was to build trust and relationships, changing the patterns in the ways that they communicated with each other. What evolved were learning patterns, as they adjusted to the sharing of power and knowledge.

Different communication styles can be a difficult obstacle to overcome in building trust. As an observer of the intricacies of this process, Pierce smiles as she remembers:

> It was kind of humorous to recall some of the earliest conversations because there was not a whole lot of listening. Rather, it was a lot of advocating. One person would put a statement out, and then another person would put a different statement out but pretend they had built upon one another. They were afraid to be completely open and were mainly advocating their own positions. Then it became completely different. Where there was open space in the conversation, there was listening and actual learning. And most important, there was now mutual respect, trust, and learning. In the beginning, the mood was, "Give me the agenda and let's be sure that we build it tightly because I don't want to waste my time here." Later it became, "Let's build more time and space into our agenda so that we can just have conversation and exchange learning on what's really important to us now." And the remark-

able thing about it all is that these were the same people who used to rush in and out. Later, after the Leadership Council meeting, we would schedule a dinner. This was social time, starting about 6:00 P.M. and continuing as long as they wanted it to that evening. There was no agenda and no one else but themselves in conversation. And that became one of the most important mechanisms for relationship building.

The structure of the Leadership Council was tested from its earliest inception. As the relationships of trust between the senior managers of the company slowly evolved, strategic initiatives demanded immediate attention.

The process that developed from the pressure to change themselves as well as the company created a triple-sided role for the leadership team.

One role was as council members and as part of the community of leaders that shares the interest of transforming the company. The team shared power and learning to create a vision around that mandate.

Another role for each was as leader of his or her particular organization (e.g., Shell Exploration, Shell Services, Shell Chemical).

The third role broke the tradition of territorial "silos" of information. In the past, as leaders of their own organizations, there was no need to share information except on a profit and loss basis. Now each of the management team members also sat on the board of another member. With these interlocking boards, information flow and the increase and exchange of mutual respect was ensured. These internal boards of the various divisions of the organizations met on a quarterly basis with the business leaders who were the CEOs of each particular business unit.

These multiple roles fostered an atmosphere of shared power and learning, which ensured that the senior teams of each business unit became exposed to that cultural change. Slowly but surely, the atmosphere of increased fearlessness and the new management approaches trickled down through the organization.

The role of Linda Pierce as executive director of the Leadership Council was one of executive coach, facilitating each leader's personal development as well as their relationships with each other. As she explained,

An example would be where two of the team members who each led their own organization did not have a good relationship. My responsibility to them would be to coach each of them in order to make their relationship more productive. Another example would be to provide the leader with the space to reflect on what he intends to create as his legacy. Then the issue to decide is: Are you achieving the results that you want to support that legacy? If not, then the challenge was to be a thinking partner with them regarding what they might be able to do differently.

One of the important issues in any leadership team is what George Fisher calls "not getting with it."

At Shell, people who can't get with it were treated with compassion. The Shell culture did not enjoy public beatings or embarrassment, and the feeling has been that there should always be an honorable way to exit from a changed situation. According to Pierce,

> There is a lot of compassion for people who have been good soldiers—but in a different world and a different time and style. The ideal case is when these people are able to come to that conclusion themselves and make an individual choice to opt out, either to move to a different assignment and still make a contribution or to take themselves out of the Shell system. Although some would say we have been *too* patient, in the end we want people to make their own choices, and we have to balance that with the need to make business results.

This is the same dilemma that Fisher encountered at Kodak:

> I would do it again. Even though we did the major cost cutting only after a number of years, we gave people three more years of employment and allowed some of them to decide to leave on their own. The interests of all the "publics" must be balanced—shareholders, employees, customers, the community, and suppliers. These kinds of situations require a great deal of humanity and compassion.

Shell Oil is part of the Royal Dutch Group. The major initiative for the Royal Dutch Group is called The Group of the Future. One of their mandates is to "build a better world." Another is to understand what it will require to compete in the twenty-first century. As a company, Royal Dutch Group spends more money around the globe than any other company in the world. Their intention is to do that not only for business success, but also to build a better world and thus become a supporter and advocate of sustainable development. This means paying attention to the sustainability of the environment, the planet, and society in general. This goal, especially after the tragedy of September 11, 2001, is even more pertinent, positioning Shell as a good global and community citizen.

A key element in attaining this goal will be the identification and nurturing of leaders who can translate this vision to multiple levels of the organization, in all its diverse operations, so that the philosophy is integrated into the day-to-day activities of The Royal Dutch Group worldwide. This process is starting slowly, and Shell will encounter many of the cultural and country-specific challenges of communicating knowledge, even though core values are stated and a vision is shared.

Linda Pierce has been with Shell for 32 years. She has seen the change begin to accelerate over the past decade:

> One of the major changes is to transition from the focus on capital assets of the 1980s to the focus on people. Shell's journey to devolve power and share it is based on the fact that leaders cannot actually give away power unless there is some confidence and investment in those people to have the capability and competency to use that power effectively. Shell's Learning Center has been an example of the belief in people. Another management process is the job posting, whereby, instead of leaders planning the careers of their employees, individuals are left to manage that for themselves and can transfer into any area within Shell by seeing what jobs are available. Of course, mentoring is offered to assist in this area.

The sharing of power and learning is at its zenith in a joint venture. Two or more entities come together and merge or create a management team. This means that two or more corporate cultures will come together, sometimes with a resounding crash, as processes compete and styles differ. It is particularly challenging when overlapping activities require rationalization and lead to the inevitable cost cutting and terminations.

At Shell, nevertheless, the environment for shared learning has been extended to alliance partners. According to Pierce, "As we've gone into our joint ventures, we recognize the need to make space for those who are leaders of joint ventures only partly owned by Shell. That creates the opportunity for a council of leaders to come together by choice, to learn and to build competitive advantage just by spending time together.

The Shell USA joint venture with Texaco, Equilon, posed many of these challenges. It is only one of what Shell calls its new and evolving *networked organizations,* and another Leadership Council was created to connect these leaders with each other and with the existing council members. Of course, as the oil industry continues to consolidate and as competitors and collaborators change dramatically, plans for networked knowledge sharing have to be reevaluated.

The concern still remains this: At what point will knowledge transfer actually constitute the education of a competitor? No one has defined that yet. The parameters will evolve over time, but that learning opportunities transpire from bringing leadership teams together from Shell organizations is indisputable. It also creates an atmosphere of collaboration and *perception,* "getting into the head" (see Chapter 11) of those who constitute the internal customer, a key quality of Ten Essential Traits managers. *Penetration,* or building personal equity, another element relevant to the Shell leadership councils, is discussed in Chapter 7.

The environment for shared learning embraces risk. As Jo Pease, associate director of the Shell Learning Center, explained,

> I think that Shell has been willing to face risk all along. But that has been technological risk—for example, getting an offshore lease or drilling an offshore well. And what we see today is a very different kind of risk. It's more of a risk to say what I think, a risk to say I don't have all the answers in this world.

The Shell transformation has not been easy. Jerome Adams, who was on the business transformation team and was also creator and leader of the remarkable Shell Learning Center, likened it to a massive geopolitical shift:

> I can only compare it to peristroika and glasnost. Once you see the new, there is no way to go back to the old. At Shell, there is no way to go back. People in the past wanted to be part of Shell because we were the technology leader. Now and in the future, it will be the

conditions and the environment that they find inspiring—and that we will be a learning organization. This means that the products and services we offer will evolve over time as customer expectations and market conditions change. Shell is becoming a place where Maslow's self-actualization can actually be met in a variety of ways. The transformation process is fragile. However, even though it is a huge undertaking, Shell has put this initiative into real action, through the Leadership Council and with the Learning Center and now with further change initiatives.

Phil Carroll saw in Jerome Adams a remarkable resource, a leader with The Ten Essential Traits who could influence the entire Shell organization. Even though Phil Carroll has left Shell Oil USA, Jerome Adams has remained. As a good example of a Ten Essential Traits leader, he continues to contribute his talents to Royal Dutch Shell's reorganization of its global group.

Adams is no stranger to difficult and fragile tasks. He pioneered the assimilation of women into the cadet corps at West Point and dealt with leadership issues of men and women in the Army. He worked with General Electric to create leadership programs to reach from the first level to the level of general manager at the company. He built a learning center for TRW, then contributed to creating a different culture at USF&G in a turnaround situation. It was then that Phil Carroll convinced him to come to Shell. According to Adams,

> My task and that of folks who are my colleagues has been to try to capture best practices and then share those with other members of teams and other locations. More important, however, with regard to the Learning Center, employees could always come there and speak from the heart without fear of retribution. They could discuss what I call the "undiscussables." They could think differently about the way they solved business problems. The absence of fear was key. Then learning and knowledge sharing can really happen.

The Shell Learning Center was a place for The Ten Essential Traits managers to foster growth in all areas of the organization.

Adams said it simply: "The bottom line is that Shell has demonstrated a true capacity to look at learning principles as a primary vehicle for leveraging change." Thousands of executives went through the Shell Learning Center. Not all of them were Shell employees. The company opened its learning opportunities to many of its partners, even its competitors, Texaco, Mobil, and others. The philosophy is that if the joint ventures and partnerships that Shell shares inside and outside its industry benefit by learning, then the individuals, the enterprise, the partner companies, and the community will also benefit. According to Shell executives, sharing learning and diminishing fear of the unknown will result in benefits for all.

A vehicle in addition to the Learning Center that contributes to knowledge sharing at Shell Oil USA is the Stories Book.

Sixtus Oechsly, executive director of corporate identity for Shell Oil, played a most unusual role at Shell. His job was to discover what Shell stood for—to its customers, to the general public, and to its employees. As Oechsly explained,

> Shell has the second most recognized logo in the United States, second only to the Olympic Rings, yet when asked what the logo means, most people said, "Gee whiz, I think they sell gas!" So my job became to help the organization discover its true identity— what it stood for. Then, once that identity was discovered, to put in place mechanisms like storytelling that make it real. And once that was done, to create a campaign including media relations, investor relations, and advertising to help our publics actually see it. That's what I do. I see myself in the role of ritual elder for Shell. It is my responsibility to collect all the stories that comprise the myths, the culture, the memory of Shell. In the same way a tribe is reunited and recommitted to each other when the tribal elders tell stories of olden times in moments of tribal crisis, so we need to be able to refer to the Shell tribal stories to renew ourselves.

Shell used several thousand employee focus groups to understand how Shell employees saw themselves. One characteristic was *relentless*. When Shell employees accomplish something, they almost have to grind it to dust. Another characteristic was *caring*. This means caring about each other and the communities in which they work. They have a high sense of responsibility, both locally and globally. Also, *humility* is an attribute of the Shell family. My personal experience in providing services to Shell and presenting seminars for hundreds of Shell executives over a number of years through the Learning Center has led me to conclude that this is a company with a high level of integrity and style. In short, Shell is a class act!

Oechsly asked Shell employees, "What do you really want people outside Shell to think of you?" In his own words, here's what he found out:

> They said what we want most of all is for people to count on us. So we went to what we call the Communicators Forum at Shell. It is a group of 80 people from all across Shell, and we asked them how their direct constituencies in all the business units of Shell would be most able to relate to "being counted upon." It ended up being far simpler than you would imagine. We held a contest and asked for the employees of Shell to write a story, in 200 words or less, about how they have counted on Shell or seen someone else count on Shell. We offered them a month to do this. We got 500 stories. We appointed an independent judge, chose 15 finalists, and sent the top three to the Olympic Games as a reward. Then we compiled the stories into a book. People have written to me saying that they keep the book on their desks and each day read two more stories to inspire them. People now talk to each other about the stories. So communication and lore about Shell is spreading. And so are the values.

The process of shared learning and power sharing clearly provides a payback to the organization. Processes can be improved in all parts of the company through the advances in one part; failures can be leveraged through learning, as can the creation of a legacy of knowledge.

But what about The Ten Essential Traits? Jo Pease has this to say:

> Well, it's one thing to lose your job tomorrow if you also lose everything you've worked for over the last 20 years, and you don't get a good retirement package because you've left two years before that magic date. It's another thing to say, well, if I lose my job tomorrow I can take with me everything I've worked for, and in addition, I know that my skills are marketable because I know what the market is.

Shared learning and power give knowledge workers the most valuable asset of all—increased know-how, not with regard to confidential matters that must remain with the company if they leave, but in value added to their own skills and competency. Now *that's* something you can take with you.

The organization benefits, and so does the individual, and thus so does the community—win, win, and win again.

Before leaving this characteristic of fearlessness, it is important to mention that many people have real, valid, and understandable fear for their personal safety and the safety of others since the September 11, 2001, tragedy in the United States. In many parts of the world, people are all too familiar with this fear, but in the United States it is a new experience for most of us. That is a different kind of fear from fear of failure in an organizational sense. For many of us, it is a fear we are managing, yet somewhere deep inside us, a new reality has been created. In this context, fear may actually be part of the survival instinct and may help us deal with certain circumstances in that it creates a need for movement or action. It is when fear creates inaction or paralysis that it can be harmful.

This valuable quality of fearlessness is especially compatible with the next one, described in Chapter 3, "Completion: The Ability to Compete."

Fearlessness: Action Items

Now that it is clear why fearlessness is important, how it manifests itself, and how organizations can help it foster, let's discuss some strategies for developing this competency.

To Develop Fearlessness in Yourself

- Conduct a "fear audit."

  What makes you fearful in your career?

  How is that fear expressed?

  What was the last risk you took, and what was the result?

- Get to the root of the tasks and responsibilities that evoke fear—probe deeper with at least five "whys" to your fear.

- Imagine what is the absolute worst thing that can happen as a result of the activity. It usually isn't as terrible as you might imagine.

- Show fearlessness by speaking your mind in a logical, business-oriented manner, scripting it out first to ensure comfort and professionalism.

- When confronted with a daunting fear, make a list of what the benefits are and focus on those rather than on the negatives.

- Make a commitment to yourself to accept at least one new opportunity, however large or small, each month.

- Review some of the risks you have taken recently that have succeeded. What made them work? How can you incorporate those techniques into other potentially fearful situations?

To Enable Fearlessness in Others

- Examine your managerial, departmental, and organizational mechanisms for addressing failure.

  Do they censure?

  Do they encourage?

  Do they ignore?

- What usually happens to people who fail in your organization? Is the feedback positive or negative?

- When a failure occurs, do not ask, "What went wrong?" Ask, "What did you learn?"

- Reward the learning, do not punish the failure. Be open about these rewards, and communicate to others that failure is permitted.

- Establish a learning mechanism by co-opting existing avenues such as quarterly meetings, company newsletters, and intranets.

Completion:
The Ability to Complete

You need to empower the people at the edge of the organization with systems that are very convenient and work in the same way as the people who use them. The reason that 99.9 percent of collaboration within and between enterprises happens using e-mail, phone, and fax is because they match the rhythm of how people work. People have different temporal and media requirements, and certain media are much more effective than others for different processes—some transmit emotion more effectively.

—Ray Ozzie, techno-visionary, CEO, and founder,
Groove Networks, at Esther Dyson's Annual PC Forum

The Ten Essential Traits leaders get the job done. They do it by collaborating, creating, and managing teams across all organizational functions, often in many locations. They are interested more in getting results than in protecting a series of processes. (See Figure 3.1.) Ray Ozzie and Groove Networks are creating the technological potential to help people work better together. Ozzie also knows how to get results, whether in helping to develop what is now known as Lotus Notes or in facilitating a myriad of other technology breakthroughs. He is a Ten Essential Traits leader of great stature.

Although obviously needed and deceptively simple, the *ability to complete* is a set of complex skills that, unless managed properly, will result in a lack of results. In today's incredibly fast-paced business

Personal Characteristic	Organizational Environment Needed	Example of a Management Process for Implementation
1. *Fearlessness*	Permits failure	Shared learning and shared power
2. *Completion:* Ability to complete; has patience and is flexible	Results-oriented with process freedom	Horizontal, project-oriented management processes with cross-functional and multi-locational teams

Figure 3.1 The Ten Essential Traits: The Larraine Segil Matrix

environment, The Ten Essential Traits managers are better off taking action than overanalyzing. They realize that it is rare to have enough information for completely balanced decision making times of intense change. The Ten Essential Traits manager realizes the importance of task, project, and idea completion and does not let roadblocks impede his or her progress. In the same way, a manager with The Ten Essential Traits must go beyond simply spotting the elephant in the room. Without action to move it out and replace it with value, elephant spotting becomes a giant complaining session rather than a change mechanism. The completion characteristic ensures that elephant spotting transitions into action with results.

When bridging the gap between yesterday, today, and tomorrow, the stresses placed on all employees for speed and adaptability are balanced by the pressure to complete what is worth doing. The Ten Essential Traits managers stand out for many reasons, among which is their ability to complete. They are seen by their peers, managers, subordinates, and outsiders as can-do people who are dependable and responsible. They are fearless in that they will take ownership. Most important, The Ten Essential Traits managers have a clear understanding of what completion means and know that the definition may change depending on various externalities (time, money, people, resources, etc.).

An interesting twist to this characteristic occurs when the *leader* or *manager* is the elephant in the room. When that person doesn't complete his or her part of the responsibility and is not particularly dependable or reliable, few are willing to discuss or even identify the problem for fear of repercussions. The worst-case scenario is when the team leader or senior executive is the one who has the inability to complete—the elephant in the room that no one can do anything about. We address this further in discussing the inability to complete later in the chapter.

The ability to complete in a world that operates at Internet speed is a quality made up of many components. These can be organized into a diagram, as shown in Figure 3.2. Keeping in mind the Pareto analysis (80 percent of the benefit comes from 20 percent of the activity), you should focus your attention and resources where they can do the most good.

The Ten Essential Traits managers continue to grow and improve the ability to complete during their life experience, whether they're dealing with one project or a multitude of activities ranging in importance and scope. In today's connected society, multiple technological tools exist to enhance these skills, and various software tools for project management and other related activities are now expected to be part of normal work competency.

However, the ability to complete is much more than a software program. Multitasking, for example, is a mind-set that means managing multiple projects, often unrelated, with different priorities and schedules, as well the relationships that go with them. The agendas of those involved in various projects need to be understood and, especially in a team environment, may have to be negotiated to a partial consensus in order to execute. Resource allocation issues may change and priorities for individual and corporate agendas may need to be rebalanced. All of these issues (some of them contradictory) must be

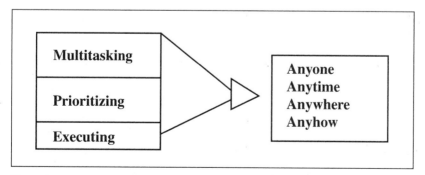

Figure 3.2   The Three Inputs of the Ability to Complete

coordinated and prioritized. This is another manifestation of a networked environment in which interlocking and related capabilities must be rationalized and leveraged.

The Ability to Complete

Let's examine the three inputs of the ability to complete (refer to Figure 3.2) in more detail.

1. *Multitasking* involves the following tasks:
   - Project identification
   - Milestone setting (intermediate and ultimate)
   - Determination to succeed
   - Relationship management
   - Agendas, both corporate and personal
   - Team building and evangelizing
   - Resource balancing and budgeting
2. *Prioritizing* can be seen to include the following tasks:
   - Project characterization as high-, medium-, or low-priority corporate goals
   - Team selection and modification according to priorities
   - Adjustment for corporate, market, and/or technology changes as execution evolves
   - Totally new event reprioritization or project modification
3. *Executing* can be seen to include the following tasks:
   - Goal adjustment and project redefinition
   - Follow-through (supervisory or actual)
   - Success metrics
   - Reporting processes up and down
   - Rewards

Increased need for speed and faster time-to-market requirements dictate that all these activities be undertaken simultaneously, flexing and changing according to circumstances. The ability to access the capabilities of others within and outside the organization or group will be essential to the success of executing fast.

Looking at the tasks of a manager with The Ten Essential Traits who is competent in this area is best illustrated by the chart in Figure 3.3.

Multitasking

Project identification requires scoping out the project. What is the background? What are some of the expectations? Who does what to whom and when? In the multitasking environment The Ten Essential

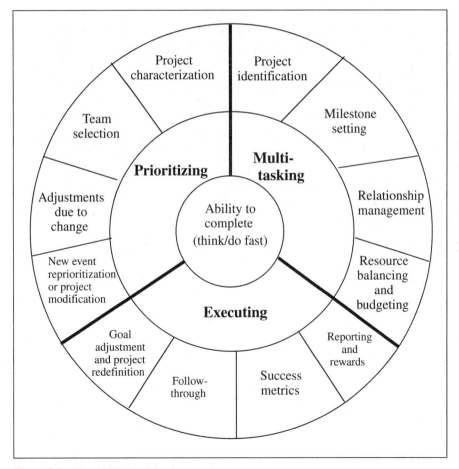

Figure 3.3   The Ability to Complete

Traits managers understand the importance of project ID in order to create the project guidelines and to resource it correctly.

Resource balancing and budgeting is the natural outcome of project scoping, because The Ten Essential Traits managers are often in positions where too much is asked of too few resources—a natural phenomenon in the business arena. The time/resource/expectation dynamic is an ongoing responsibility of The Ten Essential Traits managers, which often means making difficult decisions where there are no totally right answers. The manager must call on his or her fearlessness to address those difficult decisions and move forward.

Setting intermediate and ultimate milestones is essential once the project identification and scoping and the resource decisions have been faced. The Ten Essential Traits managers stand apart in their determination to succeed in completion, even if completion does not bring success. In a recent interview, George Fisher, former chairman and CEO of Motorola and Eastman Kodak, talked to me about the definition of success and the importance of intermediate milestones:

> It's important to redefine how you measure success in certain circumstances. Setting a goal, for example, during an exploratory period and saying that you have to reach it by a certain time can be dangerous—because you are prejudging that during the exploratory period you will come up with a positive answer. If, on the other hand, you set milestones, it might simply mean making a decision at a certain point, such as, "Do we take this further?" Then people can have success along the way even if the end product doesn't get into the market. This is especially important in the R&D world, where people often forget to define intermediate milestones of success. People need reinforcement much more often than every 24 months in a two-year development project. They need intermediate reinforcement so they can feel good about what they have done. Then, even if the conclusion is a negative one, the fact that conclusions were reached can still be seen as a success of sorts.

Relationship management is a key success factor in the ability to complete. It is rare (except in some research functions) that anyone works alone. Agendas of others and conflict with personal or corporate agendas can sabotage even the best project management process. I have developed a methodology and software, called Partner

Relationship Management (PRM), to analyze organizations and individuals for the best planned relationships.[1]

Nevertheless, one of the critical components of the ability to complete is recognizing and co-opting (creating cooperation with) others to participate in the completion process. The Ten Essential Traits managers know who they can collaborate with and where to get buy-in. The Ten Essential Traits characteristic of penetration and building personal equity, discussed in Chapter 7, plays an integral role in the relationship management process.

Prioritization

The prioritization phase of the ability to complete flows naturally from the multitasking phase.

Project identification now becomes *project characterization,* which means placing the project in a high-, medium-, or low-priority category. This will clearly affect the resource allocation, in both time commitment and amount. It will also affect the next activity, which is ongoing, *team selection and modification,* according to present and changing corporate priorities. The Ten Essential Traits managers recognize who make the best team members (other Ten Essential Traits managers!) and are not afraid to change the dynamic of the project team as needed. They evangelize as they go, co-opting the involvement of others.

All these activities change as the execution evolves. This is because, as time passes, the organization changes, the market changes as competitors reposition, and technology changes.

Sometimes an entirely *new event* happens. This is so important that it requires a totally different approach. For example, when WorldCom set out to acquire MCI, even though the U.S. and European antitrust approval process took time, all projects were reevaluated from the moment the acquisition was announced. For some at MCI, it meant treading water and keeping their heads low until project priorities were decided. The Ten Essential Traits managers took the initiative in creating specific milestones and project priorities. This produced especially cost-effective solutions, because WorldCom's track record with other acquisitions involved some slash-and-burn techniques of cost cutting. These actions improved their chances for survival, although there were no guarantees.

Execution

The execution phase of the ability to complete requires skills in *goal adjustment and project redefinition* over time, but more important, the essential skill of *follow-through.*

Those broad-strokes folks who have difficulty with the details required in follow-through will, over time, defeat their ability to progress and learn. Although oftentimes the follow-through processes can be shared or even delegated, it is a critical part of The Ten Essential Traits competence to know what follow-through is required and, if it becomes the responsibility of others, to ensure proper execution.

No execution phase is complete without the creation of *success metrics* to measure progress so that project team members or intermediate and ultimate goals can be readjusted as needed. These will vary by project, but should involve both *quantitative* and *qualitative* metrics. Has the project reached its intermediate or ultimate goal? Was learning perhaps one of the softer goals, and was that reached?

In addition, the execution phase requires a *reporting process,* both up and down. The Ten Essential Traits managers understand the need to co-opt. This means communicating with those to whom they report, with those in their lateral teams, and with those who may report to them. This constant communication feedback mechanism ensures the lowest level of misunderstandings. It also increases the potential for *shared learning*—an essential management process and outcome from the *fearlessness* characteristic discussed in Chapter 2.

Rewards come up often in discussing The Ten Essential Traits managers. But rewards need not always be monetary. In many cultures outside the United States, as well as in some subcultures within the United States, money is an insufficient reward. Abraham Maslow's hierarchy of needs shows self-actualization at the top of his pyramid. For The Ten Essential Traits managers, most of their needs fall in this category. This means that factors such as job satisfaction, recognition (including group or even whole company, depending on country culture), future potential (e.g., greater research freedom, higher visibility within the company or industry), intellectual satisfaction, and general corporate (or even community) environment play a large role in rewards valued by these leaders. Monetary rewards are only part of the equation.

PRT, a company in Barbados that offers software programming services to companies worldwide, has addressed these needs. The company's programmers come from over 40 countries, and every Maslow-identified need is taken care of. New employees are met at the airport, and all amenities are taken care of, including housing, new bank accounts, trips to markets and stores, schooling for children, and frequent community get-togethers. The work environment is sublime, as is the living environment, and rewards of this kind make up for the 10 to 25 percent differential in gross salaries that could be earned comparably in the United States. The real difference is that employees can save 30 percent of their gross income, because utilities, housing, schooling, and other amenities are free. PRT exceeded $100 million in annual revenues in 2001—another indication of the The Ten Essential Traits at work in an unusual environment, where employee turnover is no more than 15 percent (far less than the industry average of 40 percent).

The elephant in the room was spotted and addressed by PRT: the fact that most employees want to be part of a family at work, not just a vehicle for generating revenues or profit. The company supported a lifestyle that recognized the largest problem of an immigrant—trying to belong. PRT identified the issue, addressed the problem, and filled the space with valuable benefits. The results are a low turnover rate and corporate deliverables.

The preceding characteristics comprise the ability to complete. They constitute an important personal characteristic required of an individual who is evolving into a Ten Essential Traits managers.

This characteristic will join the other nine as part of an approach that you can use to evaluate yourself personally and others in your organization.

The Inability to Complete

The lack of results is the most noticeable deficiency in any leader or manager. The repercussions of such paralysis can be devastating not only to individuals, but also to the longer-term competitive viability of an organization. Those reporting to leaders or managers who are unable to complete may mutter to themselves about the inadequacy of their leaders, but rarely will they raise the issue in an environment where their complaining could be misinterpreted by those senior to the managers in question. Thus the problem becomes an elephant in the room.

One food processing company that we are working with is suffering from this very problem. The cross-functional, cross-divisional team, a hardworking group with a good representation of The Ten Essential Traits, is hampered by a group leader who is fearful, bureaucratic, political, and lacks the ability to complete. No one talks about his lack of competency. Yet it's clear to everyone that he is unable to take risk, so the team mandate, which is to explore new opportunities and alliances, is hampered. Good people are becoming frustrated and soon will want to leave the project. Finding a way to create a 360-degree feedback process is essential for survival. The future of the organization depends on the insights developed by the strategy group and implemented by the line organization members who are involved in the development of new alliances and acquisitions.

A 1990 *Harvard Business Review* article, "Commercializing Technology: What the Best Companies Do" (Nevens, Summe, and Uttal), still holds true today. The authors studied companies in the United States, Europe, and Japan and found that leaders in technology commercialization could be identified by certain statistical parameters:[2]

- They commercialize two to three times the number of new products and processes as do their competitors of comparable size.
- They incorporate two to three times as many technologies in their products as do competitors.
- They bring their products to market in less than half time.
- They compete in twice as many product and geographic markets.

All of these items are directly related to the ability to complete. But what happens to those people, and consequently to their organizations, when completion is not achieved?

The authors of the article share the story of Xerox Corporation, a company that dominated the copier market for years. During its halcyon days of the 1960s and early 1970s, Xerox held an 82 percent market share and developed products in four- to seven-year cycles. Xerox's competitor, Canon, saw a tremendous opportunity in the midrange copier market, and from 1976 to 1982 it launched 90 new models of copiers. Xerox struggled, losing half of its market share as it plodded along with a model aimed at the same market. It missed the mark.

Why? Clearly, the Xerox project leaders and teams were lacking The Ten Essential Traits. They did not embody or practice the ability-to-complete the characteristic. First, they failed to identify the project priority—the importance of this venture to the overall performance of Xerox was tremendous. Second, the Xerox team was not able to identify the key objectives of the project, a critically important piece of the ability to complete. The product was too expensive for the midrange market and unreliable in quality. Xerox did not get the job done.

In the meantime, Canon continued to develop technology innovations and commercialize them swiftly, introducing eight different low-end and midrange copiers.

Could this be the fundamental cultural reason why, in 2001 and 2002, Xerox is now facing a major cultural change? Even though development cycle time has been reduced over the past year, the company has lagged its competitors and suffered terribly. Not only has it been painful for the employees, but also for the citizens of Rochester, New York, who have struggled with the travails of the Kodak downsizing and are now dealing with the problems of the once proud Xerox. It could be said that Xerox moved from the stage of intelligent arrogance in the late 1960s to the stage of arrogant stupidity in the late 1990s. Only now, in 2002, under the steady leadership of CEO Ann Mulcahey, is it beginning to turn around.

The inability to complete the development of a new printer on time could result in a 31.5 percent decrease in profits for Xerox. This is one of those situations where The Ten Essential Traits leaders must be able to identify the main objectives of the situation and act on them.

We've been discussing the bottom line impact of the inability to complete, but how does it manifest within individuals? In truth, the danger of a leader who is unable to complete goes far beyond the lack of outputs. A noncompleter will quickly lose credibility and will be seen as neither dependable nor responsible. Perhaps most damaging is the fact that this reputation will infect all areas surrounding that person—laterally to colleagues, downward to reporting employees, and upward to executives. The inability to complete fosters a lack of trust from all sides, and the so-called leader becomes ineffectual. Any existing team environment breaks down, because collaboration and delegation are seen as "dishing out the dirty work" that the noncompleter cannot accomplish. Resentment may prevent the whole team from reaching its goals. After all, why should they work diligently to protect the ineptitude of the noncompleter? Conversely, because nothing can be trusted to the noncompleter, the team members may burn out from trying to do everything themselves.

The inability to complete in individuals often shows itself in excuses: "I tried, but . . ." The Ten Essential Traits managers, in contrast, achieve the end result by pursuing any and all avenues necessary to reach the goal. They do, however, balance their determination with another of The Ten Essential Traits: *integrity*. (See Chapter 10.)

The inability to complete, like fearfulness, will cause paralysis. The manager who lacks The Ten Essential Traits is faced with too many tasks, none of which can be properly prioritized or executed, and becomes completely overwhelmed. Not knowing whom to access for assistance, this person is eventually either relegated to a courtesy position (with no power or responsibility) or removed from the organization altogether.

A less severe side to the noncompleter (but problematic all the same) is the manager who is all vision and no execution. Such managers may be highly intelligent and have tremendous ideas, but the lack of execution and follow-through makes them impotent. Although initially inspirational, these managers lose their luster as they gain the reputation for "all talk and no action." Eventually, they, too, will be passed over.

How can an organization enable the ability to complete?

Organization Characteristic: Results-Oriented with Process Freedom

The manager who has the individual characteristic of ability to complete thrives in a results-oriented organizational environment. These results must be clearly articulated.

Cathleen Black, vice president for Hearst's magazine division, knows that it is her responsibility to her direct reports to outline expected results: ". . . You have to be very clear about what your expectations are, what your goals are, what your objectives are, and where you want to take the company. And I think we communicate that effectively and our people know what they have to do in order to produce." She adds that her executives "know exactly what they have to do every day, so they don't need me to look over their shoulder every day." Hearst Publishing has established the essential environment for the ability to complete by communicating the expectations and then letting The Ten Essential Traits managers accomplish them.

The Ten Essential Traits managers are very adept at reprioritizing changing expectations—as long as the new expectations are communicated. Hidden targets frustrate self-motivated managers immensely because they work very intelligently and diligently for completion. To find out too late that the definition of completion and success has changed will frustrate managers who have The Ten Essential Traits. They will adapt to the new scenario, but hidden agendas over time work to reduce credibility, and since The Ten Essential Traits managers value honesty, their respect for such an approach will diminish over time.

A fertile environment for the ability to complete means that an organization rewards results in a fashion that is appreciated by the receiver (as mentioned previously, monetary rewards may not be enough). In addition, consistent follow-up must occur, but the methods for doing this are flexible. Organizations may create feedback sessions, team analysis of performance, continuous redefinition of project success (readjusted as the circumstances change), or other processes. The key is that processes must be able to evolve and change over time. The *result*, not the process, is the focus. If the process is not flexible, it creates a roadblock and becomes ineffective. Then The Ten Essential Traits managers will ignore it, circumvent it, or leave.

With this results-oriented reward system, the organization must hold its leaders accountable. The Ten Essential Traits managers are astute: While watching their own progress and process, they are watching the performance of others. Managers with The Ten Essential Traits notice when results are taken lightly and if lack of results bring no penalty. When, despite memos or performance reviews, results are not taken seriously, these managers move on to other organizations where their accomplishments and contributions will be considered valuable and where all managers are held to the same standards.

What kinds of organizations manifest these characteristics?

They are often high-growth companies, especially those with sales organizations or an emphasis on sales growth. Mature organizations that have low or negative growth may have difficulty attracting or maintaining The Ten Essential Traits managers. My research shows that mature and declining organizations score lowest on the The Ten Essential Traits (Larraine Segil Matrix).[3] Stellar managers often leave these companies to join organizations where they feel more appreciated and are free to achieve results without bowing to bureaucracy and politics.

In addition, those same mature organizations that are trying to re-create a growth environment must do so while cutting costs. As they struggle to make their cultures adaptable and change-oriented, they must create and sustain the kind of environment that rewards results-oriented performance while leaving the process flexible. Since many of these companies are moving from a process-heavy and constrained bureaucratic culture, the challenge is to create different metrics for performance. Unfortunately, the people that these organizations need are The Ten Essential Traits managers—the very ones most frustrated with staying there.

Eastman Kodak, referred to earlier, is a classic example of this challenge: bloated by bureaucracy, sustained by a paternalistic culture, and left behind by its technology choices. When George Fisher took over Kodak, his challenges were daunting. He first identified the elephants in the room—low morale due to diminishing self-esteem, fear of the digital age, multiple layers of bureaucracy, and more.

He also plucked the low-hanging fruit and sold off activities that were a distraction for the company, reducing debt and refocusing on the future of "Taking Pictures Further." Change came slowly—so slowly that after three years, some analysts were predicting the demise of the company and the de-deification of Fisher. However, Fisher's intense competitive spirit, coupled with the basic foundations of a fine company and huge brand equity, would produce a different outcome. Huge cost savings and even more intense refocusing improved results so much that in 1998 the stock price again soared. Yet Fisher stayed cautious and concerned. His caution was well placed. The stock has sagged again, and so have analysts' predictions. In his interview with me, Fisher commented as follows:

> A big part of the transition of the Kodak culture was moved to a more performance-oriented culture, where measurement is taken on actual results. And not just business results, although we were doing that very well (when I left). Continually and increasingly, you don't have the luxury of saying, "I can grow just for growth's sake and not work the cost side and the growth side simultaneously." In fact, if you don't take the attitude that it is necessary to work both, you will add layers of cost to the organization. It is essential to work both, even in companies that are growing aggressively.

The organization that Fisher was trying to create is one that encourages The Ten Essential Traits approach, a key element of his own personal philosophy. This cannot thrive in organizations that are highly political. Kodak was. Fisher admits that internal politics was a critical element of the culture that needed to be changed:

> There was a lot of that in Kodak, as in all big organizations. What we had to do was get everybody focused and aligned on making Kodak successful. We needed to bring about shocking change in order to create a cost-competitive structure, to have products coming out much faster, to be more leadership-oriented. This kind of change is uncomfortable but necessary, and it shakes up the political connections that are not good for the organization.

But even within this uncomfortable time of change, The Ten Essential Traits leaders are emerging at Kodak. More than ever before, they understand the goals, and they have the freedom to use the necessary means to reach those goals. Unfortunately for the market analysts and shareholders, the change has been too slow. Kodak's stock in 2001 languished at all-time lows. Despite additional management changes, more restructuring, and deeper cost cutting, the company's top-line growth in its competitive market has suffered. Only the very nimble will survive the digital wars. And Kodak drags along too much baggage for even a Ten Essential Traits leader like Fisher to remediate.

Process freedom does not mean no process. On the contrary, it means choosing the right process in order to get the results.

Shell is another example discussed earlier. In the five years under former CEO Phil Carroll (now CEO of Fluor Corporation), Shell transformed itself, providing many examples of how to create and nurture The Ten Essential Traits leaders/managers. Before that, the company was hierarchical and bureaucratic, and processes were rigid and specific. Jo Pease, assistant director of the Shell Learning Center and long-term Shell employee, recalls the old days:

> Viewgraphs were everything. You didn't dare go to a meeting and not have viewgraphs. In fact, no one asked questions, since discussion or disagreement was not encouraged. This is definitely not the same organization it used to be. Now, if you don't encourage discussion and listen well you are outside the norm.

Recently, Royal Dutch Shell has changed its global structure, which has affected Shell USA, and it is not clear whether The Ten Essential Traits changes brought about by Carroll (and continued in part by former CEO Jack Little and his successor) will continue or recede.

Hormel Foods in Austin, Minnesota, is beginning to show awareness of the need for The Ten Essential Traits approach. The company, being very results-oriented, is building the environment where The Ten Essential Traits leaders can accomplish their goals. David Dickson, group vice president for Hormel, tells the story:

> One of the things that is unique here at Hormel is that three times a week, if you are in town, you come to a meeting—all of the officers of the company. (It's almost a religious commitment!) We have representatives from all the staff groups, representatives from all the divisions, and we sit and talk about the business. We discuss what's good, what's bad, and what's difficult. Every Wednesday we have to report on our results for the previous week. So we're up in front of the whole group saying, "My sales are up 20 percent" (or down), and it's an amazing incentive when you have to do that weekly in front of your peers. In addition to that, we take notes at those meetings, and then those notes (at least the ones that are not confidential) are disseminated widely throughout the organization. A discussion where the CEO makes a point at 9:00 A.M. on Monday morning probably gets out to every sales district in the company by 10:30 A.M. It is an amazing results-oriented process and communication system that keeps us all working together as a team.

The ability to complete is expected from the leaders at Hormel. It is not just a competency. It is part of the ethic of the company. Dickson explains further:

> This is a company with the old Midwestern work ethic. All the officers in the company start work at 6:00 A.M. every day, five days a week. We don't work real late—till 5 or 6 every night. We used to work every Saturday morning, too. Now we only do that part of the time. It's a hardworking culture here at Hormel.

It is expected that those in the company will fulfill their responsibilities. However, Hormel has traditionally been somewhat hierarchical, and fearlessness was not a greatly rewarded quality. Some of that is changing, although change is not yet uniformly embraced throughout the company. The new CEO of Hormel is also changing the speed of innovation and the speed of information flow within the company. David Dickson, as a leader with The Ten Essential Traits, is a major senior contributor to the company. He and others within Hormel have spearheaded the creation of innovative strategic alliances in the area of ethnic foods, both as product line extensions in the United States and in different geographic locations, such as Spain, Mexico, and China.

Yet Dickson would be the first to admit that The Ten Essential Traits approach may be challenging in different cultures. As an example, he mentions Poland:

> In Poland, there is a need for strong leadership in order to motivate people to perform. They don't have incentive systems like we do, so that method of reward is rather foreign to them. Although delegation is a good thing, and one would hope that Ten Essential Traits leaders emerge, when you're running a business in those areas of the world, there has to be a strong authority who makes the tough decisions. The fact is that many people there are motivated by "carrot" and fear, and that is the only combination that works to make a company successful there.

The concept of The Ten Essential Traits must incorporate both fearlessness and the ability to complete. Some country cultures that have only recently evolved from command-and-control leadership styles will be slow along this road. However, understanding The Ten Essential Traits will enable those who show promise to be identified and encouraged, even though the majority of employees in a given country or region may be unwilling or unable to participate.

Dickson summarizes his perceptions of The Ten Essential Traits as follows:

> Here at Hormel, it is a matter of coming in, making your presentation, getting your resources lined up, and going for it. We are given a pretty good opportunity to run our own show and call our own shots. There are lots of resources here if you need them in finance and legal—brilliant guys, and we work well as a team. But there is no question that the Generation X community is going to demand better execution of The Ten Essential Traits here at Hormel. They want to be given the tools and then turned loose.

Unless Hormel makes adjustments, it will lose its younger Ten Essential Traits managers, who are fearless and focused on completion, but are asking for more freedom to get the job done.

Management Processes: Horizontal Project Management

Many management processes are related to this personal characteristic of ability to complete. These are found in organizations that are results-oriented and allow for process freedom. By definition, the orientation is to achieve the result, not to fixate on the process.

It is important to identify the processes that are relevant and worthy of improvement and attention. Many firms have found that dramatic process improvement does not translate into better business performance. Peter G. W. Keen, in *The Process Edge*,[4] states that businesses can even decline and fail at the same time that process reform is dramatically improving efficiency, saving time and money, and improving product quality and customer service. He posits that it is important to identify the processes that are not only salient, but also those that *create worth* (i.e., *economic value*) for the firm.

A management process commonly used by The Ten Essential Traits managers who exhibit the ability to complete is *horizontal project management*. In most organizations, this is a process that meets Keen's definition of being both salient and of worth. This is the kind of process that can return more to a company than it costs. It is what

Keen calls a *process asset* (as opposed to a *process liability*), and it will link up with corporate strategy and finance when executed efficiently. It is the kind of process that drives *commitment* and *emotional vesting* (Chapter 4) in The Ten Essential Traits managers, because competent execution of the process can improve both profitability and productivity.

In its best form, horizontal project management processes will include a commitment to collaboration and teamwork in order to complete effectively, another component of the networked environment. Lateral team selection with a variety of functional skills is not a new concept. Managing it is the challenge. It requires many of the same skill sets as multitasking, prioritizing, and executing. Flexibility of process choice and use is the key.

The ability to complete and the management of projects—indeed of the whole company in a horizontal fashion—is especially important in the era of electronic commerce.

Jeff Bezos, CEO of Amazon.com, put it this way in an interview on Primedia (the network that carried my satellite television programs):

> In the Amazon.com world, we are using technology not just to help readers find books and customers find products. We are using it to help books find readers and products find customers. You can go in both directions.

This requires a completely different look at the retail process. The ability to complete demands a horizontal structure, a way of analyzing and serving customers' needs at warp speeds. Jeff Bezos explains:

> There are at least 100 to 1,000 really great books out there that each person could relate to. The issue is how to connect the book with the reader. It means using mapping technology to understand the customer and then to deliver the books as quickly as possible, even quicker than the customer thought possible. And we have been able to apply this to other products, too.

In this environment, employees of companies must evidence all the qualities of Ten Essential Traits managers and become network centers of leadership themselves. They must meet the specific customer focus of the company as well as the speed of customer decision making. Then they must meet the customer request. There is no time for intricate processes. There is huge demand for flexibility and interconnecting leverage, where the complementary skills of many people with different capabilities and functions come together.

Horizontal project management at Amazon.com extends even to its customers. In order to execute an idea properly, Amazon.com knows the value of bringing in the ultimate expectations setter: the customer. As Bezos explains,

> . . . The cycle of experimentation is so much shorter. So, for example, a little promotion we did was to give away a thousand dollars' worth of books, and we toyed with the question, "Should it be win a book a week for a year or win a thousand dollars' worth of books? Which one would work better? And you don't ever have to debate or guess about anything like that online. You try it both ways, and within an hour, they [your customers] give you the answer.

As discussed earlier in the chapter, The Ten Essential Traits managers know whom to co-opt to achieve results.

The Ten Essential Traits fuel companies that compete in the electronic community toward continuing, renewable success. Regardless of eBay's stock price fluctuations, it has surpassed Amazon as the classic example of what's new and what works in e-business, experiencing huge growth and success in just a few years—clear evidence of fearlessness and the ability to complete. Companies such as Amazon and eBay also evidence two more of The Ten Essential Traits: *perception* (Chapter 11) and *energy* (Chapter 9).

Management Processes: Cross-Functional Skills

In research done by Nevens, Summe, and Uttal (mentioned earlier), the authors found that high-performing companies emphasize a set of skills different from companies less successful at the technology commercialization process. They value cross-functional skills, whereas other companies focus more on functional strengths. The research found that structures and habits of companies work against the development of cross-functional skills. Most of the activities of organizations are function-specific, so there has to be a concerted effort to design links between various functions. Nevens et al. found that "superior commercializers strive to build an extensive network connecting R&D, manufacturing, sales, distribution and

service, and they organize around products, markets or development phases rather than functions."[5] Job rotation and training can
contribute greatly to easing the silo mentality of functional differ-
entiations.

Cross-functional networks and teams are not only characteristic
of companies good at commercializing technology, they are a sys-
temic necessity in organizations that create and nurture The Ten
Essential Traits. Results orientation means crossing over into every
function of the organization and coordinating with other Ten Essential Traits: *energy* (Chapter 9) and *penetration* (Chapter 7).

Ability to Complete and Fearlessness

The fearless Ten Essential Traits managers will try many things—
but without the ability to complete, their value diminishes. Spotting
the elephants is only the first step. Moving them out and introducing
value to replace them is the action that must be taken. That action
will be supported by the willingness to fail, the desire for new challenges, and the desire to be on the move—always learning, challenging, and progressing. All these qualities are significant, but the
ability to complete is the key to making fearlessness relevant and
valuable.

Completion: Action Items

To develop this highly visible competency, you should consider the
following techniques.

To Develop the Ability to Complete in Yourself
- Be sure you understand the definition of *completion* for each
  responsibility. It will probably encompass several different factors, each with a different weight.
- Are you completing with the interconnecting capabilities of
  others? Are you taking advantage of the human skills that
  could enhance your effort? How are you sharing capabilities
  with others?
- Objectively review your past performance. What didn't you
  complete, and why?

- Initiate project management systems for yourself:

  Educate yourself on project management techniques through literature or seminars.

  Access project management tools such as software programs.

  Learn about and interface with existing internal project management mechanisms

- Periodically review projects against the list of expected results.

- Be open and innovative to solving the seemingly impossible.

- Reward yourself and your team for completion, even for milestones. You'll experience the positive impact it has on morale and future results.

- Never say, "This cannot be done." The Ten Essential Traits managers find the way to do it, with integrity.

- The interrelationship of *results* and *process* will affect the comfort level of The Ten Essential Traits managers. How results-oriented are you? Does your organization allow for process freedom? To what extent?

To Enable the Ability to Complete in Others

- Set clear goals and communicate them.

- Inform managers/leaders of changes to objectives immediately.

- If goals stretch out more than six months, set periodic milestones.

- Hold all leaders accountable for results.

- Interconnect the capabilities of team members. Reward them for flexible behavior that leverages off the skills of others in addition to their own.

- Analyze your internal process structure. Is there only one way for each type of project? If yes, is that necessary?

- Apply the Keen test to each process in which The Ten Essential Traits managers are engaged. Is the process *salient* and *of worth* and therefore a candidate for improvement?

- Examine the reward system currently in place.

  Is it flexible?

Does it factor in milestone achievements?

Is it tied to the outlined results?

Does it connect to the network concept?

Consider expanding the current reward system to include non-traditional methods.[6]

4

Commitment: Being Emotionally Vested

People will be most creative when they feel motivated primarily by the interest, enjoyment, satisfaction and challenge of the work itself— and not by external pressure.

—Teresa Amabile, Ph.D.,
Harvard University
School of Business

The Ten Essential Traits managers care intensely about what they do. They give more than nine to five, more than the status quo—just simply more. For those with The Ten Essential Traits, commitment is about emotional vesting, perseverance, and passion. (See Figure 4.1.) The sense of reward they derive from their accomplishments feeds more than their pocketbooks: It feeds their souls.

Being Emotionally Vested

Emotional commitment is critical for effective use of The Ten Essential Traits. The word *emotion* is one used with restraint in business. It is often equated with weakness and instability. Emotional vesting does *not* mean losing emotional control. Nor does it mean burdening your coworkers or superiors with emotional problems. Emotional vesting means that the individual has the capacity to have strong and passionate expectations for positive results. It means working with commitment and using multiple resources, including small work groups and internal alliances. It means not clocking in and out on a

Personal Characteristic	Organizational Environment Needed	Example of a Management Process for Implementation
1. *Fearlessness*	Permits failure	Shared learning and shared power
2. *Completion:* Ability to complete; has patience and is flexible	Results-oriented with process freedom	Horizontal, project-oriented management processes with cross-functional and multi-locational teams
3. *Commitment:* Emotionally vested	Encourages individual contributions	Small work groups and flexible work behavior; fun

Figure 4.1 The Ten Essential Traits: The Larraine Segil Matrix

rigid schedule but rather as the workload and projects demand. Vesting in the activity means that the desire for success is high. And so are the rewards.

Jo Pease, team leader for customer focus of the Exploration and Production Division of Shell Oil Company, describes it this way:

> The concept is to come to work and be all that you can be. So it's saying to you as an individual, "Don't leave part of yourself at home." We once had a corporate poet here who told this wonderful story. He said, "Have you ever wondered why people leave the car window cracked open when they come into work? In Houston people say that it's because of the heat. The real answer is that you've left 40 percent of yourself in the car. You brought 30 percent of yourself to work, and the other 30 percent never got out of bed in the morning." Shell is in the process of a transformation that will increase the percentages of what comes to work with people in the morning.

Emotionally vesting means bringing your hopes, dreams, aspirations, and skills to work and finding an environment in which they can thrive for mutual benefit. It is a personal investment that The Ten Essential Traits managers make in their activities so that the compulsion to excel increases.

The elephant in the room for some companies is the lack of enthusiasm that is evident in the work environment. This is often the case in government offices, where many people are not emotionally vested in their work. Energy is low, enthusiasm is minimal, and lunch hour and breaks are important escapes. I have also observed this attitude in many retail store employees, whose main focus is break time and whose primary goal seems geared more toward escaping work than doing it. However, retail and government environments that focus on The Ten Essential Traits are different.

Nordstrom's has for some time epitomized the ideal of committed employees who serve customer needs. Bruce Nordstrom, chairman of the board and the third generation of family in the business, told me in a recent conversation, "We are just country shopkeepers really, shoe salesmen by trade. Once you have fit and satisfied customers with their shoes, you can satisfy them on lots more as well." Then he quoted from Elmer Nordstrom's small book, written to document the Nordstrom story for family members and employees: "The better we treated our people, the better our people performed."[1]

This is the Nordstrom way and one of the secrets to their success. They have taken their family commitments to each other and applied them to their business. Another example of the family value system is found in this quote from Elmer's book:

> When we approached Everett about becoming president, he gave it some serious thought. He knew that in many companies, the oldest brother became president and remained president, relegating the younger brothers to positions down the line. But Everett insisted on a different plan. "I'll agree to be president for now," he said, "but only if we agree to rotate the titles." Occasionally people would ask us our titles and we sometimes had trouble remembering who was who on that day. We had to know when signing papers, but that's the only time the members of the team needed a title."[2]

Nordstrom principles incorporate many of the ten traits of versatile leaders. Commitment to family, employees, and customers is one of their most compelling characteristics.

The U.S. Postal Service is an example of a government institution that has been changing its energy level. Many of the newer buildings offer light, modern fixtures, and self-serve options that reduce long lines. Training has improved the way the customer-facing employees deal with the public, transforming a stereotypical dead-end job into one of pride and satisfaction.

It is true that today's business world demands more of us as individual contributors.

Larry McManus, when he was area manager for the western United States for Ericsson, was very candid with me in our interview. He discussed the vast diversity of the Ericsson organization and the importance of individual contributors.

> It is difficult to get something moved through a global organization when you only have 8,000 people in the United States. You have to step into the global box of over 100,000 employees worldwide, and there are many places to go for resources. This year alone I probably dealt with managers of six different countries, spanning Fuji, China, Spain, Italy, Sweden, the United Kingdom, and Ireland, which makes one's network very powerful. And yet at Ericsson you do feel as though you have some leverage as an individual.

The emotionally vested Ten Essential Traits managers answer that demand with enthusiasm, verve, and commitment. Why would they do that? Primarily because of the multitude of returns the investment will bring—not just monetary returns, but recognition, increase in knowledge and skills, and personal gratification. An organization built by The Ten Essential Traits leaders will offer these various types of returns.

Cal James, CEO and president of Kaiser Permanente Company's Permco, was ready to retire and surf when the opportunity came along to lead the organization. Faced with numerous challenges that will unfold throughout the next chapters, James was intrigued by the opportunity.

> The organization was multilayered, and the key was in bringing every part of our group face-to-face with the internal customer. In such a complex organization, it required completely rethinking the way we did business—and doing it fast.

Cal James knew that the only technique that would work would be to create an intermeshed team of networked Ten Essential Traits managers who could reinvent the business and struggle to overcome the bureaucracy that would resist massive change. He threw himself totally into the task, not only during the workweeks, but also by volunteering on the weekends in various community service projects alongside his employees and their families. In this way, Cal James was able to expand his emotional vesting to encompass activities that diminished feelings of isolation and loneliness that may occur as the careers of Ten Essential Traits managers take them away from their families.

For The Ten Essential Traits manager, an emotional investment is an essential part of the ability to complete. This compulsion to excel, coupled with fearlessness, leads to the ability to complete, particularly with projects and visions that seemed impossible.

The David and Goliath story of Southwest Airlines epitomizes the connection between emotional vesting and results. From its conceptual beginning on a cocktail napkin, through intense legal battles to get off the ground, through fierce competition from also-ran airline strategies, to a day-by-day commitment to its vision, Southwest Airlines would not be the best airline to work for in America (according to *Fortune,* January 12, 1998) without its legendary stable of committed employees. CEO Herb Kelleher describes the investment Southwest pilots made during the high jet fuel prices in the early 1990s:

> I wrote a memo to our pilots and said, "Fuel is just going sky high, we've got to cut back." And in one week our costs went down, just like that. Now, let me contrast that with the consultant who wanted to set up an incentive program whereby pilots' pay would be increased to the extent they conserved fuel. Our guys just did it on their own.[3]

This emotional investment and commitment by a leader/manager with The Ten Essential Traits creates a positive and important impression on customers, both internal and external. It is no surprise that Southwest Airlines is famous for its customer service. And its employees feel part of an extended family.

Yamaha Motor Company is an interesting example of how one organization is actively connecting emotional vesting and customer satisfaction.

Yamaha Motor Company, manufacturer of motorcycles, analyzed what differentiated its product from that of its competitors. Dr. Hiroshi Yamagata, director of research at Yamaha, in a joint article with Dr. Ikujiro Nonaka, professor and director of the Institute of Business Research at Hitotsubashi University in Japan, describes the evolution of Yamaha's core competency with respect to motorcycles:

> In 1992 we began a new transformation movement, Yamaha Customer and Community Satisfaction (Yamaha CCS) to reflect our

changing emphasis. . . . CCS means the creation of a space in which both the user's satisfaction and Yamaha's deep dedication are realized. The slogan of the Yamaha CCS movement is "Having Deep Excitement Is My Vocation."[4]

A clearer statement of emotional vesting would be hard to imagine. Yamagata continues:

To create customer excitement for our products we must clarify the knowledge and technology that we will build into Yamaha products. Further, we hope to find deep satisfaction in our work through the process of creating these products. This is a kind of tacit knowledge. When we achieve deep satisfaction with something we are involved in—whether it is work or play—the experience affects us deeply, in a very personal way, often in a way we cannot express. This is tacit knowledge.

Yamagata's description supports the need for The Ten Essential Traits managers in a knowledge economy. Knowledge work, by definition, requires a personal investment.

Teams and Affiliation Needs

The team process of emotional commitment and bonding is an important part of applying The Ten Essential Traits.

Small and family-owned companies embody emotional vesting in many ways. Commercial Lithography is one such family-owned business in Kansas City, Missouri. The Pfeiffer family started the company, and several generations of family members have modernized and updated operations to make it a valued supplier of printing services to a number of companies, not the least of which is Hallmark, another family-held company. Admittedly paternalistic, Commercial Lithography prides itself on the fact that as visitors tour the sophisticated facility equipped with German printing presses, multiple generations of employee families will be introduced as they pass through. As Bill Pfeiffer Jr. said to me during one such tour, "This place has been home for many besides myself and my family. Having people committed to the enterprise, as well as to each other, is key."

However, The Ten Essential Traits are not always the norm in closely held businesses. Often, you will see very rigid hierarchies in family-owned businesses that prevent individual contributions and vesting from others. In addition, the familial relationship to the business does not always guarantee the needed professional management skills.

Ready Pac Produce in Pasadena, California, is one that is succeeding. The business was started by Dennis Gertmenian. His father owned a small vegetable and grocery store in Pasadena. One summer, Dennis worked in the store to give his father a well-earned vacation. A very important customer called Dennis one day and said, "We don't have time to clean and chop the vegetables you sell us. We need you to do it. If you can't, we will have to find another supplier."

Dennis was in a quandary. He knew that his father did not offer that kind of service. He also knew that losing their most important customer would not please his father. So Dennis made a decision. He found an old bathtub and scrubbed it thoroughly. He took a large knife and started chopping, cleaning the vegetables in the tub and then packaging them in plastic bags for delivery. The customer was delighted. Dennis's father was not.

"We don't do that," he said. "If you want to do it, go and set up your own business." That is exactly what Dennis did. Today, Ready Pac Produce is a leader in its industry, having created a market niche that did not exist before—fresh, cleaned, chopped vegetables and salad ready for the table, available for restaurants and food chains as well as the ultimate consumer. The business will exceed $1 billion by the end of this year. As it grew, Dennis Gertmenian recognized that even though he and his early team embodied some of the The Ten Essential Traits, it was difficult to manage without the network approach of leveraging off the skills of others internally and externally. He has brought in managers from larger organizations and considers this an important check and balance on his decision-making and idea-creating processes. Not all of them have been able to adapt to the commitment, fearlessness, and penetration needs (Chapters 2 and 4) of the company. More managers have followed who understand the need to network and create alliances, both with customers and suppliers, and the challenge continues to be maintaining these characteristics while growing both the top and bottom lines.

Many Ten Essential Traits managers within large organizations want to create a family environment. There is a need to ensure that others in the organization share the same passion and commitment. Remember, The Ten Essential Traits managers are very savvy about looking around them. They try to gauge the commitment of others to determine whether the organization is a breeding ground for other Ten Essential Traits managers. Such an environment will evolve into small family units.

The virtual corporation is a business model built on such pseudo-family ties, and the movie industry is another good example of such a structure. Various contributors to the moviemaking process join together for a common purpose—making the movie. Each brings his or her special expertise and passion for quality and creativity. When they disband (commonly known as the *wrap party*), cast and crew often liken it to saying good-bye to members of the family.

The Spider Network (see *FastAlliances: Power Your E-Business*, Wiley, 2001) is a business model showing the interconnectedness of organizations that create alliances in order to be flexible and compete in global markets. People who excel in building those networks are The Ten Essential Traits personalities.

Affiliation needs are high for Ten Essential Traits managers. They require building ties that create a feeling of belonging, along with the feeling of independence and freedom, a challenging combination. Yet that is exactly what the knowledge worker requires, the push-pull of affiliation and flexibility.

Joerg Agin, who ran the Entertainment and Imaging Division of Eastman Kodak, believes that affiliation is often the key to inspiration:

> I have seen it at Kodak, and also in my prior activities at Universal. Part of leadership is having a vision of where you need to go. It has to be credible. You have to communicate it and you have to demonstrate it. If you do that, then you get people excited. People fundamentally want to succeed. They want success. They want to wear a T-shirt with their group on it. They want to belong to something and be praised for achievement. Kodak has had an organization called Imagination Works, which created that kind of feeling. It's important to have an innovative environment. Belonging to something exciting has a very seductive attraction, not just money.

Balancing Work and Personal Life

For some Ten Essential Traits managers, the work affiliation and emotional vesting can encroach on home life. Then work and personal life become out of balance. Although periods of imbalance are normal, when they become a way of life, smart organizations provide opportunities for change. Large law firms, for example, have traditionally offered multimonth sabbaticals to their partners. The hope is that renewal will avoid the burnout that occurs from the hundred-hour workweeks that are normal for that profession. Hewlett-Packard in its early years had corporate policies deliberately directed at this issue. David Packard said, "Situations arise in which people have personal problems that temporarily affect their performance and attitude, and it is important that people in these circumstances be treated with sensitivity and understanding while the problems are being resolved."[5]

Since the pivotal events of September 11, 2001, in the United States, the immediacy of life, its fragility, and the value of meaningful work is even more important. Ten Essential Traits managers need to temper their emotional vesting and commitment to include work, family, and community—and their often delicate interrelationship— as life's priorities change. Thousands of executives, police, emergency workers, and firefighters perished in the criminal attack, and for the first time many young leaders and managers between the ages of 25 and 40 reflected on their own mortality. The average age of those who died that day was 32. Many were Ten Essential Traits leaders in the making, moving into the growth years of their careers. My e-mail newsletter goes to thousands of executives worldwide. The outpouring of support was immediate. Many of the readers are in the same demographic as those who died. This tragedy caused everyone a moment of reevaluation. Commitment was focused on community, family, and work, in that order. This has created a changed reality in many organizations. Ten Essential Traits leaders and managers must be aware of this need and act thoughtfully.

Creating balance is the subject for an entirely different book. However, it is worthy of note that part of being a manager with The Ten Essential Traits (and the accompanying accountability and responsibility) is also finding a way to detach from the work environment in order to recharge and renew.

Valerie Salembier, publisher of *Esquire*, has an unusual way of doing this: She manages a Rotisserie League Baseball Team. Valerie explains, "This is a statistical betting league for those of us who always wanted to own a baseball team but couldn't afford the $400 million to buy one!"

Whatever their avocation, The Ten Essential Traits managers find stimulation and renewal by giving back to the community and by engaging in activities outside the workplace. Management gurus talk about *corporate* renewal all the time, but equally important is the *personal* renewal necessary to keep The Ten Essential Traits managers from burnout.

The Emotionally Nonvested Leader

A leader or manager without passion will be seen as emotionally nonvested in the organization. In my book *Intelligent Business Alliances,* I categorized certain kinds of managerial personalities as fitting into various life-cycle stages of the organization. Those most commonly found in the high-growth stage of a company, which I call the *hockey-stick stage,* are warrior managers. They are also emotionally vested. The managerial personality type generally the least emotionally vested is the *politician,* who is most often found in declining companies. Thus, lack of emotional vesting can be a leading indicator of a company on the road to decline. The Ten Essential Traits managers will not stay long in that environment, since their commitment is integrally related to their ability to vest passion and emotion into opportunities that will reward them in many different ways. The process of corporate turnaround must take into account this critical characteristic.

The Environment for Emotional Vesting

Some shortsighted companies may rationalize a high level of emotional vesting by individuals as an excuse not to be concerned about the organizational environment. If employees love their work, they might say, then the working conditions will not matter. That is a very dangerous rationalization, though it may work in the short term. But as pressures of growth and market changes cause work to be restructured or redefined, the environment and the corporate culture will become a more compelling factor in attracting or retaining people. Lack of attention to a consistent corporate culture is certain to drive away emotionally vested leaders and managers. An organization must make a continued and concerted effort to create an environment that allows emotional vesting to take root and grow.

What is common in highly political and bureaucratic organizations is that the emotional vesting is psychologically beaten out of people. Eventually, they protect themselves emotionally from such hurt by not giving their all to making success happen, individually or organizationally.

Trident Data Systems is an entrepreneurial company in California that develops software and solutions for the security industry (some of the applications are classified) throughout the Americas. Company founder Fred Lukas is a man with deeply held beliefs about the need to understand and serve customers, but, just as important, about the need to make a work environment where Ten Essential Traits managers thrive. He said it this way:

> Growing this company is all about valuing people's careers—not just creating jobs, but rather a place where people can invest themselves and not only give the company their best, but also get the best out of their jobs.

Nurturing an environment that keeps emotional vesting high is a challenge for highly technical and research-oriented organizations, where the staff inherently loves their work. DuPont, creators of nylon and Lycra, could have easily locked away its 3,500+ R&D professionals in its Experimental Station in Wilmington, Delaware. As Dr. Joseph Miller, chief technology officer and senior vice president, Research and Development, explains, "Our people insist that it is their work rather than their environment that satisfies and motivates them."[6] In turn, DuPont provides them the freedom to control their own work and the encouragement to provide individual contributions to the larger organization ($40 billion plus in sales) through their discoveries.

Fun and Emotional Vesting

One important way that organizations can foster emotional vesting is through fun. Trident Data's human resource director, Krista Carlson, explains the importance of fun. "If you don't have fun while you're on the job here, then maybe you should find a position where you will have fun. We think that the whole idea of enjoying yourself at work is essential—that means being really committed."

Emotionally vested employees add real passion and quality to the work product and customer orientation at Trident Data Systems because they consider their work to be fun. Clearly, when something is fun, you can hardly wait to get back to it each day. Productivity soars, and so does creativity.

Valerie Salembier, publisher of *Esquire*, was clear in her vision for this characteristic:

> The *Esquire* staff is incredibly committed to what we are doing, but it's also fun. We've created a work environment where there is a whole lot of laughing going on. There are so many ups and downs every single day, it is like a big roller coaster ride. As such, one needs to make sure that the people on the team are enjoying what they do so that they can leave at the end of the day happy. All of us believe passionately in this magazine—and because of that, we can create the best product and do the right thing for the customer.

Per Olof Loof, senior vice president of The Financial Solutions Group for NCR Corporation agrees:

> It is so important that you enjoy what you are doing, that you enjoy your interaction with your customers and the interaction with the people around you. It's essential that you create a diverse team of people that actually like to be together.

Arie de Geus, learning theorist and former coordinator for Group Planning at Royal Dutch Shell, said it well:

> Fun in an organizational context is a necessary prerequisite for learning, particularly the type of strategic learning that is the source of an organization's competitive advantage.[7]

Emotional vesting increases proportionally with the opportunity for creative expression and independent thinking and development. Creativity is really a tool for realizing the passion that The Ten Essential Traits managers feel. They will be depleted and eventually leave organizations where creativity and affiliation is a low priority (see the quality of *energy*, Chapter 9).

Office Design and Emotional Vesting

The Ten Essential Traits managers are expected to be emotionally vested in activities, not in the territoriality of the placement, design, or size of an office. Interestingly, this goes against the anthropological history of humankind, which is fundamentally territorial. However, emotional vesting is shifting from the physical to the intellectual—a natural evolution in the knowledge economy.

New terms have now entered the vocabulary for these office designs. *Free-range teaming* is the term used to describe "the freedom of movement and expression in open space that supports a collaborative work culture."[8] Another term is *hot-desking,* a technique used at Ericsson in all their locations worldwide. It means that space is claimed on a first-come, first-served basis. Employees arrive at the office, select from available wired workstations, plug in, and log on. At Ericsson, conference rooms have two uses: for meetings and as a quiet place where people can work without interruption (a common issue with hot-desking). Cisco uses the hot-desking method, too. *Hoteling* is another method common to Cap Gemini and Ernst & Young. Employees book reservations for office space with a company concierge who then assigns the employee to a workplace, switches the phone lines, places the employee's personal belongings there, and adds a nameplate to the door. Space can be reserved by the day or the hour—a kind of instant office. This is the trend, and for some Ten Essential Traits managers the adjustment will take time, certainly for the post–World War II baby boomers. It can, however, be quite liberating and create a clearer focus for commitment and emotional vesting—in the work activity rather than in the office size, position, or furnishings!

Centralization versus Decentralization

Organizational structure can have a tremendous impact on emotional vesting. A decision that all organizations in the developed world are now wrestling with is whether to centralize or decentralize. Although the trend in the early part of this decade has been toward decentralization, along with that goes the push-pull of a trend toward the integrative rather than the dominant. This means that organizations are pushing The Ten Essential Traits into the field, but still want a unified theme, corporate strategy, and belief system to permeate and interconnect the entire organization. Never before has emotional vesting been more critical. There is no longer central headquarters' dominance. Many organizations are mixing product groups and geographic regional divisions in a matrix reporting system where commitment and enthusiasm has to come from the middle down and the bottom up, while vision, overall corporate image, and brand positioning come from the top down.

ABB has been a global leader in the decentralized, think-global-act-local trend for the past decade or more.[9] Every division of the organization considers itself at the center of the universe. This mentality will help build a place for The Ten Essential Traits managers to thrive, as they commit themselves to the goals of the division rather than the intangibles of the headquarters.

NCR has reorganized along these lines. Per Olof Loof reflects on some of NCR's challenges in the recent past:

> During our history of 114 years, the country manager has managed each country. They have basically ruled that domain. They started products and ended products and did deals or not, depending on how they felt they could best serve that country. Now, in today's world, that is not a sustainable model, because the investments you need to make in product, software, and people are way too big for even the largest country. So we took away that structure. It was a decision that the senior management team developed with a lot of help from the NCR board. All the country managers from one day to the next went away. And we had no transition time. The trick was how to do that, since the country managers were good people, but we had to make the change, we had to convince a country manager to cut his area of responsibility, sometimes to 30 percent of what it had been. It was very difficult. We have to explain what we were trying to achieve. The explanation was this: If I am a customer of NCR and I talk to my sales representative, I want to be sure that all the 38,000 people at NCR are right behind this individual. And I want my problems solved quickly. We had two days before we went live with this announcement. Each member of the senior management team, the five division heads, had a list. We talked to every country manager and said this is the change that will happen in two days. We will not cut your salary; here are some

of the good things and here are some of the difficult ones. There are some people who did not want to work within the new organizational model, and they have left. But there really has not been a huge exodus of people. It is really working now.

What NCR has done is to ask for a commitment from its country managers. The honesty and speed with which information was relayed showed that NCR was committed to its leaders and to finding solutions. Now it was asking for the same consideration. In turn-around situations, it is imperative for organizations to gain buy-in immediately and to discover who still has an emotional investment in the future of the organization.

There is no doubt that quality of commitment and emotional vesting will be sorely tested at NCR and that continually rewarding The Ten Essential Traits will increase the company's competitiveness and ability to attract and retain quality people. As Lars Nyberg, NCR's CEO, said,

> It is absolutely crucial that we get a culture in this company where people feel motivated, where they are challenged, where they can grow and where they are reasonably well rewarded and therefore feel confident working at NCR and will opt to stay. Without those kinds of people, we will never make it.

One of the trends futurists have been predicting for the early 2000s is the increasing importance of small communities, both real and perceived. This goes along with the decentralization trend and reinforces the affiliation need of The Ten Essential Traits managers discussed earlier in the chapter.

The enormous success of Starbucks is evidence of the small-community trend. In the long-standing tradition of the European coffeehouse, Starbucks has created a place where people can hang out, be recognized by the employees, and have their coffee preferences called out even before they acknowledge that is what they are there for! Employees are trained to create "the Starbucks experience," not just a perfect cup of coffee. The perception is that the customer matters—the barrista knows him or her by name and coffee preference. The result is a visit frequency for the Starbucks buyer *averaging 23 times per month*—and closer to 29 for its high-use customers. What retailer wouldn't yearn for those kinds of numbers!

In the first benchmarking study on sales and marketing alliances, in which I was selected as the subject-matter expert through the American Productivity and Quality Center (APQC) in Houston, I chose Starbucks as one of the companies worthy of study.[10] Its alliances with companies such as Barnes & Noble, Host Marriott, United Airlines, and others are based on the expectation that its partners understand and buy into the Starbucks culture, its belief system vis-à-vis the customer, and its perception of service. Starbucks is discussed again in Chapter 11, about perception.

The small-community idea, however, is key to the company's successful business model and is trend-appropriate for the times. The Ten Essential Traits approach is also part of their model—pushing initiative (and rewarding it!) into the hands of those who have direct contact with the customer at the store level. As the environmental characteristic, Starbucks' excellent benefits package attracts a workforce that has more loyalty than those normally found in the fast-food, restaurant, and beverage industry. As a result, employees are more emotionally vested in the organization, and they value the flexibility that the high-growth company offers.

Encouraging Individual Contributions

Encouraging individual contributions means listening to those with ideas and stimulating and rewarding the energy of creativity. In countries where the culture supports a group rather than an individual belief system, the individual will align with the group, so that small groups serve the same function as individuals in exhibiting this characteristic. This environment is closely related to two other characteristics: *energy* and *sense of urgency* (Chapter 9).

All of The Ten Essential Traits can exist in some parts of the organization and not in others. The Ten Essential Traits are at their best when they infiltrate up and laterally from multiple points within the organization rather than being implemented as companywide initiatives from above.

General Motors

What is beginning to happen at GM is extremely hopeful.[11] After more than three decades of decline, General Motors still holds the record of being the world's largest company. It is difficult to both effect and measure change in an organization of that size (over 600,000 employees, larger than the governments of some countries).

The organization has restructured to become a company that designs, assembles, and markets cars and light trucks but makes few of the parts. The sought-after result is to change the corporate culture. This will mean that, instead of being a company of warring tribes (a phrase often used to describe Motorola in the late 1980s and early 1990s), in which divisions are pitted in battles against each other (sometimes for the same customer, other times for corporate resources), GM will expect a spirit of collaboration between divisions. Marketing managers will be expected to cooperate to avoid duplication of effort.

In order to overcome a legacy of emotionally nonvested middle managers and poor labor relations, change has to be biological. It must come from the very core of the organization. How can this happen?

The beginning is already in place.

GM boasts a highly productive and efficient subsidiary in Brazil that has created flexible and mutually rewarding relationships with its suppliers—alliances that share risks among vendors and purchasers alike.[12]

The Brazilian subsidiary, however, has discovered and nurtured the hidden weapon, the very purpose of one of The Ten Essential Traits: It has a workforce that is *emotionally vested.* Imagination and individual contributions are welcomed into the small work groups and supplier committees that ally with each other so that cost savings and ideas are shared, learning is disseminated, and middle managers and others feel as if their contributions *are* making a difference. And indeed they are.

Can GM integrate the success of The Ten Essential Traits from its Brazil operation into its worldwide operations? It depends on the NIH factor—namely, how territorial is each group? How intense is the cross-divisional rivalry? How deeply will it resist the "not invented, manufactured, or thought of here" syndrome, which is often one of the largest elephants in the room? And how will fearlessness play out across geographies and product groups? Will failure be permitted? Will learning be transferred? GM doesn't need another major consultant-driven initiative. Using the evidence that is flowing out of Brazil, the company has the starting point defined, but The Ten Essential Traits require a commitment to continual improvement—for individuals as well as for organizational environments.

Another part of GM is the E-GM activity. When it was created in the early days of the Internet boom, the expectation was that the e-business, fast-time-to-market culture and customer-centric approach of this division would ultimately transform the entire organization. E-GM hired and nurtured The Ten Essential Traits managers and hoped that their success and influence would work to transmute others into the responsive, technologically savvy culture that permeated the group that developed OnStar well in advance of many other automakers and marked their territory in the e-economy. Although the Internet bust may have de-emphasized this strategy, there is no question that GM has integrated its online strategy into online supplier and customer management.

Hewlett-Packard

Hewlett-Packard has embodied the philosophy of commitment and emotional vesting and the value of individual contributions since its inception. As early as 1938, the company instituted a profit-sharing plan, which paid everyone a bonus as a percentage of their base pay. As David Packard put it, "We wanted to recognize the contributions of each individual, not just a special group." Even though future profit-sharing plans took different forms at the company, David Packard and Bill Hewlett were determined that the philosophy be sustained. "To this day," according to David Packard, "Hewlett-Packard has a profit-sharing program that encourages teamwork and maintains that important link between employee effort and corporate success."

This desire for emotional vesting started at the most senior management levels at Hewlett-Packard. David Packard said it clearly:

> A high degree of enthusiasm should be encouraged at all levels; in particular, the people in high management positions must not only be enthusiastic themselves, they must be able to engender enthusiasm among their associates. There can be no place for half-hearted interest or halfhearted effort. Bill Hewlett and I have had a strong belief in people. We believe that people want to do a good job and that it is important for them to enjoy their work at

Hewlett-Packard. Closely coupled with this is our strong belief that individuals be treated with consideration and respect and that their achievements be recognized . . . to create an environment in which people have a chance to be their best, to realize their potential, and to be recognized for their achievements.

David Packard shares a personal story of emotional vesting within the company:

I was walking around the machine shop accompanied by the shop's manager. We stopped briefly to watch a machinist making a polished plastic mold die. He had spent a long time polishing it and was taking a final cut at it. Without thinking, I reached down and wiped it with my finger. The machinist said, "Get your finger off my die!" The manager quickly asked him, "Do you know who this is?" To which the machinist replied, "I don't care!" He was right and I told him so. He had an important job and was proud of his work.

Hewlett-Packard has pioneered many employee benefits. One of them is flextime. As early as 1967, the organization instituted a policy that says that an individual may come to work early or stay late as long as they work the expected number of hours. As David Packard says,

Flextime is the essence of respect for and trust in people. It says that we both appreciate that our people have busy personal lives and that we trust them to devise, with their supervisor and work group, a schedule that is personally convenient yet fair to others. Tolerance of the differing needs of individuals is an element of the HP way.[13]

After early evidence of competency in The Ten Essential Traits, Hewlett-Packard lost its way, then reinvented itself to recover its former glory (an ongoing challenge). Lew Platt recognized that the elephant in the room was creeping inertia and lack of tight communication and integration with the new market realities. He saw that the job required not just a good elephant spotter (he could do that), but someone who would actively move the elephants out and bring valuable change into the organization. Platt set the stage through the bifurcation of the organization into two companies. Then he appointed a committed Ten Essential Traits leader, Carly Fiorina, as

CEO to re-create emotional vesting and develop the flexibility and customer orientation that will maintain and grow HP's position as an integral part of the Internet-speed world. Fiorina's initial presence in almost every potential market that could be of interest to Hewlett-Packard (an almost Gatesian empire-building focus) has meant that the company is now competing aggressively in every market where its products are sold. The metamorphosis has happened mainly from within. Fiorina has morphed the dormant Ten Essential Traits managers into energetic examples of what HP could be. Can they deliver on her promise? The answer is not clear.

Fiorina's gutsy move in making an acquisition bid for Compaq has been challenged by the family foundations and shareholder representatives as not being "the HP way."

In an article for a recent e-mail newsletter sent to thousands of executives, I wrote a fantasy letter to the children of Mr. Hewlett and Mr. Packard, as follows:[14]

Dear Hewlett and Packard Heirs:

I know how painful it is to lose a powerful father. I did. I also know that preserving his memory is critically important, and a part of the mourning process. So how do children preserve a parent in perpetuity? By refusing to recognize the parent has passed on. Unfortunately, you and your siblings are fighting a war of biblical proportions in the futile and destructive hope of preserving the Bill and David Way. This is no longer the HP Way. The market has changed, the business has changed, the survival of this company is challenged—and it is time for your beloved fathers to pass on. Hanging on to the past with the rationalization that this is good business practice is but a rationalization of loving children who are not ready to say a final farewell to their beloved parents. The problem is that hundreds of thousands of jobs and families are dependent on the right decision being made. So the grief of the few, just your two families and your pain and reluctance to accept the passing of your fathers, as well as the way they ran their business, is putting on the altar of sacrifice the well-being of the many—the employees and dependents of both HP and Compaq. The rationale is that the integration will obfuscate and confuse management of the combined companies, deflecting their attention from market issues. But management has been quite explicit about their aggressive integration plans, many of which have been months in the development. Another rationale is that Compaq would drag HP deeper into the consumer PC business. This also is not supported by either Compaq's stated strategy or HP's future goals.

This hurts, I know, especially when motivated by the deep emotional desire of a child not to say goodbye to a strong, dominant, and always present father—who is personified in the company that continues to hold his name.

It is time, children, to say a sad farewell. Put the emotional ties into the family context; take them out of the business environment where they have no place. Let HP go forward, not backward. Survival of both companies could be at stake—as are the lives of hundreds of thousands of their employees and suppliers. These interests are the very ones that your fathers stood for—you would do them proud by supporting this deal.

With respect (I might even be doing the same thing if this were my father),

Larraine Segil

Making change happen (whether at HP, Compaq, or your organization) is going to require the emotional commitment to do difficult, often painful things. Not everyone will be happy with the moves made, or even with the short-term results. But the long-term cultural change with deep commitment can be made—staying the course.

Much of the success of these ideas for all organizations, however, will depend on the management processes in place to allow for individual contributions, creativity, and decentralization.

Management Processes

If your organization scores low on The Ten Essential Traits, the following management processes will help, especially if your employees are scoring higher than the organization.

Small Work Groups: Meetings

In small work groups, individual contributions are more easily recognized and rewarded. The challenge, however, lies in the greatest destroyer of corporate productivity—the meeting. More hours are wasted and initiative dulled by this process than any other corporate activity. Another result of certain kinds of meetings, certainly the interminable kind, is the diminishment of emotional vesting.

In the *show-and-tell meeting*, affiliation will blossom along with emotional vesting. Some of the other meeting models described here have the effect of "dumbing down" to a common denominator, which means diminished innovation because of decisions by committees that pander to the average. Conversely, the small work group model seen in show-and-tell is an offensive tactic to combat meeting inertia. Many organizations misunderstand meeting strategies. Most meeting models are good at informing. The show-and-tell model is good at doing. Managers and team leaders should strive to conduct Show-and-Tell meetings whenever possible.

Show Time

Here the goal is informing and selling a concept or series of activities—a showcase of sorts. The audience is generally large. This means that members are there to be sure they are not left out, and after a fairly short period of time, their need to be there diminishes. Sometimes this kind of meeting is a way for senior management to give inspirational messages, a kind of rally, and part fun as well as part serious information.

Show Up

This is the meeting where people show up in order to be seen to be in the loop of information sharing, but really have little to contribute beyond being able to say the constituency they represent has been informed. Often a huge waste of time, but politically valuable.

Showdown

This is a smaller meeting and for the purpose of real decision making, although most of the decisions will have been made prior to the meeting via internal lobbying and co-option.

Show Off

This is for the manager who wants to show off or highlight the performance of one group to other groups. It is generally not very long and, in order to have impact, should be well planned. If not, it will create derision rather than admiration.

Show-and-Tell

This is the real workhorse. It is a place where learning is transferred. The ego of the members is not an issue, and the genuine work is created, delegated, and executed. The processes include analysis, planning, execution, and correction. Teamwork is valued, as is value creation for the enterprise and for the group and its activity. The agenda will be defined by the group members, and small working teams (sometimes no more than two) will move forward with energy.

Composition of the Work Group

The composition of the work group should include a variety of skills and approaches in order to develop *creative tensions*.[15] This is a mix between comfort-reinforcing stability and conflicting challenge. Research has found that the average time that a group has worked together significantly impacts its technical productivity.[16] The long-term stable technical group apparently becomes too self-secure, diminishes outside technical contacts, and decreases its performance. Thus, changing the work group composition may be constructive. However, a caveat exists where the overarching culture values the group over the individual. In Japan, for example, the sense of harmony, or *wa*, is key to group dynamics, and confrontation is destructive of *wa*. Changing the group dynamics too often could upset the sense of *wa* in group-oriented cultures to the point that it becomes counterproductive.

Flexible Work Behaviors and Culture

One of the greatest gifts an organization committed to The Ten Essential Traits model can give to their Ten Essential Traits managers is *flexibility*. Freedom to express their emotional vesting on their own time and in their own way is essential. Hewlett-Packard has one of the lowest turnover rates in the dynamic high-tech industry, only 5 percent in 1997,[17] even though former CEO Lewis Platt confessed to HP employees, "I can't offer an easy job. Jobs are not easy here. I can't offer short hours. The hours are not short here. But I can offer a lot of flexibility." Tremendous flexibility in work hours helped combat what Platt referred to as "invisible burnout," where employees show up physically but not mentally. The early excitement of the Carly days enabled The Ten Essential Traits managers to recommit themselves to the corporate mantra, and long hours became the norm, not the exception. After the struggles with the shareholders regarding the Compaq acquisition, with Fiorina's job in jeopardy, even Ten Essential Traits managers are laying low. Nevertheless, it is indisputable that over the past decade, with the advent of advanced communications technologies, flexible work environments in many organizations have become more common.

The work behaviors of individuals vary greatly depending on their formal education. Another key factor is their cultural background and life experience. The differences are easy to see when people of different cultures work together.[18]

Power and hierarchy, for example, are viewed differently in India, which has a more hierarchical culture. That means employees feel comfortable with the antithesis of The Ten Essential Traits model— namely, being given explicit instructions on expected behavior. In the United States in many organizations, explicit directives that expect obedient behaviors are not common, because the U.S. perspective on power and hierarchy is more egalitarian, leaning toward participative and collaborative management styles.

Time has a vastly different meaning for those in Germanic versus Latin American cultures. Those with German or Swiss backgrounds are more likely to consider the start time for a meeting to be the one stated, so being late would be offensive. Those from Mexico or Saudi Arabia may consider the relationship aspect of the meeting to be far more important than the time set for commencement, so being late is not insulting. In China, however, attendees will most probably arrive early, since being on time is often considered to be almost late!

One must be careful of creating stereotypical expectations, because many subcultures exist within the dominant culture. Nevertheless, common characteristics can be described for most cultures. An example of a subculture in the United States is the Native American culture. The dominant culture of the United States considers that we generally have control over our environments and so can have quantitative as well as qualitative expectations of people and events. This may lead to conflict, which would then require resolution. In some circumstances in the United States, conflict is even considered to be a healthy way to "get it all on the table." In Native American cultures, however, the general belief system is based on a concept of harmony, and conflict is to be avoided and ameliorated. Of course, many country cultures hold this as their dominant belief system (e.g., Japan, Thailand).

Overall, an elephant that commonly enters the room in cross-cultural situations is the lack of true understanding and allowances for the values of the cultures of all parties. Spotting the elephant is one thing, making those allowances and changes is quite another. There are many books, courses, and now, thankfully, executives who have experienced living in multiple cultures and who are adept at making this happen effectively. The Ten Essential Traits managers would do well to expand their horizons to become culturally sophisticated and knowledgeable. It's a matter of becoming educated about and experiencing that which is different from your own way of doing things.

Communication is an important issue for The Ten Essential Traits leaders—and never more important than across different cultures. Some cultures communicate directly and verbally (United States and Canada), whereas others prefer indirect and nonverbal approaches (Japan). When a work group includes people of different beliefs regarding communication (and different styles, tones, and body language), misunderstandings are rife.

The Ten Essential Traits model requires flexible work behavior. That includes learning the ways of other cultures and understanding that information must be communicated using a variety of vehicles—verbal, nonverbal, situational, deductive, indirect, and direct. Sometimes passive behavior speaks as loudly as action.

Since multiculturalism is a way of life in North America, it is likely that some of these cultural elements (and many more) will be reflected in the work behaviors of small work groups and teams and will therefore impact directly the effectiveness of The Ten Essential Traits managers and their characteristics of commitment and emotional vesting. People of different cultures will manifest these characteristics differently. Some will be vested as they relate to the group rather than as an individual. Work behaviors in countries that reward groups rather than individuals can nevertheless be included in the The Ten Essential Traits analysis.

Dominique Gaurdie, CFO of Shell Oil and also of the Planning, Finance and Investment Services Group of Shell came to Shell Oil from Royal Dutch Shell. He has lived the culture challenge, having been born in France and worked in Norway and Scandinavia. In fact, continues to be multicultural. Gaurdie offers the following observations:

> Let's take two values, trust and doubt. My experience in the United States is that you would tend first to trust and doubt afterwards. In Europe, at least in my own experience, you doubt everything from day one. It takes years to build some sort of trust. The second thing in the United States is that if you have a problem, you will always find somebody telling you, "I will fix it for you." There is an obsession to fix problems. In Europe, if you have a problem, and you come to me saying you have a problem, I will probably say, "Yes, I hear what you say. You have problems, but I also have problems. So you are better to deal with your problems and I will deal with mine." So that's a very different way of doing business.

You can see the potential danger explained in the preceding quote. Without an understanding of the European culture, Gaurdie may be seen by a U.S. Ten Essential Traits company as not emotionally vested because he expresses doubt before jumping on the bandwagon. Or he might be labeled as a nonsupporter because he doesn't rush to help solve others' problems.

Gaurdie suggests that flexibility is key to understanding in cross-cultural encounters:

> It is always very important when you come to a new country or new business environment to try to understand how it works and operates. It would be very presumptuous to say that since I am coming to Shell Oil that 20,000 employees should adapt to me. I must understand how this organization works and hopefully bring my own experience as my value-added contribution. My first job here is to learn and understand. Then to give input from my own experience. There is no question that it's a challenge being French in a Dutch company working in a U.S. environment—it takes a bit of energy at times to be heard!

Indeed it does! And all of Dominique Gaurdie's considerable skills and those of his colleagues in Shell Oil work well together as they take the organization into a new era of governance using The Ten Essential Traits model.

The Ten Essential Traits Work Behavior Models

For flexible work behaviors to succeed and thus foster emotional vesting, organizations must recognize that work behaviors come in many different forms, all of which can be successful for The Ten Essential Traits managers. In other words, there is not only one way to work in order to successfully apply The Ten Essential Traits. We offer three work behavior models: *back-end load, front-end load,* and *long-distance runner.*

The Back-End Load

In the model shown in Figure 4.2, even though goals are understood in the beginning, the implementation of work begins only at the eleventh hour. This means that the tasks involved will probably require a high level of intensity, overtime, huge adrenaline flow, and high stress in order to produce a quality result on time. This can be extremely aggravating to those with different work patterns and can impact the schedules of support staff who handle the service needs of this behavior, but for some, this is the most effective way to be creative and productive.

Here's an allegory: Two executives have to travel on the same day at the same time. One arrives at the airport an hour before, goes through interminable security checks, and checks in, sitting calmly waiting for the flight. The other arrives late, is delayed by security, and arrives at the gate at the last moment, leaping over the widening

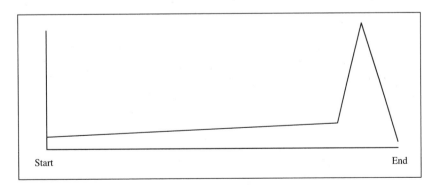

Figure 4.2   Back-End Load

gap between access ramp and airplane, barely making the flight. Both arrive at their destination at the same time. Who is right? You might argue that the late executive left no time for unexpected contingencies. Or that the other executive wasted valuable time sitting at the airport. Who is wrong?

This kind of behavior is exposed to risk in the event of the unusual, which, because of the short time for execution, could impact the ability to complete. In addition, where other team members fall predominantly into the other two work behavior styles, there will have to be an educational process regarding team member contributions, both substantively and timewise. For example, early team or work group discussions would include time management of team member contributions, leaving certain activities for the end. This could make some team members nervous if this is their first experience of working with a back-end loader, but as soon as the back-end loader proves capable of delivering quality in time, his or her behavior will be accepted. The alignment of group expectations is essential. Otherwise, some will consider the back-end loader to be a freeloader!

The Front-End Load

Another kind of work behavior is the front-end load, depicted in Figure 4.3.

Here the individual will start with tremendous enthusiasm and effort and achieve a great deal in the early days of the activity. Over time, this effort wanes, and as the work nears completion, it tapers off drastically. This results in a multitasking situation. Whereas the

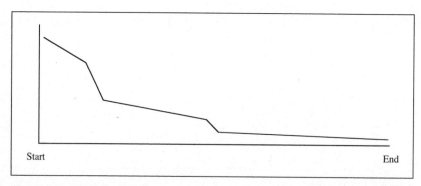

Start   End

Figure 4.3   Front-End Load

back-end model goes from one crisis scenario to another, the front-end loader starts off with a bang only to lose enthusiasm over time. In the multiple-activity scenarios, the front-end loader tends to feel overwhelmed. If there are many priorities, the ability to complete will depend on a high level of organization at the start of projects to plan the workload accordingly.

The Long-Distance Runner

The long-distance runner is the most even-paced of work behaviors, as shown in Figure 4.4.

With work spaced out equally over time, the long-distance runner is predictable and will easily work in organizations that require PERT charting and milestone development (most commonly, aerospace and pharmaceutical development). One danger inherent in this mode of work: Because the long-distance runners are clearly visible throughout the project, there is a temptation to load them up with extra tasks, the reason being that at any one point along the project timeline, they have the clearest view both backward and forward.

The Ten Essential Traits managers will struggle with this characteristic when the work behavior of a colleague does not mirror theirs. Yet the end result may well be the same, and for some, the behavior described allows them to contribute their best. It may even be a worthwhile exercise to ask team members in an initial meeting to choose which work behavior model they find most comfortable, then plan workloads accordingly. Often, the elephant in the room will be this difference in work style, which at the end of the project may fade

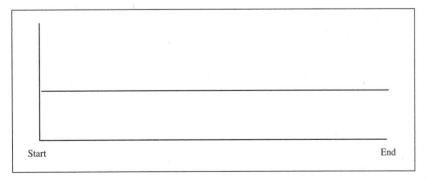

Figure 4.4 Long-Distance Runner

away if the results are satisfactory. If, however, the work style difference is the reason for failure, the elephant should be identified and
discussed so that consensus on work style can be developed to
replace him.

Trying to change work behavior can be effective in organizations
where training is offered in the initial stages of new employee orientation. The Ritz Carlton Hotel Company very effectively trains
employees in its philosophy that all of them are "Ladies and Gentlemen Serving Ladies and Gentlemen," whether they are serving external or internal customers. Chapter 11 focuses on the service
orientation of the Ritz Carlton organization.

As a supplier of consulting services to the Ritz Carlton Hotel
Company, I was required to go through its new employee training and
orientation. The experience was essential to learn the culture and
belief systems, as well as expected work behaviors. One such behavior is that, when a customer has a problem, the employee to whom he
or she communicates that problem owns it until it is resolved. If a
customer is walking down the hall of the hotel and says to a maid, "I
have not yet received my luggage [room service, FedEx, etc.]," it then
becomes the responsibility of that maid to communicate the problem
to the correct resource and follow up until it is resolved. Of course,
this may be difficult to manage, because the normal responsibilities
of the maid continue, but taking ownership is part of the Ritz Carlton
culture. You can see it in the way employees, when responding to a
question such as "Where is the restaurant [health club, pool etc.]?"
will lead the guest there, not direct them.

These work behaviors mean that the entire organization is working in tandem to deliver a coordinated, consistent message and that
The Ten Essential Traits managers are empowered to take actions
that depend on team response, but are self-directed in accordance
with expected outcomes.

In organizations that aspire to incorporate The Ten Essential
Traits, there is a delicate balance between training employees to
behave in culturally acceptable ways and maintaining the freedom of
The Ten Essential Traits managers to interpret, adapt, and execute in
individual and creative ways.

A key skill that is rarely taught, however, is the ability to recognize
and manage different work behaviors without placing value judg-

ments on them. Remember from Chapter 3 that organizations committed to The Ten Essential Traits concept allow process freedom. The final evaluation depends on the results. Was the process contributive rather than disruptive (which is one of the risks run by frontload work behavior)? The Ten Essential Traits managers grow and improve this capability over time. It will become even more important as the number of Generation Xers and Yers increase in the workplace.

Those who are not Ten Essential Traits managers will have difficulty managing the variables caused by different work behaviors. This will impact the completion quality as well as the quality called *energy* (Chapter 9). Energy decreases when high performers are forced into work processes that stifle their creativity. If they are unable to perform at optimum productivity using their own work behaviors, this could be a good indication of the need for work behavior change. At this point, it is appropriate for leaders with The Ten Essential Traits to recommend training.

Commitment and emotional vesting imply a commitment from both the individual (who must be ready to give more than the explicit job function requires) and the organization (which must be willing to allow that personal investment to flourish).

Commitment: Action Items

Commitment and emotional vesting are characteristics that can be developed internally and nurtured by the organization. Here are some strategies for doing so.

To Develop Emotional Vesting in Yourself

- Conduct an audit of your emotional investment.

    Where does your investment lie—in the organization as a whole, in your division, in your team, in your project?

    What is the degree of that investment—high, medium, low?

    What affects your level of emotional vesting?

- Make two lists: What things in your *personal* life are you passionate about? What things in your *professional* life are you passionate about? Consider integrating and cross-pollinating items on these two lists.

- Get involved in projects (even if they are not part of your assignment) that you feel passionately about.

- To assess the balance between your work and personal life, log the hours and general activities devoted to each for two weeks. Find three areas where you could improve this balance for yourself; then do it as a group activity for your team.

- Has your value system regarding work and family/community life changed in the last 12 months? If so, list the changes you have made to implement the value decisions—for work, family, and community.

To Enable Commitment and Emotional Vesting in Others

- Analyze the size of normal working units for your organization. If they include more than five people, can they be divided into smaller groups to create more intense emotional vesting?

- Create an atmosphere where fun and individuality can flourish. This might involve workspace decor, music in the workplace, spontaneous rubber band fights, surprise outings with the team, and so forth.

- Assess the kinds of meetings your organization holds (see "Small Work Groups: Meetings" subhead earlier in the chapter).

    Are the roles of each of the meeting participants defined? Are expectations for each participant verbalized?

    In meetings, does the first statement define the goal of the meeting? Does the last statement review what was achieved and suggest next steps?

- Recognize individual contributions, particularly in new ways.

- Talk to and communicate with your employees about meaningful work. Find out what holds meaning for them individually and collectively. Communicate these insights among the employee community.

- Examine the organizational structure. Is it changing? Is it centralized or decentralized? Have you adjusted the role of your group accordingly? Have these changes been communicated?

- Train for cultural differences.

CHAPTER

5

Inspiration:
The Ability to Motivate

If you try too hard to improve your failure rate,
you become afraid of your inbox, terrified by the
proposals made by authors and their agents.
You end up having either no output or a book
that is so bland that no one will want to read it.
Discovering J. K. Rowling has reminded me of
the sheer fun of knowing long before anyone else
that you have something that will change the
world.

—Nigel Newton, chairman and CEO,
Bloomsbury Publishing PLC, London, England,
publisher of The Harry Potter Series[1]

ndependent publishers generally have a difficult time successfully competing with the market share and distribution power of the giants. However, Harry Potter's success has been so huge that Bloomsbury Publishing PLC has succeeded where others have failed. Newton's inspiration in taking unknown authors and his ability to attract and inspire key editors who are not only willing to take risks, but are entrepreneurial as well, has meant that this independent publisher is making its presence felt globally. (See Figure 5.1.)

Inspired Leadership

Valerie Salembier, publisher of *Esquire* magazine, has been an inspired leader from her earliest beginnings. When the late Katherine Graham (former chairman and CEO of the *Washington Post*) one

Personal Characteristic	Organizational Environment Needed	Example of a Management Process for Implementation
1. *Fearlessness*	Permits failure	Shared learning and shared power
2. *Completion:* Ability to complete; has patience and is flexible	Results-oriented with process freedom	Horizontal, project-oriented management processes with cross-functional and multi-locational teams
3. *Commitment:* Emotionally vested	Encourages individual contributions	Small work groups and flexible work behavior; fun
4. *Inspiration:* Inspires and communicates vision; motivates	Access to internal and external people networks	Constant visibility and accessibility

Figure 5.1   The Ten Essential Traits: The Larraine Segil Matrix

day asked the president of *Newsweek* why there were no female salespeople, Salembier suddenly found herself moved from receptionist to *Newsweek*'s first female salesperson. Thus began an illustrious career. Salembier moved on to become advertising director of *Ms.* magazine, then senior vice president of advertising for *USA Today,* eventually taking the helm of *TV Guide,* the *New York Post, Family Circle,* and *Quest.* Not least, she served as vice president of advertising for the *New York Times.* Salembier shared some of her perspectives with me:

> In the earlier part of my career, I micromanaged, because I am a control freak. Now that's a hard thing to admit. I have had to force myself throughout the years to stop doing that . . . if you hire good people, you are hiring them for a reason. The reason is because you trust their integrity and vision and their creative spirit and their willingness to get the job done. You have to be the inspiration and the cheerleader.

Cathleen Black, president of Hearst Magazines and Salembier's boss, added the following in our one-on-one interview:

> I have to be clear in my sense of expectations. I am president of the division, there are 16-plus magazines in the family, and the publishers of each magazine, like Valerie, are all looking to me for

guidance and direction. But they don't need me looking over their shoulders every day. It is the role of the top executive to raise the bar so that everybody really is producing and knows that you are inspiring them to be even more than they thought they could be.

"Pushing the envelope" is a recurring theme suggested by many Ten Essential Traits managers who are able to see the elephant in the room. Becoming an elephant spotter and then replacing the elephant with value is the outcome of having an abundance of The Ten Essential Traits characteristics. This ability can be observed in many of those people who wish to rise to positions of leadership in their organizations. Organizations that offer freedom for The Ten Essential Traits managers to apply their philosophies will beckon them. Valerie Salembier was enticed by *Esquire* and could not resist:

> This magazine is an American icon. It is 66 years old and deserves a place not only in past history but in the future. That means that our editor, David Grainger, and I have to work very well together. We both report to Cathleen Black and are very dependent on each other for many things. This means that we have to inspire each other in many ways.

Cathleen Black applies her style of penetration, being "of the people," to the inspirational role that she sees herself playing:

> I have always felt very comfortable in saying to whomever I reported to, "Let's get together at the end of the week and spend an hour together." And I had a list of things that I wanted to talk about, and we spent the time. It's information that is occasional, and wasn't every week that I would meet with whomever I reported to—only when I had a list of issues about which it was important to take their time. That is what I expect of those who report to me— the idea is that I know what's going on and there are no surprises.

Motivation is a key element of the characteristic of inspiration.

Renee Lewin, associate publisher at *Esquire*, has known Valerie Salembier for many years, having worked with her at *USA Today*. Here's what Lewin has to say:

> Valerie motivates because she has three strong attributes.
> First is her undeniable sense of humanity. She is so unlike many senior executives who are in the corner office and who are inac-

cessible in many ways. She is extremely real as a person, not just to me, who deals with her every day, but also to the lowest person in the organization. She is the first person to admit being vulnerable. She also admits her mistakes, celebrates successes, and knows everyone by name, as well as their birthdays. When you have to spend as much time as we do at our offices, you want to spend it around someone that you know is not just a facade.

Second is her work ethic. There is nothing she will not do to get the job done. She will clean out a stock room if she has to. And because she sets that kind of standard, it's an unspoken expectation of everybody around her. And people simply rise to the occasion when they see their boss working that hard. And finally, she embodies teamwork. She really does believe that everyone at every level has a contribution to make.

Kevin Martinez, another member of the *Esquire* team, puts it this way:

Imagine if you were to walk into an enormous amusement park where there is an incredible ride. And this ride would bring you up to 100 miles an hour and spin you and swoop you, and you would be going down and up, and you'd be exhilarated and scared at the same time. Then you would pull in at the end of the ride, and a guy would come over to you, and you would look up at him, and your eyes would be spinning in your head, and your hair would be standing on end (or what's left of your hair), and he'd look at you, and you'd look at him, and he would say, "Let's do it again." And that's what it's like to work with Valerie Salembier on a day-to-day basis.

This characteristic has another side to it that is not often discussed in organizations. That is the *enticement factor.* People like to work where they can feel inspired or motivated, where they are part of a larger and important picture. This enticement factor had a lot to do with the migration to, and exodus from, the dot-coms. The enticement to leave traditional firms and go to the dot-coms was the promise of more freedom, less structure, and more money. The enticement to return to the traditional organizations was more security, more structure (and less chaos), and a steady paycheck rather than risky options.

As economic cycles wax and wane, managers struggle with the

issue of saving employee costs by downsizing in a labor market that is demographically expected to be tight for many years to come. Consider this:

- The years from 1998 to 2001 saw labor shortfalls unknown in the history of the United States for the past 30 years.

- Although in 2001 the unemployment rate rose, it is still under the historic levels seen during previous economic slowdowns. September 11, 2001, events caused an upsurge in New York unemployment and had a chilling effect on the economy as a whole. The jobless rate will probably rise, even as the economy begins to grow more aggressively, suggests David A. Wyss, chief economist at Standard & Poor's, a unit of *Business Week*'s publisher, The McGraw-Hill Companies. "Even if we get unemployment up over 5%, it won't free up more nurses or computer programmers," he concludes.[2] The skilled workers will continue to be in short supply. More jobs will be demanding more workers, who will need to be college-educated and skilled. Finding, attracting, and retaining skilled workers will be more difficult than ever before.

Becoming a Ten Essential Traits organization is critical, not only to make change happen now, but also to position the organization for the future.

To offer an inspiring place to work, to motivate people to work smarter, happier, and more productively—these are the reasons everyone is searching constantly for the many ways to reward, inspire, and provide opportunities for innovation. Books and management consultants who promise to do that are in great demand.

Can you inspire your employees? Only if you can inspire yourself. If you come to work every day with a sinking feeling in your stomach and are either bored with what you do or irritated by it, the people who work with you will sense the truth about your feelings, regardless of your words. Motivation and inspiration cannot just be the talk; they also have to be the walk. This is one of the most prevalent elephants in the room for many organizations. Lack of inspiration shows up in low energy and clock watching, as people just try to get through the day.

Uninspired Leadership

Recently, I was with a team of midcareer people from a company that has been through three mergers of "equals" (a myth because there is always a controlling culture). They were bright, dedicated people. However, their leader (not present, evidently thought the group needed inspiration but she did not) was a bureaucratic and, frankly, completely boring individual. Not everyone can be a comedian, or even have a good personality, but "lighten up" is the phrase that comes to mind. If you are going to deal with people (as opposed to staying isolated in a laboratory somewhere), you have to develop the interpersonal skills that make relationships worth having. Even laughing at yourself is appropriate behavior if you are known to be quiet or reserved. And fun is inspiring in itself—it creates team bonding, respect for others, maturity if presented with the latter, and a chance for people to refresh themselves and their environment.

This group told me a story about a parrot that one of them had brought to work. (The employee had to take delivery from the pet store before the weekend and had no time to take it home before the end of the day.) This parrot was rather talkative, and everyone on the team who came to meet it mentioned the name of Helene, because there was a fair amount of trepidation about how Helene (their manager) would react to the parrot.

Right on schedule, Helene came in and made a disparaging remark about the parrot. For whatever reason, our feathered friend seemed to like the name Helene. Maybe the parrot had heard it before or had heard it once too often that day. For the rest of the afternoon, the parrot screeched, "Helene, *Helene.*" Helene was not amused. However, the group members were doubled up in hysterics. What a missed opportunity! Had Helene seen the humor in it all, she could have made a disparaging remark about herself such as, "Well, at least someone here pays attention to me," or some other comment to show she was human. Instead, she mumbled and grumbled about rules and animals and birds and corporate decorum and so on.

You can bet that Valerie Salembier would have handled this one far differently! The *Esquire* employees are clear about her sense of humanity and inspirational example. Inspiration doesn't have to be a brilliant thought or a motivational speech—after all, not many of us can do that on the spur of the moment! It can be something mundane to show that we are vulnerable, that once, maybe a long time ago, we were children who played all day, that we are willing to recapture that sense of fun.

The organizational characteristic of inspiration, accessing internal and external networks, recognizes that few of us are able to create unique and different ideas continually without brainstorming with others. Information transfer from all kinds of events and people helps to exercise our brains, to stimulate thought, comparisons, and solutions, and even to raise problems we had not previously contemplated. Information transfer also educates—and no one should ever stop learning.

Inspiration and Productivity

The real definition of *productivity* should be value added per unit of time worked, rather than total number of hours worked. The Ten Essential Traits approach increases productivity by inspiring and motivating value-added work. What is that? It's the opposite of busywork, which is work that makes an employee look busy, but the output is not valuable. This concept means that all processes and activities have to be examined from the following point of view:

What value does this activity add to the enterprise?

I was speaking with a very senior scientist who participated in one of my programs recently. He's from an organization known for its brilliant thought leadership in a variety of scientific arenas. He was complaining about the latest initiative to come down from on high. "I look at all these forms that I am filling out, and I say to myself—what on earth am I doing this for—where is the possible value to the organization or to my activities?"

Unfortunately for this organization, the elephant in the room is the lack of leadership at the top of the organization and a perception that there is too much talk and no walk. When mandates for corporate initiatives come down from on high, they are met with cynicism and resistance.

Inspiration is empty without the productive acts that follow it. Yet most organizations bury their employees in repetitive, boring, and nonproductive, form-filling busywork. In an era where the cost of personal and organizational interaction has been reduced to lower levels than ever before—due to intranets, collaborative software programs, and technology that enables all types of digital connections (video programming and more)—busywork should be reduced. For example, the Partner Relationship Management (PRM) system[3] is a software program for creating and managing alliances between divisions and groups within an organization as well as with external partners and suppliers. It can dramatically reduce the communication costs between those entities and reduce busywork. The Ten Essential Traits managers use internal and external networks of partners and other relationships to exchange information and leverage off each other, at lower cost and with higher value per unit of time worked, due to the immense access to resources available.

A good example of this is seen in the virtual organization. This is a model of loosely connected and allied organizations, all of which contribute to an agreed-upon goal that will be a separate enterprise from their own, very often with a separate brand. One of the partners takes a lead position to manage the enterprise. All partners contribute expertise and competency.

An example of an extremely successful virtual organization is DirecTV, started within the Hughes Satellite Division, first as part of the Hughes organization and then as part of General Motors. The attractiveness of DirecTV to NewsCorp and the Murdock empire, as well as to EchoStar and others, is a clear indication of its huge success. In this business model, intense use of outside resources turns an inspired idea into reality. The original partners for DirecTV were Warner, MCI Worldcom, Thompson, and others. Each contributed their competencies to the idea, and Hughes managed the enterprise and the brand. The internal and external networks and resources enabled the idea to take hold and become successful. The original founders, who were The Ten Essential Traits managers in a large organization, had been given the opportunity to be innovative and different, and so built an enterprise of which Hughes and GM were proud.

A good example of the stresses and strains of making fundamental and structural organizational change is Shell Oil USA.

Over the past five years, Shell Oil USA has attempted to create a series of virtual organizations out of internal functions such as human resources. Shell Services was created for that purpose, and this company became the outsourcing option for all Shell divisions. This meant that they would have to compete with other outsourcing providers contracts that they were not assured of getting. There is nothing like a real taste of competition to get the mind focused! This brings about shocking change to organizations, which some people may not be willing to accept and consequently will move elsewhere.

The Inspiration Process

The approach to inspiring yourself and your employees can be broken down into a three-part process:

1. The first part consists of a brief exercise.
   - Identify what you love to do.
   - Find a way to include that in your work habits or approach.
   - Ask those on your team or who report to you to do the same.
2. Reward those who do this with recognition.
3. Spread the word about what you and they did.

Here are three examples that were provided to me by an outsource manufacturing company, a software developer, and a telecommunications company, respectively:

1. *Outsource manufacturing company.* One midlevel manager was a photographer on the side and spent a lot of time thinking about his hobby. At work, he was in the finance department. In that role he related often to those in other functions in the organization. Most people did not see him as a person with an ability to see creative solutions, but rather someone who often said no. The constraints of his position frequently required that response. His solution was to create a series of photos that expressed his points of view. In contrast to handouts or speeches or even PowerPoint presentations, the photos increased his coworkers' understanding of him as a whole person (not just as a number cruncher or a naysayer). This acted as a learning tool for the internal services that he offered. Sometimes he used humor with the photos to assist in his communication process. Instead of grimacing when he entered a meeting, people would ask,

"What's on the photo menu for today?" He was also perceived as more creative than he had been given credit for, and his performance improved (as did his enthusiasm for his work). Finally, he looked forward to coming to work. Instead of thinking about home while he was at work, he spent some time at home thinking about how to communicate his next set of work issues using his hobby of photography.

2. *Software company.* The midlevel manager was a new employee and part of the staff/support team to the sales group. To her dismay, she found that not only was her job not highly regarded by the salespeople, but that the company was in a continual act of reorganization and restructuring, so the salespeople had given up trying to know who was in which job. She had to find a way to make herself known to the salespeople she was supposed to support and to gain their respect for her ability to add value. Her actual job was to evaluate and implement sales training programs for the sales staff. Unfortunately, the sales team continued to see her as overhead (which of course she was!). She tried to apply some of The Ten Essential Traits to her position and looked for inspiration! When trying to come up with what she could do that was different, she returned to the passion of her youth—playing tennis, a game of individual skill that required concentration and agility. She decided to create a game that would act as a grading system for the various sales programs. She hoped this would add something different to her internal training and open the door for further conversation. The game system she chose was Hangman (commonly known to most), which she adapted to explain why one program might be more valuable than another. If a sales program contained more than 15 management buzzwords, it failed on the noose of consultant-speak and was replaced by another program that provided clearer language. She also created a series of quizzes, which made the communication process more fun.

3. *Telecommunications company.* This company was an outgrowth from one of the former Bell operating companies and, as such, was still rather hierarchical, which meant that The Ten Essential Traits managers had a tough time surviving there. The only way to make change happen was on a local level, bypassing the politics of senior management that still threatened to choke off innovation and growth. One mid-senior-level executive came up with a competition that would connect the internal, same-site working groups at the

midlevel in the organization. They were asked to come up with a team song and mascot that would communicate to other groups within the organization what they did. This acted as a communication mechanism for the internal network of those who served each other—information technology, human resources, marketing communications, legal, finance. The competition would be held on a Friday in the company cafeteria, with free lunch for all who attended. The winners would have a page on the company web site to show employees at other locations what they did and how. It worked so well that other team leaders really bought into the idea, adding their own concepts, and the program was adopted companywide. Needless to say, The Ten Essential Traits manager gained personal recognition as a good corporate citizen, leader, and motivator of people, which was very helpful in her career.

Constant visibility and accessibility is one of the management processes that make The Ten Essential Traits managers good at applying this characteristic. It is also one of the most difficult, because if you commit to a Ten Essential Traits role, those who report to you will watch you all the time—even when you are not thinking about them watching you. They will also hang on your every word, which means that careless words could send a whole group or division in an inappropriate direction. One of the responsibilities of leadership is visibility and accessibility. Ensuring that The Ten Essential Traits managers are not hidden behind closed doors but are seen and heard often is one of the most effective ways to communicate the vision of the organization to those who are responsible for implementing it: the people in the middle of the company. Corporate security issues that require some organizations to keep their senior managers on the proverbial top floor, away from the rest of the company, may ensure their personal security, but it is dangerous for the future of the organization. This means that management by walking around will require very long hours, full weeks, and lots of traveling for senior executives in large organizations, especially those in turnaround.

Visibility is critical. When leaders are not visible, *that* becomes the elephant in the room, as expressed to me recently by a manufacturing team representative: "Oh no, you never see the suits round here—they wouldn't dream of dirtying themselves on a manufacturing floor. I did see the corporate jet land the other day—but we never see those guys here on the line."

People want to know that their leaders are working hard. That doesn't mean they have to physically see them all the time. There are other ways. One Kodak divisional president told me that he was impressed and somewhat surprised when he found regular voice-mail messages from CEO George Fisher that had been sent after midnight. The Kodak voice-mail system indicated the time the message was received, so there was no mistaking that the CEO was systematically going through his voice mail and e-mail, not only in response to routine business matters on a 24/7 basis, but also to proactively generate ideas. Most of the CEOs that I work with never take a day off. They may take vacations, but they are never completely out of touch. This means that they handle voice mail and e-mail daily, even when sailing or traveling with their families on vacation. That fact alone motivates employees, who strive to measure up to high standards set by The Ten Essential Traits leaders in the organization. I certainly believe that taking time off from work is key to a balanced life—but some positions are so heavy with responsibility that to get the position and all its perks requires some trade-offs. Besides, for many CEOs it *is* what they love to do the most. The organization *is* their inspiration.

Balancing inspiration, constant visibility, and accessibility with the internal and external networks is an important challenge. No one has it quite right.

One of the most important aspects of leading with The Ten Essential Traits is learning from what others are doing. Networks and associations are critical to those who are new in leadership positions. They can also be beneficial to those who aspire to leadership positions.

Many CEOs join industry associations, CEO roundtables, alumni and university boards, and boards of other companies. The benefits are tremendous, although the time drain can be substantial and must be managed. But with the thought in mind that no person is an island and that there is much to be learned from others who are wiser, older, or more experienced, inspiration is greatly enhanced by these formal and informal networks.

When I was CEO of an advanced materials company that pro-

vided products and services to the aerospace and electronics industries, I lived, breathed, and thrived on thinking about and running the
company. Because it was a turnaround situation, there was even less
time for a balanced life. And I loved it. What really helped me to gain
some perspective was networking with other CEOs in an association
for CEOs of technology companies. My roundtable consisted of about
14 CEOs from a variety of companies, and we met monthly to share
insights and advice.

One of those CEOs was Fred Lukas, founder and CEO of Trident
Data Systems, a company featured at various points in this book. All
of us envied Lukas because he was the most organized of the entire
group. He had created an amazing company of outstanding Ten
Essential Traits managers in a niche market (security software,
mainly for government uses) and at that time was contemplating selling the company to his employees. The privately held company has
over $100 million in annual revenues, and Lukas saw to it that the
next layer of management and all those below were vested, inspired,
had fun, and earned very good money. Because of his management
style, Lukas was able to take off Tuesday and Thursday afternoons to
surf, ski, play tennis, golf, or whatever the season called for. An
Olympic-level athlete and champion skier, Lukas lived well. We would
tease him about it—yet all of us envied his ability to delegate and let
go. Amazingly, the company thrived, as The Ten Essential Traits leaders saw what they needed to do, took the responsibility, and no one
needed to clock in and out to ensure that tasks were completed.

Fred Lukas made it a personal commitment to make the most of
every moment of his life while he could. Perhaps he had a prescient
insight into his future. Just a few short years ago Lukas was diag-
nosed with multiple sclerosis, which has progressed quite rapidly.
Now in a wheelchair, he continues with his upbeat, proactive Ten
Essential Traits ways—growing orchids, taking classes and watching
from afar the company he started, now being well run by those he
employed who, due to his foresight, became the owners and sold the
entire company recently at a nice profit.

Becoming inspired at work means making the most of our short
and precious time on this earth, since most of us spend a good deal
more time at work than anywhere else. The story of Fred Lukas's success in so many areas continues to be a good lesson for all of us.

Another executive, whom I was not privileged to know, but whom I have read and studied about for some years, is Konosuki Matsushita, founder of a company by that name. His success has been phenomenal, especially in a small island nation like Japan. His success had to do with a strength of will and tolerance for pain that few others could have lived through. His early years were driven by entrepreneurial zeal that differentiated his small company from his competition. He also had a strong customer focus, an obsession with productivity and keeping costs low, and a willingness to take risk to improve products developed by others. Service and mass-production techniques were supported by total commitment and belief in his employees. Consequently, Matsushita created a team of Ten Essential Traits managers never before seen in a Japanese organization. He expected his people to perform miracles—over and over again. And, amazingly, they did. His culture was hugely adaptive, able to withstand the stock market crash of the late 1920s and the depression years, as well as World War II and the rebuilding of Japan. John P. Kotter, author of the definitive book on Matsushita, has this to say:

> Globalization and ambitious plans forced employees to search constantly for superior methods and to keep growing themselves. To reinforce these tendencies and to ensure that the company's success did not create a rigid and arrogant environment, he tried tirelessly to inculcate the kind of continuous improvement that is driven by humble hearts and open minds. . . . He pushed himself and others out of comfortable routines, took risks, reflected humbly on successes and failures, listened carefully, viewed life with an open mind, and tried to draw from the collective wisdom of others.[4]

Sounds a lot like Matsushita identified the elephants in the room (the comfortable routines and risk-averse behavior) and moved them out of there by using The Ten Essential Traits matrix, doesn't it?

The success of Matsushita may not be possible for everyone, or even desirable for some. But the tenets of his success and belief system are foundational to good, inspiring leadership and a balanced combination of The Ten Essential Traits characteristics.

These few examples are designed to help you find the hidden inspiration in your team and in your organization.

Inspiration: Action Items

- Are you doing what inspires you (and what you love) as part of what you do every day? If not, how can you insert some of what you love into your job?

- Do your direct reports or team members act as though they are inspired every day? Ask them to do the same exercise you did.

- What tells you and others that you are inspired at work and that you get a kick out of what you do each day? Find a way to communicate this. If only you know it, you are missing a huge leverage opportunity. People around you will become more productive and inspired when they know you are!

- What tells you that your employees feel the same way? Encourage them to communicate their areas of inspiration to others.

- Do you belong to associations that enable you to meet others in your industry or community? Take one tip or good idea from your association with others in these roles and communicate it to a member (or all) of your team. Ask them to do the same.

- How visible are you to your direct reports?

- Create a physical environment where you can be seen or communicated with quite easily.

- Set up times for social or lighthearted interaction with team members (Friday pizza, weekly breakfasts, or some comparable event). Our anthropological beginnings as tribal creatures have predisposed us to relax when eating (or taking walks), and these activities seem to create an atmosphere that enhances communication.

- Are you living each day as if it were your last? Before September 11, 2001, that question may have sounded dramatic to many Americans—we now know it could be true. Make sure you make your work activity into something that inspires you or others. If you don't, it's just work, and no one ever said that they regretted not working enough. It's uninspiring work that causes regret.

6

Assuredness: Knowing What You Want

I know what I don't *want—that should work to tell me what I do want, right?*
—Executive, in a strategy and corporate visioning session

oes *assuredness* mean raw ambition? Not at all. Rather, it is the clear focus and personal definition of individual intent and the coordination of that intent with the goals of the organization. (See Figure 6.1.) The Ten Essential Traits managers know what they want to achieve— and they focus on doing so. Although the quality of their work is an overriding consideration, they have an ability to home in on the specifics of their jobs in a way that is energizing and self-fulfilling.

"I am not a big believer in long-term career and life plans," says George Fisher. "I think these kinds of plans are seriously flawed in a rapidly changing time. To a certain degree, I believe in a predictor-corrector model of life, like Magoo, who bounced off one wall after another just because he couldn't see. I don't think that is a bad understanding to have of life, since it causes you to continually adapt. But it is important to know the things that are fundamentally important to you and to strive to achieve those and be the best you can at them."

It is not necessary to have a long-term plan for your life. Most of the time, it will be changed by events. People and events beyond your

Personal Characteristic	Organizational Environment Needed	Example of a Management Process for Implementation
1. *Fearlessness*	Permits failure	Shared learning and shared power
2. *Completion:* Ability to complete; has patience and is flexible	Results-oriented with process freedom	Horizontal, project-oriented management processes with cross-functional and multi-locational teams
3. *Commitment:* Emotionally vested	Encourages individual contributions	Small work groups and flexible work behavior; fun
4. *Inspiration:* Inspires and communicates vision; motivates	Access to internal and external people networks	Constant visibility and accessibility
5. *Assuredness:* Knows what he or she wants	Opportunities for advancement and reward	Career progression process

Figure 6.1   The Ten Essential Traits: The Larraine Segil Matrix

control and even outside of your expectations will influence your life's directions, good and bad.

A number of CEOs, when asked at what point they decided to become CEO of a major company, gave answers similar to that of George Fisher:

> I never aspired to be CEO, it just happened, rather like Magoo. I took one step at a time, always tried to do my best at every point along the path to make my people and organization a success. Other people control the situations that make a CEO, so there's not much you can do about it except to always do your best at whatever you are doing.

There will come a point, however, when a life direction shines clear. In a 1973 performance review, Jack Welch stated that his long-range goal was "to become chief executive officer of General Electric Company."[1]

How do you find out what you really want?

Sometimes it's easier to decide what you *don't* want, what you are *not* good at. For many, it is a lifetime quest to find what they are good at. A lucky few discover a talent early in life and develop it over time.

For those who are multitalented, the challenge may be greater. Lack of focus can take someone with huge talents and send them down a number of paths with no end. There is a delicate balance between focusing too soon, thus limiting personal and intellectual growth, and not focusing enough, which produces unsatisfactory results. The way to balance these qualities is greatly enhanced by incorporating the earlier quality *ability to complete*. In that way, The Ten Essential Traits will be enhanced, because no matter what the focus or how experimental or short term the goal, the ability to complete will bring process, organization, and measurable results to the activity.

An important technique, however, is *visualization*. This psychological approach will help clarify what you really want. By visualizing what a day in the life of a particular career might be, not the fanciful, imagined role but the reality of such activity, it may become clearer that this is exactly what you *don't* want. Many lawyers who spend years working their way up to become full partners find that when they achieve their goal they are as unhappy as when they were young associates—only richer. The belief system of Generation Xers is a direct result of their baby boomer parents. Many have deliberately set out to define a different set of values and lifestyles, where personal fulfillment is of more importance than the acquisition of material wealth.

A wonderful example of visualization occurred recently in the popular-music industry. A small girl who used to sing for her father and the other members of her family dreamed of one day singing professionally with her father. Unfortunately, he died at a young age and she could not fulfill that dream. As she grew into young womanhood, her beautiful voice took her every place she had hoped for in a shining career, but her dream to sing with her father never left her mind. She visualized it again and again. And the day came when technology was able to make it happen. The woman is Natalie Cole, and her father was the unforgettable Nat King Cole. *Unforgettable,* the album in which technology blended their voices, is indeed unforgettable, the realization of a dream. It sold to baby boomers, postindustrialists, and Generation Xers alike.[2]

Regardless of your profession, your job description, or the industry you're in, the visualization technique can be of enormous, almost prescient, assistance in creating scenarios for the future.

The father of corporate scenario building is Pierre Wack, a planner who worked with Ted Newland, Napier Collyns, and finally Arie de Geus in the London offices of Royal Dutch Shell, in a newly formed department called Group Planning. Their colleague, Peter Schwartz, has this to say in his book, *The Art of the Long View:*

> Scenario thinking is an art, not a science. You will find yourself moving through the scenario process several times—refining a decision, performing more research, seeking out more key elements, trying on new plots and rehearsing the implications yet again. The order of the steps may be muddled; in some cases you may start with a plot line first and ask yourself, "If this plot is to take place, what decisions am I likely to want to make?" Or you could start with a new finding based on research: "If this possibility becomes a fact, what scenarios could it set in motion?"[3]

Thinking ahead and projecting different scenarios for the future is not as foreign as it might feel. Dr. William Calvin, author of *The Cerebral Symphony* and *The Ascent of Mind,* believes that scenario planning is as old as humankind. He says, ". . . We humans are capable of planning decades ahead, able to take account of extraordinary contingencies far more irregular than the seasons."[4] Calvin believes that the part of the human brain that controls speech is also the part involved in ballistics. Ballistic prowess—the ability to hit animals with thrown rocks—was apparently an important survival skill for early humans. The abilities to think ahead and make small talk are side benefits of marksmanship. The capabilities involve preplanning.

Sports psychologists have created an entire profession based on this concept. The idea of running through the motions of an activity in one's head is key to its final perfect execution. Athletes prepare for their moment of glory concentrating intently as they do the movements over and over again—in their heads as well as with their bodies. This involves the ability to judge and amend past movements and adapt and improve future ones. Scenario planning involves the same skills.

The Ten Essential Traits managers will go through the process of scenario planning in many different ways. The process will be applied to their career goals and ambitions, to the projects on which they work, to the organizations within which they work.

For the highest-level Ten Essential Traits leaders, the process is one of creating a vision for the organization. As described in Chapter 1, The Ten Essential Traits process is one of creating a vision, giving people the tools, and then getting out of the way—George Fisher's stated goal for Eastman Kodak.

Joerg Agin, who ran the Entertainment and Imaging Division of Eastman Kodak, described it this way:

> When change did impact Kodak, its leadership team at that time did not quite know how to accommodate the change. The team before George had the smarts and the intelligence, but did not have the experience to know how to confront the conditions in the market. [This was the elephant in the room.] George Fisher had a vision that could accommodate that change. It was clear to him. He said, "These are the circumstances that occur in the market-place and this is what I would do about it given the core strength and competencies of the company I am asked to lead."

How did George Fisher develop that vision? Agin saw it clearly:

> It came from his being in markets that were highly competitive. Motorola is very much on the leading edge of technology, not technology for the sake of it in a research sense, but technology as it is practical and applied in the market. In his role as CEO of Motorola, I think that George really felt that he was abreast of change and knew what the key drivers were for change. That helped him articulate a vision of how change would affect us at Kodak. It was natural for him to articulate a path forward because he had that visioning process.

What is the visioning process? Agin continued:

> It's understanding the dynamics of what is occurring in the mar-ketplace and figuring out how to work through those dynamics—not the ones that are wishful thinking, but those that are real. It means understanding where the junctions are in the road and choosing the ones you must take.

Visioning, or visualization, is exactly that. The Ten Essential Traits leaders must do this for themselves as well as for their organizations. What are some of the techniques to help you do this? We return to the words of Joerg Agin:

A smart individual always maximizes their associations with people inside and outside their industry. You always learn something; you also learn who to listen to and why. George had a platinum Rolodex—he was well connected in many industries and purposefully did that to create relationships and maintain contact with people. Then he can get the kind of information that he needs to make up his mind about things. He runs ideas by people he can trust, couples it with his own ideas, then adapts his vision.

For leaders with The Ten Essential Traits, creating a vision is fundamental, but the key to implementation is communicating that vision effectively so that other Ten Essential Traits managers can make it their own and execute it. Says Agin,

> One of George's core strengths is leading people toward a vision that they will believe is their own. He has a way of working with people to make them feel that they are important, they are contributors, that they are there because they have a role to play and are very integral to the organization. In my case, I knew that George was there if I needed him, and I knew that he didn't want me to call him on a day-to-day basis to run the organization. That is what he has entrusted me with, so I would never jeopardize his confidence in me. But if I did need him, he was there, and he was there for the tougher things, too. He is a visionary whom you have to respect. He gave me a lot of independence.

How does a manager or leader with the ten essential traits spread his or her vision?

Agin reflects on the sense of near panic that existed at Kodak when George Fisher arrived:

> People had never lived through and thrived in an environment of change. Now along comes George with a high degree of confidence, not panicked at all, and says, "Clearly, you ought to be happy with where you are and the kind of capabilities that you have. I can take those and make you feel better about how to amortize them against the future opportunities that we have." George said, "Why are you beating up against imaging? You have an asset you haven't even begun to utilize yet. Let me show you how to do that. We have a lot of core competencies here. We don't have to run out and try something new and do acquisitions or change the nature of our business." So here was an outsider who had every

reason to believe that the digital domain is going to be dominant. He had come from Motorola and loved some of our competencies. By doing so, he gave people a lot of faith and belief. It's taken us a little longer than we planned, but we are on the road.

One of the frustrations of this quality of assuredness is that sometimes, even though it is clear what you want, a great deal of patience is needed to get there.

George Fisher had a vision of where he wanted Kodak to go. He understood what it took to do that. But even he could not control the changes in the market, and adapting a large and still-political organization like Kodak is like turning a destroyer on a dime. Joerg Agin ruminates:

> He knew what it takes and went through the rigors of making sure everyone in the organization was committed to making that happen. He dedicated the resources and he had the patience to wait. That was one of his most important capabilities. He had patience. He could ride the roller coaster. He realized that there are highs and lows and he has been there before. There was no reason to panic. He never lost sight of the end and the vision.

The analysts, market makers, and shareholders were not so kind.

Creating an organization steeped in The Ten Essential Traits has required patience at Kodak. It hasn't been a straight-line improvement, as no fundamental change can be. Joerg Agin verbalizes how he experienced Fisher's Ten Essential Traits approach at work.

> He liked to express it to you this way. "I like to create organizations that think for themselves, that run themselves in very competitive situations. That's why we are hiring people to do that, and that's really what I want you to do." He may say to you when you present your report to him, "Hey, that's not my product road map, that's yours. I didn't tell you to do that. You told me to do that. That's why I am hiring you—to make those decisions and then to do it." Then he gives you this guilty kind of thing, but in a nice way. "You know, it's not my numbers; it's your numbers. I trusted you, and that is what you have come with. Now, as a result of that, here is what we are going to have to do, because you didn't deliver against your numbers." In this way, there is not only responsibility there is also accountability. I think that he honestly believes that George Fisher will not run a successful organization. It will be run by the people

whom he entrusted and empowered to do that. Internally, he will work that belief, and you will always know that he hired you to do the job that you are supposed to be doing. He does not want to do the job for you. You really feel that here is a leader who has entrusted the people to run the company, and those same people are expected to be part of a team and to contribute in their particular area. But he expects you to be very competitive and dynamic in your own right, and when you need him, he is there.

The best way to describe the experience process that combines both the Magoo approach and the Ten Essential Traits experience is visually (see Figure 6.2).

1. Experiment.

2. Experience.

3. Analyze and react.

4. Think and plan.

This process is like a Slinky toy made up of the preceding elements. It changes, is dynamic, can be viewed from many different angles and perspectives, and can climb up and down, sideways, and around. However, its essence always remains the same. It must be the most flexible it can be, yet still have substance and measurable results. That is why the think-and-plan mode is integrated into the process and does

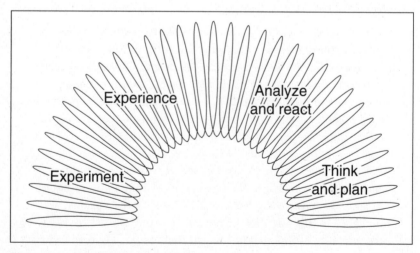

Figure 6.2   The Experience Process

not necessarily come first. In fact, sometimes the best and most creative thought comes from brainstorming or from something that was initially a mistake or a failure (e.g., 3M Post-it notes allegedly came from the failure of a newly invented adhesive to bond well). Clearly, this kind of process works especially well in energetic organizations that have *yes*-type cultures (Chapter 9). It is a continuous learning process.

There are no value judgments along the road of this Slinky process; no one point is better than another. But with a vision, the opportunities will pop higher into participant awareness as the treasure hunt for ideas and their modification goes on.

The most effective use of this process, therefore, is after a vision has been created or is in development, because this will give some direction and strategic intent to the activity.

Verbalizing the Unspeakable: Spotting and Discussing the Elephant in the Room

One of the most difficult aspects of the quality of *assuredness*, or knowing what you want, once you think you've identified it, is learning how to verbalize your intent. Unless you can do so, as a leader and manager with The Ten Essential Traits you run the risk of making the wrong decision for the right reason. In other words, you know you want to make change happen, but you can't quite decide what the specifics of the changed situation would look like, so you make a decision that doesn't quite do it.

This is tantamount to seeing the elephant, knowing it must leave, leading it out, and then scratching your head and saying, "Now what?" Then you may do something that attracts alligators instead of elephants, which is sometimes better than no decision at all. After all, elephants do make a huge mess. Other times, this could take you in the wrong direction (alligators are pretty slimy creatures, after all), and it may take a while to self-correct. Although this is a good learning experience, surely there is a more efficient way?

There is, but it requires practice.

It is seen most clearly in the example of Yamaha Motor Company. Yamaha realized that its core competence, the thing that differentiates it from other motorcycle manufacturers, lay not in producing motorcycles per se but in creating deep satisfaction in its customers' lives by the production of consumer goods such as motorcycles.[5] By making this distinction, Yamaha uncovered the flow of the engineering process technology that enables the company to achieve its goal of creating satisfaction in their customers' lives. Yamaha may have consciously or unconsciously been developing this capability in the past, but after it was verbalized the company actively began to foster the development of this capability in the organization. It is called *knowledge engineering,* or as it is known in Japan, *Do-Shinka engineering.*

What is Do-Shinka engineering?

Yamaha requires its engineers to have a thorough understanding of motorcycles and also of Yamaha. They must be able to design a solid product with the most up-to-date features. However, according to Dr. Hiroshi Yamagata, director of research at Yamaha, that is not enough:

> In addition to these traditional engineering skills, they must bring a high degree of personal expertise to the Do-Shinka engineering process. For example, Do-Shinka engineers must be expert riders who can personally evaluate the motorcycles. This process involves more than simply test-driving the motorcycles. Do-Shinka engineers must have a deep personal understanding of the experience of riding a motorcycle. Moreover, being able to access this tacit knowledge is the key to Do-Shinka engineering . . . the engineers must be able to articulate their deeply personal experience of riding a motorcycle and they must be able to do this in a way that the other engineers in the development group can understand and build on.

Clearly this is the most difficult part of knowing what you want. How do you verbalize it? Some might say, "I'll know it when I see it." But how do you teach and measure that? In product and service development, that is not enough. Yamagata continues, "Externalizing these deeply personal experiences is a difficult, abstract task, but it is a critical part of Do-Shinka engineering, because *the outcome of Do-Shinka technology is a product that will create a particular image or feeling within the user.*" How do you do this?

One way is through collaboration between the designers and the customers, which means that they merge and combine their tacit knowledge—that special set of feelings that each experiences in their use of and reactions to the product. But this goes far beyond listening to customers and incorporating their suggestions, needs, and wants into the product. Yamagata continues:

> ... Customers often find it difficult to describe what they feel when they ride a motorcycle. This seems counterintuitive because the customer naturally knows what he or she is feeling. But because such knowledge is usually tacit, stored in personal mental models, the Do-Shinka engineer's ability to articulate what it means to him to ride a motorcycle helps the customer to articulate the individual experience of riding a motorcycle, and this is not a simple skill. Engineering is a logical process, and creating an elegant concept is an artistic endeavor. It is not easy for engineers to develop a common language that they can use to share their personal experiences. But this is where the role of the Do-Shinka engineer really begins ... they must understand how mental models work, how to build trust with the customer, how to share personal experiences in a way that will elicit the customer's experience. They must be capable of understanding and deeply synthesizing their own and the customer's reactions and feelings about how the products should look, perform, and make them feel. Thus the heart of Do-Shinka technology at Yamaha is the convergence of tacit and explicit knowledge.

The Ten Essential Traits manager must do the same. He or she must strive to understand how people think and process information, how to communicate in the way and manner that the receiver of the information will understand and internalize, how to create and grow feedback mechanisms, and how to verbalize better, clearer, and more appropriately for both audience and circumstance.

Apple Computer in its early incarnation was masterful at merging tacit and explicit knowledge. The aficionados of the Macintosh were devoted not only because of functionality but also because the tacit understanding between engineers and users that went into the development of the Mac made them feel as if someone understood what they needed. Then Apple stopped merging the tacit knowledge of the customers with that of its engineers. The company brought in those who had little appreciation for the tacit knowledge that resided in the organization or the changes in the marketplace or the competitive challenges. That, combined with some strategically dubious decisions, almost led to the company's demise. Founder Steve Jobs is listening again, and, among Mac disciples, hope is rising.

Organizational Characteristic: Opportunities for Advancement and Reward

In order to provide The Ten Essential Traits managers with self-realization (i.e., offering an environment in which to see whether there is indeed a fit between what they want and what the organization needs), a series of opportunities for advancement and reward must become part of the corporate culture. This is normal for most companies and becomes part of performance evaluations and reviews.

What is not so normal, however, is an organizational environment that allows people to reinvent themselves.

Shell Oil has recently instituted a job search process called an *open posting system*. This enables employees to decide for themselves where and when they would like to transfer, change jobs, improve skills, and so on. In other words, it is not left up to a supervisor to plan the career path of an employee. All the available jobs in the organization and its various divisions are made available to everyone electronically. In the past, employees stayed within a particular division and business function.

The idea is reinforced by one of Shell Oil's former CEOs, Jack Little:

> When we started this open posting system, it allowed people from E&P [the Exploration and Production Group] to move into Shell Chemical or to one of the Shell Professional firms. This has gone a long way to reinforce the idea and belief in people. We have said to employees, "You, as an individual, bear some of the responsibility of developing yourself. You have to personally take that initiative." The open posting system helps people to chart their own career paths and to move into parts of the business that they may have some affinity for.

Shell Oil now provides the opportunity for Ten Essential Traits managers to reinvent themselves, to put themselves into the flow of future growth, if they so desire, instead of remaining stuck in the past. It transfers responsibility for advancement to the individual, a large step in The Ten Essential Traits emancipation for the entire organization. Of course, there's a tendency for groups to try to retain their good people. So be it. If there is a market internally for good people, as there surely is a market externally for them, then this kind of internal striving for excellence paves a clear pathway to reward for all concerned. The job search open posting internal process at Shell Oil has transferred the balance of dependency from the hierarchy to the individual or small group. That move, among others, will attract and retain Ten Essential Traits individuals.

This movement by Shell is a reminder that organizations cannot pigeonhole people. Most people entering the workforce now will retrain and reinvent themselves multiple times in a career. Sometimes this will be the result of external factors (e.g., disappearance of an industry due to technology advances or global competition) and other times due to lack of emotional vesting in what they do every day. I left the practice of law for the latter reason and have never looked back. I moved into the world of business, where I am deeply emotionally vested.

This is a story often repeated as people move through corporations. For example, recently a CPA working as a controller was involved, almost by accident, in a large software project. He immediately became emotionally vested in that arena. Consequently, he finally knew what he wanted, after years of asking himself, "Is this all there is?" In addition, that level of certainty gave him the confidence to be fearless in his quest. With enthusiasm, he spoke to the CEO of the company about his desire to develop further expertise and to add to the company competency in a different area. However, the organization could not flex with him. After repeated efforts at coaxing change, he left the company and joined another as a financial software consultant.

The company he left could have benefited from his expertise, and he would willingly have trained someone to fill his place. However, the organizational flexibility was not there.

In other circumstances, this CPA may have come to the conclusion that no matter how flexible the organization, he was at the wrong place and needed to leave. Knowing what you want may mean exactly that. There is no fault to be allocated here. You may need to move because you want to change industries, and even the finest company in the wrong industry is counterproductive for you if you cannot realize your goals there.

Many times, leaving an organization can be the right move to increase maturity and capabilities. Hewlett-Packard has a value-added approach.

David Packard offered the following:

> Many companies have a policy stating that once employees leave the company, they are not eligible for reemployment. Over the years we have had a number of people leave because opportunities seemed greater elsewhere. We've always taken the view that as long as they have not worked for a direct competitor and if they have a good work record, they are welcomed back. They know the company, need no retraining and usually are happier and better motivated for having had the additional experience. Some people have left HP and started their own companies . . . we respect their entrepreneurial spirit . . . and are flattered that in building their companies they have adopted many of the management principles and practices embodied in the HP way.[6]

Fred Lukas of Trident Data Systems is a former HP employee. As his company now exceeds the $100 million mark, he recalls,

> I give Hewlett-Packard a lot of credit for the way we built the culture and values of Trident Data. I learned a lot from them about treating people with dignity and respect, valuing people's careers and not just creating a job but getting the most out of their jobs. A lot of what we do is the HP way. Moreover, it's doing what you think is right and what you would have done to you. I get back the loyalty that I give.

Just what is the HP way?

It became a clear manifestation of its founders *knowing what they wanted.* David Packard and Bill Hewlett thought often, long, and hard about how a company like theirs should be organized and managed. "We thought that if we could get everybody to agree on what our objectives were and to understand what we were trying to do, then we could turn them loose and they would move in a common direction." They created and published seven objectives, which became known as "the HP way." They are described in David Packard's book by the same name and quoted directly from that text.[7] Since I mentioned earlier that Carly Fiorina's actions were interpreted by the families as changing the Hewlett-Packard way (although she denies it and says rather that she is augmenting it), I am sharing the tenets of the "HP way" here to let you decide for yourself:

1. *Profit:* To recognize that profit is the best single contribution to society; and the ultimate source of our corporate strength. We should attempt to achieve the maximum possible profit consistent with our other objectives.

2. *Customers:* To strive for continual improvement in the quality, usefulness and value of products and services we offer our customers.

3. *Field of Interest:* To concentrate our efforts, continually seeking new opportunities for growth but limiting our involvement to fields in which we have capability and can make a contribution.

4. *Growth:* To emphasize growth as a measure of strength and a requirement for survival.

5. *Employees:* To provide employment opportunities for HP people that include the opportunity to share in the company's success, which they help to make possible. To provide for them job security based on performance, and to provide the opportunity for personal satisfaction that comes from a sense of accomplishment in their work.

6. *Organization:* To maintain an organizational environment that fosters individual motivation, initiative and creativity, and a wide latitude of freedom in working toward established objectives and goals.

7. *Citizenship:* To meet the obligations of good citizenship by making contributions to the community and to the institutions in our society which generate the environment in which we operate.

The Ten Essential Traits are identified, rewarded, and encouraged by such a culture. Only when HP temporarily lost sight of some of these beliefs (in the early 1990s), overlaying the organization with multiple decision layers and bureaucracy, did they waver from this path.

"We have a set of values," David Packard said, "deeply held beliefs that guide us in meeting our objectives, in working with one another, and in dealing with customers, shareholders, and others."

Fred Lukas of Trident Data Systems has learned them well, as have hundreds of thousands of HP employees before and after him.

Value systems reach beyond an organization and its employees. Many organizations contribute to their communities as well.

Target (a subsidiary of Dayton Hudson) contributes substantially to the communities in which it operates. Being a good citizen is a part of being a customer-oriented company and being in the customer's head (*perception*). (See Chapter 11 for more on Target and this characteristic.)

Shell Oil gives, too, not only in terms of corporate grants and working with banks to create minority business financing, but in individual ways. Says Jerome Adams, former leader of the Shell Learning Center and part of the Business Transformation team,

> Important at Shell is the silent work that's done with those who are less advantaged or privileged. This isn't some corporate mandate. There are basically small groups at a plant or a location working on something with the community that will make a difference. And as Royal Dutch Shell is working on the credo of Shell making the world a better place, our work in the community is part of that.

The HP way defines as one of its objectives the *field of interest*. The environment that supports this Ten Essential Traits quality of assuredness can offer opportunities for advancement and reward in ways that "keep it under the radar," also called *the stealth approach*. This is what happened when Hughes Communications created DirecTV.

James Ramo (son of the legendary Cy Ramo, founder of TRW) was working for Hughes Communications, in charge of the C-Ban Satellite sales group, selling products to the cable television broadcast industry. For example, companies (e.g., Home Box Office) have to buy satellite transponders to deliver their signals to cable companies around the country. Hughes Communications was a leader in that business.

James Ramo recalls how it all started:

I was calling on one of the providers to the cable TV industry, and I said to the guy who was buying our transponder, "You know, the cable industry isn't taking a whole lot of your programming. What you really need is a powerful satellite to bypass the cable operators so that you can get directly to the consumers." He got really excited, and that was how it all began. We created a joint venture with that company and a couple of other media companies, and we were all set to go when there was a massive capital crunch, and our partners were so highly leveraged that they couldn't provide the capital to finance the venture. Now we had an FCC license but no media partners and no capital. So three or four of us got together and said, "Okay, let's do it." Of course, Hughes didn't know the first thing about this business, but they said, "Go pay your way and we'll finance this." Paying our way means that since it takes three years to build a satellite, you have to pay the labor costs all the way through. That's money that has to be put up before the business launches!

Ramo and his colleagues knew the enormity of their task. However, as Ten Essential Traits managers, they also knew what they wanted. That goal was clear in their minds, and the opportunity was so exciting and revolutionary that they could not turn away from it. Ramo continues:

We found another company that was interested in buying 5 of our 32 transponders, and we sold them and therefore could consider that money as earnings. So in the first year we brought in cash flow as well as earnings and were in the black from the get-go!

With that kind of clarity and some money in the coffers, the group was inspired. They created and implemented a strategy of selling franchises. They sold franchises in urban and rural markets and, through these sales, were able to finance the business up to and through its launch phase. Year after year they delivered positive earnings and cash flow.

Then, in 1993 and 1994, management at Hughes changed. The company was now run by Michael Armstrong (currently CEO of AT&T), a visionary and results-oriented manager who encouraged The Ten Essential Traits approach instead of relying solely on an engineering focus. The change was immediate.

"Mike came in and he said, 'Hey this is a good business, let's invest in it!' " Ramo remembers.

How did The Ten Essential Traits managers make this decision become a reality?

First, they had a clear idea and knew what they wanted. Second, they proved that what they wanted could be done and showed the ability to complete. In addition, they risked failure—and the organization permitted them to do so. The organization was listening.

"This gave us the capital to do something that had never been done—to start to sell cable TV–like services with a national brand," James Ramo continued. "We were the first distribution company to create a brand, and this immediately differentiated us. We knew specifically that we had to have the product options that cable TV had—and more. We also needed a sports product that was different and so we took advantage of all the brands of the major sports leagues."

DirecTV exceeds $1 billion in revenue—a truly remarkable example of The Ten Essential Traits at work. The qualities of *energy* (opportunistic optimism) and *perception* (being in the customer's head) also relate to this story, as we show in future chapters.

The management processes that accompany The Ten Essential Traits quality of assuredness are described as *career progression*.

However this can occur in many ways, both orthodox and unorthodox.

Promotion is one traditional route. But the executives at DirecTV created an entirely new business for themselves and the organization. Because Hughes permitted them to do it, that part of the organization changed from a defense orientation to consumer products and service. In the process, these executives' careers were indelibly modified.

If the organization is open to it, Ten Essential Traits leaders/ managers can spot market opportunities and bring innovation, motivation, and culture change (as difficult as that can be) to all kinds of organizations. Again, this means identifying and moving out the elephants and bringing in value to replace them.

Communicating that kind of opportunity, however, requires more than simply assuredness, or knowing what you want. This quality, as is true of all the others, must interrelate across the matrix. A quality that is an essential partner with this one is *penetration*—being "of the people" (see Chapter 7).

Assuredness: Action Items

Personal

- Do you do scenario planning for your work activities? Your career path? Spend two hours this month doing that.

- Have you reinvented yourself in your career? How have you done that? If not, why not? How could you reinvent yourself? Brainstorm alternatives with a friend.

- Do you know what you want in life? What you don't want? What you value? Make a list of values and prioritize them. List how your values have changed.

- Are you living your values? If not, why not? How can you bring your life closer to what you believe in?

- Does your work activity support your value system? To what extent? Analyze your list of values on a scale of 1 to 10, with 10 meaning they coincide very closely with your lifestyle. If you score less than 5 on any one of your core values, it is likely that you are increasing your stress and discomfort level at work and will not fulfill yourself or your potential. This will require changing the work environment or changing jobs!

- How can you increase your knowledge of the values of those around you? Ask coworkers to do the same evaluation and exchange them.

Organizational

- Does your organization do preplanning? Does this take the form of strategic and operating plans, or is it scenario planning? Start a scenario planning process for what-ifs of any particular work project. An alliance is a good place to start—first within your company and then with the partner, if possible.

- Does the organization know what it wants? Is it clear at all levels of the company? How do you get that information? How do you internalize it and then use it to implement organizational goals? Find out and make it clear to coworkers, using informal and formal networks to communicate.

- What are the methods for organizational listening (i.e., listening to employees and their concerns)? Create a plan to increase these opportunities.

- How are organizational opportunities for advancement and rewards related to goal setting (individual with corporate)? What do you have to do to be promoted at your organization? Is it in alignment with the stated organizational goals? This is an area for remediation if the organization does not put its money where its mouth is.

- What are the organizational structures for career advancement (e.g., mentor programs, review processes, open jobs advertised across functions and divisions, networked project opportunities across functions and divisions)? Increase these opportunities.

7

Penetration: Being "of the People" and Building Personal Equity

As I look at our company and the industry today, the most successful are stellar communicators. In our company, we do a poor job communicating with the employee base. As I look at recent problems, had I communicated issues with more clarity, several problems would have been averted. I suspect most of us spend too much time "working hard and fast." We forget to talk with those around us, we forget to listen, and we rarely share thoughts and concepts. After a recent conflict with one of my managers, I'm attempting to be a better communicator. Our CEO certainly needs to do this.

—Divisional president of Fortune 500 global company
in the chemicals industry who participated
in The Ten Essential Traits survey
(with the assurance of confidentiality)

As we move to the sixth characteristic, let's briefly review the approach we are taking. (See Figure 7.1.)

The elephant in the room is the metaphor for issues that are often ignored but that *need to be addressed.* The Ten Essential Traits (Larraine Segil Matrix) comprise the delivery system to make change happen and bring positive results from that change to you; your colleagues, and your organization.

Personal Characteristic	Organizational Environment Needed	Example of a Management Process for Implementation
1. *Fearlessness*	Permits failure	Shared learning and shared power
2. *Completion:* Ability to complete; has patience and is flexible	Results-oriented with process freedom	Horizontal, project-oriented management processes with cross-functional and multi-locational teams
3. *Commitment:* Emotionally vested	Encourages individual contributions	Small work groups and flexible work behavior; fun
4. *Inspiration:* Inspires and communicates vision; motivates	Access to internal and external people networks	Constant visibility and accessibility
5. *Assuredness:* Knows what he or she wants	Opportunities for advancement and reward	Career progression process
6. *Penetration:* "Of the people" and builds personal equity; listens with respect; empowers with dignity; confident; good mediator	Flexible organizational structure	Free information exchange, communication, and benchmarking across groups and divisions

Figure 7.1   The Ten Essential Traits: The Larraine Segil Matrix

In this chapter we look again at the three parts of The Ten Essential Traits. First, we address the individual characteristics that comprise the trait of *penetration*. Second, we examine how the organization must manifest these characteristics in order to nurture and attract the kinds of individuals who learn (or already have) these traits. Third, and this is interwoven throughout the chapter, we discuss the management processes that support free information exchange, communication, and benchmarking across groups and divisions. Fortunately, many of these management processes *already exist* in your organization, all that needs to be done is to identify where to apply them more effectively.

How is *penetration* a successful management trait? The term encompasses many subtraits:

- The ability to see the whole
- A deep belief in people
- A willingness to be personally vulnerable
- The ability to see interrelated connections
- A balanced perspective between short- and long-term needs
- A balance between the extremes of toughness and humanity

Elephants have been known to pop up in many of these areas. When micromanagers are unable to see the whole—in walks the elephant. When managers and aspiring leaders are too insecure to show personal vulnerability, *that* becomes the elephant in the room. When adherence to company policy is the goal as opposed to what is right, and when the rules are just plain stupid—*that* is an elephant in the room.

Phil Carroll, formerly CEO of Shell Oil USA, is a good example of a leader who exemplifies the trait of penetration. Those who worked for him at Shell affirm that one of the most important things he did as their leader was to be inclusionary. Jerome Adams, former leader of the Shell Learning Center, has this to say:

> This is not a superficial gesture that communicates, "Let's give everyone a say but do what we want to anyway." Rather, it is a concerted effort made personally by him [Phil Carroll] to get the opinions, concerns, and issues on the table that confront the people in the organization, no matter what their title or position. This means genuinely being interested in different points of view, not just from senior management but also from those in the middle of the organization who are often more knowledgeable about what is really working or not.

This personifies the ability to have a *deep belief in people*. In addition, certain management techniques enable constant visibility and accessibility (e.g., "sign up for lunch with the CEO," visiting far-flung groups within the organization, both planned and unplanned).

Penetrating an organization to its depths enables its leaders to become educated and its employees to build trust, confident that their points of view matter.

Figure 7.2 offers a visual representation of how penetration works and illustrates how to make sure that you have the ability to see the whole.

Active Listening

Listening is a critical subtrait of this characteristic in The Ten Essential Traits matrix. Active listening is not a skill that is taught or acculturated in North America. Rather, the ability to "speak up" is rewarded. The result? North Americans are far better at talking and teaching than they are at listening and learning. The consequence of this subtrait is that those who listen well and with intelligence differentiate themselves from others.

Active listening, however, doesn't mean just being quiet so that another person can talk, then responding or communicating as though that person's contribution is irrelevant. It means having an open mind to new ideas, different ways of doing things, alternative ways of thinking. Seen in that context, active listening becomes an entirely different skill. People feel that they are being patronized and

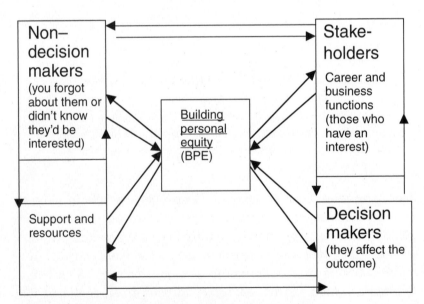

Figure 7.2   Building Personal Equity: A Continuum of Feedback

humored if the listening is merely a break in the conversation so they can "have their say." Active listening means processing the information that the speaker is giving and thinking about its relevance and applicability, an intellectual process.

Emotional Listening

The other component of listening is emotional. Anyone who has maintained a relationship with another person for even the shortest time will know this feeling. Have you ever listened to people who made you so angry, so frustrated, and so reactive that it took all your self-control not to leap off your chair and throttle them? Of course, very few of us actually behave that way. Social, moral, and criminal sanctions prevent such behavior. But in business, sometimes those who anger you the most are in positions of leadership (or authority), and convention dictates that their wishes become your desires!

What does all this have to do with leadership? *Everything.*

Understanding the basic human instincts that respond to anger with fight or flight (the essential traits of survival, anthropologically) will give you a significant edge in relating to others and will change the effectiveness of both your leadership and your management skills. Lack of awareness regarding listeners' reactions (namely, lack of sophistication about the concept of emotional listening) produces an effect opposite to that which most communication strives for—information transfer and behavior change. Those who are listening in an emotional fashion will tune out the speaker if they feel angry, intimidated, bored, or patronized.

Leaders with active listening skills (The Ten Essential Traits leaders) who understand the signs of emotional listening are able to tailor their remarks to the situation. They listen to the responses and comments of others with both intellectual and emotional awareness. Building personal equity happens when you are good at these skills and are able to move around an organization both listening and communicating effectively.

Figure 7.3 visually depicts some of the concepts we have been reviewing—for those of you who like to see rather than read.

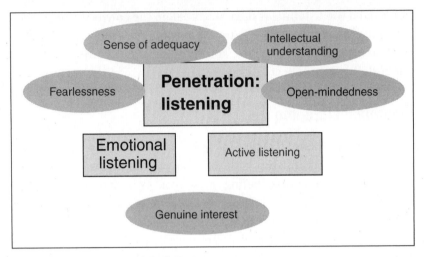

Figure 7.3   Penetration: Listening

One of the biggest concerns of all good leaders is this: *"Am I getting the bad news as well as the good news? Or are people telling me what they think I want to hear?"*

This leads to another discussion of the elephant in the room.

The Elephant in the Room

When were you last in a situation where the real issue was not discussed but, rather, peripheral issues were debated? Here's an example. One large Fortune 500 company that we were recently working with was going through its umpteenth reorganization. Employees were just tired out from trying to remember everyone's new group, new title, and new job. This resulted in endless meetings. Meetings to decide who would work on whose team, meetings to determine job titles for everyone, meetings to schedule meetings! And the main topic at every meeting was how to get internal buy-in from others in the organization regarding the new groups and titles. This would usually generate yet another meeting.

What was the elephant in the room? The fact that this company has no leadership at various levels of the organization. The CEO does a good job of broadcasting, from a 30,000-foot-high point of view, the vision for the company. That is not the problem. As you know, the

CEO is farthest from the implementation of his or her vision. In this example, the next layer of management is communicating to their direct reports via detailed memos that announce new groups and new titles using the same people. Although they may not use these exact words in their memos, here is the gist of the memos e-mailed to their direct reports:

> Create a new group with a new mandate. Move people around. Don't reduce my head count (the number of people I am responsible for), but make up a fancy job description to justify what we are doing. And don't be real specific. Leave it vague so people can come to their own conclusions.

The result is a very busy group of people. Their main activity is creating presentations to present to each other. Conference calls, meetings, off-site sessions—all of these activities take up a lot of time, since the organization is devoid of real leadership beneath the level of the CEO. And some would argue that a CEO who cannot direct his or her direct reports is ineffective.

What *should* they do? Here is another scenario.

The CEO certainly should be announcing the 30,000-foot-high vision. After all, that person *is* the policymaker and visionary for the company. It's the next layer of management that missed an opportunity. They have communicated so vaguely and their reports are so confused that they are creating even more bureaucracy to maintain their head count, power, and influence. Clearer mandates, outlining defined accountability and expectations from their reports, would create an environment of action rather than one of obfuscation. How could the CEO and the next layer of senior management communicate better? By penetrating the company at multiple levels—one-on-one discussions with middle managers; walking around; using the relationships of the past to create equity that could be leveraged for this very situation; picking up the phone, calling middle managers, and asking for their opinions or for descriptions of real-life situations with customers or suppliers. All of these actions will add a touch of badly needed reality to an organization that is chasing its tail. They are also the kinds of management techniques that make up the third part of our Ten Essential Traits: free information exchange and benchmarking.

Respect, Not Friendship

This is not the same as being "one of the guys." The objective of organizational penetration is not about friendship, but about respect. Some organizations create a Friday happy hour or pizza lunch to create social situations where everyone can mingle. This is an example of the management techniques in the third part of our Ten Essential Traits: free information exchange. Think of it as a continuum, as shown in Figure 7.4.

A small company called The Iris Group in Carlsbad, California, has taken this idea to another level. The company is in the postcard business with a highly sophisticated and digitized printing and design operation that takes the product from concept to mail delivery and fulfillment. Steven Hoffman, founder and CEO (it is privately held), noticed that hundreds of employees were leaving the company building for lunch, often driving quite a distance to find a place to eat since the company was located in a developing community without many restaurants. This time-consuming activity caused a decrease in productivity. Alternatively, some employees would bring their own lunches and eat at their desks. This resulted in no communication, little networking, and few opportunities for team and group leaders to build personal equity and penetrate the organization with new and fruitful business relationships.

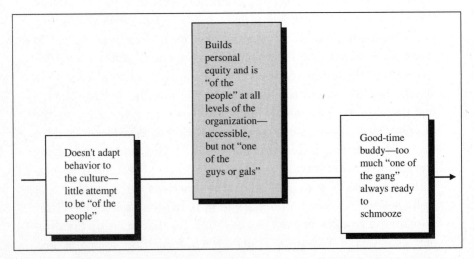

Figure 7.4   The Continuum of Building Respect, Not Necessarily Friendship

Hoffman decided to provide a soup and salad bar for employees, with fruit and cookies for dessert, thinking his employees might use this resource a few days a week and go out the rest of the time. However, this works so well that no one leaves the company during the lunch hour, employees sit together in the cafeteria and talk, less time is wasted, and building personal equity through penetration has moved into all areas of the company, dramatically increasing the effectiveness of all teams. Hoffman and his senior management team now have the ability to talk to people at every level of the company and actually know what is going on! Interestingly, this is *the* benefit that employees talk about. It has become an employment differentiator and part of the culture of this small company, which is growing by double-digit numbers annually.

Walk-Around Management

Walk-around management is not as easy today as it has been in the past. One of the reasons is the corporate security challenge that faces CEOs. Many of the CEOs I have worked with have had personal threats on their lives, and some have resorted to hiring security forces as a consequence. This has led to certain floors in corporate buildings being accessible only by invitation and slews of bodyguards accompanying CEOs who are moving around. This does not lend itself to casual conversation and walk-around management. In addition, when the CEO's executive assistant plays the role of gatekeeper, a casual conversation with the CEO becomes almost impossible.

Cal James, CEO of Kaiser Permanente's Permco Subsidiary, has taken a different approach: "I don't have a secretary, assistant, or anything else. When I got here, the job had a full-time assistant and a full-time executive assistant assigned to her. I don't need it."

Many CEOs, however, have tried to circumvent their inaccessibility by encouraging direct e-mails from anyone in the organization and by having voice mail for incoming direct calls. This means that at the end of a long and demanding day, many CEOs answer e-mail and voice-mail messages until the wee hours of the morning. It's worth it. Electronic "walking around" may be the only way left to access the personal equity network of relationships for leaders in global and multilocational organizations. Lew Platt, former CEO of Hewlett-

Packard, did what he called "an all-hands coffee talk" at various HP locations for individual discussions with small groups. In addition, electronic communications have been an important tool for Carly Fiorina during her tenure as part of her mission to change the slow-moving parts of Hewlett-Packard while retaining the golden parts of the company culture in an era of slowed growth and earnings.

Often, using management practices that give the impression that senior management has good access to information can create the perception of penetration. This perception can become reality with further effort. And the practices themselves move the organization in the right direction to support the perception of having built personal equity.

A good example is Southwest Airlines, which has a "day in the field" concept, where senior managers work with departments on the front lines. This is supported by the Front Line Forum at Southwest, where senior employees meet with senior managers (including CEO Herb Kelleher) to discuss how to improve the company. Those suggestions are then acted upon. These kinds of sharing sessions will have the opposite effect if nothing changes. In other words, the elephant in that room would be *ignoring the suggestions* that people have taken the time to contribute. (Message: "We don't really care what you think even though we say we do. Clearly, this is not a good message to give employees!)

Of course, it doesn't hurt that Kelleher is no more than four management layers away from every frontline supervisor. Another tool that helps this process comes in the form of Colleen Barrett, who currently holds the position of president and depends on a network of people to keep her up-to-date on what is going on with all employees. This provides the perception that management knows all the important events in the personal lives of their people.

Insecurity

Clearly, a leader who is insecure in his or her decisions runs the risk of communicating that problem to employees in one-on-one discussions. It's difficult to imagine that a leader can rise through the organizational ranks to a position in senior management while being insecure in his or her decisions. But it happens. Don't mistake this characteristic for humility. The most appealing trait of a leader is the ability to be humble. It generally comes from a good sense of self, a feeling of personal adequacy that enables an open willingness to learn. Unfortunately, it is one of the most difficult characteristics for many organizations that seem to institutionalize corporate arrogance—and for many leaders who see it as a sign of weakness.

Patience

What role does patience play in this characteristic of penetration? Personal equity is not built in a day or a year. It takes time. Most action-oriented people have limited patience and short fuses. Consequently, this trait will be difficult to learn and will probably be forced on them. For example, working in a large organization means constantly being willing to defer gratification. Making decisions takes time, seeing results often depends on the actions of many, and getting resources becomes a process of proof of concept, debate, persuasion, and salesmanship. Entrepreneurs are impatient by nature and prefer to control decision making, which is why there are so few entrepreneurs in large companies (at least who stay).

The increasing importance of patience is antithetical to a world of instantaneous feedback and satisfaction encouraged by the Internet environment. Yet managing contradictions is what business is now all about. This is one of them.

"Just do it." "Now is not soon enough." "Satisfaction is just a click away." These are the admonitions of a society in a hurry. Yet building personal equity takes many repeated interactions, and often it is created over *years*. Knowledge workers particularly—those who hold the intelligence assets of the organization in their heads—will carry their equity relationships with them wherever they go.

Personal equity is *not* limited by corporate boundaries or legal structures. It moves with an individual. Hence, those who patiently build multiple relationships over the years are continually creating their own databases of community. These leaders often take their teams with them to new opportunities. Building personal equity and penetrating an organization deeply is a skill that is not job-dependent, which is why I believe that it is one of the more important of The Ten Essential Traits—it travels with you wherever you go and can be one of your most treasured personal assets. All of this justifies being patient in the development of your personal equity base—and realizing that, even in a fast-moving world, the relationships in which you have invested yourself (not necessarily friendships) will be assets you tap into continually.

This was made clear to me during my many years of presenting programs on technology and alliances in China. On my first trip there in 1988 (at the invitation of the Science and Technology Commission of Beijing), a young aeronautical engineer who worked for the commission, Wang Xuezong, was instructed to accompany me and act as my assistant throughout my travels. I was also provided a car and chauffeur, a translator, and a local representative of the Science and Technology Commission in each city or province where I lectured.

We began in Beijing, and over the following weeks, I lectured in Nanjing, Hangshou, Shanghai, and Guangdong. Everywhere we traveled, Xuezong, who had until that time never been in a Western-style hotel or on an airplane, was by my side, hungrily absorbing everything he could, dogging my every step to learn as much and as fast as was humanly possible. In each place we visited, he was able to call upon his personal network of contacts, fascinating young men and women in various professions and jobs, all of whom comprised his personal equity. Depending on the circumstances, he called in his *guanxi*, a system of "favors" that enabled him to get what he needed. These favors varied from arranging for bicycles so we could ride around the mystical lake of the Hangshou region to finding out how we could observe a particular technology that was being developed to creating an impromptu dance in one of the government workrooms for all the people who had attended my lecture that day. The network Xuezong had built during 20 years of government-sponsored education and employment was a reliable source for everything he needed, from career advancement to recreation to good eating. In my continued visits to China over the next 15 years, I watched Xuezong grow, along with his networks and his ability to obtain *guanxi*. He is now deputy mayor of the capital city of a province of 200 million people—as well as president of that city's technological research and development center. He has obtained graduate degrees in the United

Kingdom and the United States and is a world traveler and global businessman. Although he still calls me his "American Mom," it is clear that the student has become the teacher.

Power, Glory, and Glitz

Certainly there is power in being a leader. And the perks aren't bad, either. But some CEOs have a different perspective. Cal James, CEO of Kaiser Permanente's Permco, says, "I don't believe in limo travel. I can't run my company that way and expect people to take anything I say seriously if I am living a different life from them. So I travel in coach with my employees."

Companies spend a lot of time on titles. They are important only anthropologically, in that we are territorial and titles define our territory for others and ourselves. "This is *mine* and that is *yours* and don't mess around on my turf" is the message. Some people love it more than others. Cal James is the exception:

> When I retire, I'm not going to miss the way people defer to me because I am the CEO. I have always hated this. I don't believe in my heart of hearts that I should be treated differently or in any special way because of my position. I want to be respected for my content knowledge and my ability to work with the team and move them forward, not because of my position.

Humility is a rare characteristic in the corporate world. Yet where it is found, is the same place that leadership will naturally find its home. Herb Kelleher, in his normal indefatigable way, describes it as "professional terminalism."

> People who emphasize too strongly the fact that they are professionals usually are not very good at what they do. What really adds up to professionalism is being very good at what you do in a very modest way. That's the way our people are. They are results oriented. Whether it's the best safety record in the world, the best customer service record in the world, the youngest jet fleet [although Jet Blue Airlines can now claim they have the youngest all-new jet fleet in the world] or lower fares, our people are really focused.[1]

Natural leaders are those who demonstrate many of The Ten Essential Traits, and, significantly, they may be unanointed as leaders. This means that they just naturally become those to whom a team will turn, those who seem to have things sorted out, or at least have a sense of what to do. These people, and you can probably think of some you have encountered in your life, are generally humble, finding their leadership to be something of an accident. Accidental leadership happens with clear talent and an above-average portion of The Ten Essential Traits. The age-old debate of whether leadership is a natural or a learned phenomenon need not be resolved. My research shows that whether leaders come about by acquiring The Ten Essential Traits or just naturally have them doesn't matter. The result is the same.

Intimacy

Intimacy is not a term we often use in business. In fact, we avoid the term and the concept because of visions of sexual harassment and more. Yet intimacy is as old as the human condition, and every organization has to define its perception of intimacy. The characteristic of being "of the people," (i.e., building personal equity through penetration) denotes some level of emotional and intellectual intimacy. One aspect of intimacy that, for obvious reasons, is *not* part of this discussion is physical and sexual intimacy. Other than that, organizations that create intellectual and social intimacy among their employees, and even with their customers and suppliers, will succeed in building long-term loyalty. I have been fortunate to be a keynote speaker at many executive retreats held by companies to celebrate their relationships with their key customers or key suppliers. They hold these meetings at five-star resorts to reward these key players in an intimate setting and to create an atmosphere of camaraderie and respect. And it works. One electronics distributor that has invited me to speak on a number of occasions tells me its annual event is so sought after that customers compete internally to see who will attend. They have to limit attendance to particular executives with whom they have the most contact. Everyone wants to come, not just for a good party, but because the relationships made with others at the meeting (not just their hosts) are enormously valuable. They are building intimacy and a feeling of belonging.[2]

Dean Ornish, M.D., a well-respected physician and author of many books, has done extensive research on heart disease. In his audio program, *The Healing Power of Love and Intimacy*, he verifies that his research has established that intimacy is good for your health. A lack of intimacy (closeness, feelings of belonging, a sense of inclusion) increases the risk and incidence of heart disease and slows the healing process. Corporate belonging is one of the reasons people stay affiliated to large (and small) organizations (see Chapter 4) despite bureaucracy, frustration, and lack of power or control.

Another aspect of intimacy is the ability to be personally vulnerable. Showing yourself to be a "real" person rather than one who always keeps a stiff upper lip can be a plus, especially for those who are running large groups or organizations. Unfortunately, this area is a slippery slope for women. Men can cry in front of others. Women cannot. Although in recent times U.S. culture has become more open to public displays of deep emotion (e.g., the Cantor Fitzgerald CEO's emotional interview on CNN's *Larry King Live* about his firm's loss of 700 employees in the September 11 disaster), women who display public emotion are generally given more criticism than men who do the same.

The result is that many women in leadership positions are considered "iron ladies" (as was former British prime minister Margaret Thatcher) for their lack of public emotion. This is changing as more women head large corporations or start their own organizations. The level of women's clout in the business world is still low. The Committee of 200 (a group of the most powerful and influential women in the corporate world) released its *Business Leadership Index* on January 24, 2002 (Chicago, Illinois), showing that businesswomen are just under two-fifths of the way to parity with men. (The largest percentage of new businesses in the United States annually, however, are started by women.) It can't happen fast enough.

Building Equity with Those You Dislike

Yes, it happens. The main challenge is not in working with someone you dislike. It is whether you or they commit to doing something and then do it. If so, you could develop a relationship that is based on a guarded level of respect even if you don't like each other.

A personal experience brought this lesson home to me when I was CEO of a company that distributed products and services to the electronics and aerospace industries. A buyer who worked for an important customer called our company to complain. After a series of unpleasant conversations with various people in my organization, I decided to intervene, even though this person clearly was out of line. It took all my self-control to not say what I wanted to. I am known for my bluntness, which, in my role as a consultant is valued and paid for, but as part of a corporate team can be a difficult trait. Honesty is one thing, diplomacy quite another. Phrasing a negative statement diplomatically is a corporate art form that Ten Essential Traits managers have to learn.

In this situation, the buyer was rude and insulting. Our customer was a very large company, and relatively speaking, we were small. I swallowed my reactive reply and instead offered one that acknowledged his frustration, enabled him to vent, and came up with a number of suggestions for fixing the problem. My main focus was to thank him for bringing to my attention something that was so important. (It was only important to him, but that's the point, isn't it?)

This tactic is what I now call a *diffusing technique*. Diffuse the emotion, turn it into something positive, like thanking someone for bringing the issue to your attention. On many occasions, angry people are diffused and disarmed by such an approach. Did I like this loud-mouthed egomaniac? Not at all ("obnoxious personality" would be an understatement). But we were a supplier and he represented a valued customer. Swallow your ego, muzzle your mouth, and do the right thing for the company.

Organizational Characteristic: Flexibility

Peter Drucker believes in building personal equity. He doesn't use that term, however, and presents it in the context of flexible organizational structures. "No one corporate structure works for all," he said recently during conversation when I was a keynote speaker at his Drucker Foundation Conference. "Flexibility is key. Know what structure is appropriate—hierarchy, flat, teams, individual contributors, virtual organization, which is a constellation of core competencies."

In my last book, *FastAlliances: Power Your E-business*,[3] I created a management tool called the Spider Network, which examines a constellation or network of partnering companies who are alternately competitors and collaborators. This is by far the most complex organizational structure, because control is not possible unless there are equity stakes, and cooperation is key. Hierarchy, as described in the early part of this book, is the command-and-control approach to management and, when appropriate, can be very effective. As can every other organizational structure. The challenge is to decide which structure to use when. That takes real leadership. Consequently, the characteristics comprising The Ten Essential Traits can assist you in deciding which type of organizational structure is correct for the circumstance, as well as how to execute it and whether the people involved will respond to and thrive under such a structure. If not, change the team or change the structure. This is particularly important when planning and implementing a short- or long-term strategy for an organization. This is known simply as *the ability to balance short- and long-term needs.*

Very often, corporate or situational crises create the need for a hierarchical structure. First, people are scared. They want someone to tell them what to do. Whether you want to label reorganizations as corporate crises or not depends on where you are in the organization. The lower you are, the less potent you feel. That is why Hans Selye (*The Stress of Life*)[4] created the concept of *eustress,* which is good stress, as opposed to *stress,* which is negative stress. Leaders and senior management may respond to a corporate crisis with renewed energy and drive, experiencing "positive stress," or *eustress,* that gives them the will and creativity to find solutions. However, those who have less control over their destinies will often go into corporate paralysis or worse, building up a load of negative stress that can manifest itself in behaviors destructive to the organization (e.g., hiding evidence of the crisis in their denial of it).

Coca-Cola suffered a crisis of brand value in 2000 and 2001, first in Belgium and then throughout Europe, due to a poor response to a local crisis, which then spread into a major concern regarding brand value and truthfulness. When bottlers in Belgium encountered various sanitary problems, management in the United States showed a U.S.-centric approach and little response. The news pundits took the problem and ran with it, resulting in a public relations debacle that took the company years to fix and contributed to a change in management. It is difficult to estimate Coca-Cola's brand value, but it is large, very large. And this miscalculation of leadership led to a hammering of the stock and a temporary diminution of consumer confidence.

What management characteristic was lacking there? If senior management had been more "of the people," if they had stored personal equity, if they had applied active listening with respect, these traits would have made a substantial difference. The elephant in the room was the arrogance and U.S.-centricity of management, which manifested itself in a number of ways. For one thing, a poor communication system existed between Coca-Cola's international operations and its U.S.-centric headquarters in Atlanta. Other factors included lack of true desire to fix the problem locally, not taking it seriously, and ignoring damage control. A senior management team who had built personal equity and been "of the people" would have had truth tellers to acknowledge the seriousness of the problem and to demand timely and culturally sensitive action in Europe before things got out of control and the media ran with the story.

It is well accepted in the world of crisis management that Johnson & Johnson takes the gold medal for its handling of the Tylenol crisis. The company's response was exemplary.

When reports came in that Tylenol packages had been tampered with, hierarchical management decisions sent the whole organization into action. Tylenol was withdrawn from all retail shelves. Product was restocked with a different top and extra precautions. Communications were direct and simple. "The customer must be protected. Do whatever it takes. Nothing is too much. Don't skimp. Make it happen. We will stand behind our product and our brand." Management showed self-confidence, active listening, and appreciation of the personal equity built by the brand within its customer base. Johnson & Johnson moved with alacrity to resolve all issues. The flexibility of the organization and the willingness to change management structures to swiftly deal with the crisis saved the brand.

Flexibility means setting up and tearing down continually. Specifically, it's the *content*, not the structure, that matters. Cal James of Kaiser Permanente Permco says it this way: "We set up and tear down teams. There is a lot of ad hocracy, setting up and tearing down task forces and work groups."

Another company that does a superlative job in this arena is Kingston Technology, a large independent maker of computer memory boards. "Job descriptions are blurred, and people are free to move between projects and take personal initiatives. There is no executive dining room, no reserved parking spaces, and the founders sit in low-walled cubicles like everyone else." This is nothing new in entrepreneurial companies or even in traditional companies who are trying to create cultural change to an egalitarian setup. However, Kingston Technology also divided up $100 million among its 523 employees when the company was sold. Now *that's* egalitarian.[5]

Another example is a Danish company called Oticon, maker of hearing aids, which took the bold step of eliminating all job descriptions, doing away with functional specialization, and disposing of resource allocation systems. Even more radical, all reporting relationships disappeared along with geographic placement of offices. The company became a roster of projects.[6]

Radical behavior as a method of change management can work. However, when an outside manager comes in with radical suggestions, he or she has to be diplomatic. Cal James again: "Because I am an outsider, employees often discount what I have to say since they don't necessarily see its relevance. So I have to package it in such a way that it doesn't come across as being unreasonable."

Herb Kelleher of Southwest Airlines is less patient. "We've tried to create an environment where people are free to, in effect, bypass even the fairly lean structures that we have in order to get something done."[7] His executive vice president of operations agrees: "I tell people, and I mean it, you don't have to have an appointment to see me. The only reason to even call is that I may be out of my office."[8] The SWZ Cutting Edge Program at Southwest has created communication connections between groups that in the past felt some animosity toward each other. Designed by a captain to improve relations between the pilots and ground crew, this program enables the pilots to work with the ground crew to learn about what goes on around the plane while it is waiting at the gate. This has been successful in building a communication network between these two groups.

The Math of an Internal or External Network

Mathematics can be applied to the structure of an organization in such a way that it supports *the ability to see interrelated connections.*

Mathematics supports the concept of six degrees of separation, which postulates that no more than six people separate everyone in the world.[9] This theory was first devised in the 1960s by social psychologist Stanley Milgram from Harvard University. Milgram randomly selected people in Kansas and Nebraska, handed them a letter addressed to people they did not know in Massachusetts, and asked them to mail the letter to an acquaintance who would bring it closer to the target. Milgram found that in each case, it took an average of only five intermediaries before the letter reached its recipient. This meant that there were six degrees of separation between the recipients in Massachusetts and the senders in the Midwest.

Two other scientists took this theory to another level. Duncan J. Watts, a postdoctoral fellow at Columbia University, and Steven H. Strogatz, a mathematics professor at Cornell, theorized that just a few well-placed individuals in a company could dramatically speed up the flow of information by acting as emissaries among floors and departments. When Watts and Strogatz did the mathematics, they discovered that it takes a very few random connections, or shortcuts, to make a small world out of a large one. Once that world is identified, adding additional connections has little effect. These two scientists applied experimental mathematics, which combines computer simulations and mathematical analysis to look at two kinds of human interaction. Watts calls the first kind "the caveman approach," which assumes that each person knows only those people in his or her immediate community. The second kind is a "random world approach," where each person is connected to others scattered around the world. These researchers combined both kinds of interaction into an amalgam, and from that came the conclusion that relatively few connections were needed to turn a large world into a small one. They further applied this model to two scenarios—the Western Electric power grid of the United States and the 235,000 actors listed in the Internet movie database. In each case, their theory held true. In June 1998, they released their findings to the world in the scientific journal *Nature*.[10]

How does this research apply to The Ten Essential Traits, and why am I telling you about it in a book on leadership? Here are the nuggets of insight for you:

1. You don't need many leaders to bring about change or influence. Communication by the right (well-connected) people at the right time to other right (well-connected) people can make huge incremental change happen. The key is to identify the right people. They will be those who incorporate many, if not all, of The Ten Essential Traits.

2. When these well-connected individuals leave a company, they can cause that company to lose its effective internal communication system, creating a time of chaos and poor internal understanding of what's going on.

The most important application of this insight is to nurture those who embody The Ten Essential Traits. They may well *be* your internal communication system, because those who are particularly adept at building personal equity (i.e., who are "of the people") will naturally become those who are well connected. Their internal networks may be one of your most valuable corporate assets.

Cal James offers his personal experience of what can happen when someone leaves an organization where his personal network, equity, and connectedness were key factors in the organization's success:

> I left a scenario not so long ago where I worked very hard to maintain relationships, and when I left, those relationships soured and things deteriorated. It had nothing to do with the work we did. It was the people who could not get along, and I had played the role of mediator and liaison, and this had kept things together, but only while I was there.

James has had a different challenge as CEO of Kaiser Permanente Permco:

I am not part of the blood fraternity, which is the group of medical doctors of Kaiser Permanente. We are an internal consulting group to the medical fraternity, and there is a high degree of skepticism about an internal consulting organization knowing anything, even though it is full of people who come from the outside. Not being part of the fraternity [*and the network of personal equity that they have built*] means I can only go so far.

A wonderful example of building personal equity and the positive effect it can have is seen in an old episode of *M*A*S*H**, a former television series about a medical unit in the Korean War. Characters B.J. Honeycutt and Hawkeye Pierce invent a fictional person by the name of John Tuttle, who does great works and is involved in all sorts of heroic activities. His personal equity is so high that everyone claims to know him and to be his friend and confidant. He dies a hero's death and his back pay (B.J. and Hawkeye convince the Army that Tuttle hasn't received a paycheck for many years) is donated to a local orphanage. Of course, the irony is that Tuttle's huge store of personal equity (which makes him such a desirable friend, colleague, leader, and employee) and the vast network of those who consider themselves in his sphere of influence were built by a nonexistent person.

Another way to use this technique is to support the third part of our Ten Essential Traits, the idea of benchmarking across the organization. So much good knowledge is developed across complex organizations—and then developed all over again at a huge, wasteful cost. By benchmarking across organizational silos, knowledge can be shared and transferred. However, the only way this can happen is by giving credit where credit is due: I call it *corporate currency*. What is the currency of intracorporate knowledge transfer? Most of the time, it's not money, although there can be budget contributions for certain research that is shared across divisions. However, most of the time it's *recognition*, giving credit where it's due—the most valuable type of intracorporate payment there is. Benchmarking across divisions or groups can dig up real nuggets of knowledge and value— to be shared only on the condition that those who do it best or who developed it are given their due. This could be in the form of personal recognition or group sublabeling—for example, the SWOT Team (Strength, Weakness, Opportunity, and Threat Team), the Fast-

Track Team. This management technique helps to implement the penetration characteristic of The Ten Essential Traits throughout the organization.

Outcomes

Leaders who invest time in developing individual relationships at multiple levels of the organization build personal equity (a store of goodwill, relationships, knowledge, and intelligence). This results in opening the lines of truth (people telling what they know and not obfuscating) and creating bonds of loyalty well in advance of a crisis, thus ensuring that communication to and from these leaders is valuable and useful information. The outcome for the employees at every level of the organization is that they come to believe their opinions count and that there is no penalty for speaking the truth. The outcome for the organization is that these Ten Essential Traits managers provide a conduit to bring about organizational change and buy-in, thus ensuring that there are no invisible elephants in the room, taking up valuable space, using up precious resources, and making a big mess that others have to clean up.

Penetration: Action Items

Personal

- Where are you in your lifelong process of building personal equity?
- Map out the relationships that you have developed in your present or past positions. Have you continued to nurture them?
- Are you a person whom others consider to be in their personal equity pool? If not, how can you prove your value and trustworthiness to others who could connect to you in this way if they knew you were there?
- What is your plan to make others aware of your value and willingness to be part of their personal equity plan? And what is your plan to build up your own penetration of the organization you are presently with?

Organizational

- How does your organization encourage or discourage walk-around management?

- Can you eliminate the role of gatekeeper? Do you have an overvigilant executive assistant? Can you institute direct communication processes via e-mail or dedicated voice mail for direct reports?

- Map the areas of the organization where it would be most beneficial for senior management to have personal equity relationships. Make sure that they devote time to creating them.

- Encourage "of the people" behavior—get-togethers, environments that encourage personal discussions between senior management and all levels of the organization (no separate cafeteria for management, walk-around management, etc.).

- Examine organizational structures and make them as flexible as possible.

- Look for areas where cross-organizational benchmarking could transfer knowledge, but keep in mind that corporate currency means giving credit, recognition, or even labeling to the originator of the knowledge.

Intelligence: The Ability to Achieve Your Potential

It is a fundamental belief of the D.A.R.E. program that there is no such a thing as a child who is not intelligent, unless there is a mental or brain disability. D.A.R.E. believes and espouses that no one must be doomed because of his or her environment or economic situation. Everyone has the ability to achieve his or her potential.

—CEO and cofounder of D.A.R.E., Chief Glenn Levant

The intelligence factor is controversial. Can you learn to be intelligent? I believe you can. There is such a thing as a lazy mind. Biologists have proven that brain cells die (as do all cells) and that only by exercising the brain can that precious yet mysterious organ be kept in as good repair as the aging process will permit.

Intelligence in regard to The Ten Essential Traits leaders is somewhat different. (See Figure 8.1.) It's an intelligence filled with insight and perspective. It has a healthy dose of maturity and a sense of self-worth thrown in. As with emotional intelligence, this characteristic includes emotional control in dealing with stress and interpersonal conflict, as well as interpersonal sensitivity and a humane empathy for others. The manifestation of this kind of intelligence is the willingness to identify others who have talent and place them in the appropriate positions where they can excel, then arrange the environment in such a way that they will not only excel, but be rewarded for so doing.

Few organizations can do this while serving over 30 million customers, all of whom are individuals with local needs and constraints.

Personal Characteristic	Organizational Environment Needed	Example of a Management Process for Implementation
1. *Fearlessness*	Permits failure	Shared learning and shared power
2. *Completion:* Ability to complete; has patience and is flexible	Results-oriented with process freedom	Horizontal, project-oriented management processes with cross-functional and multi-locational teams
3. *Commitment:* Emotionally vested	Encourages individual contributions	Small work groups and flexible work behavior; fun
4. *Inspiration:* Inspires and communicates vision; motivates	Access to internal and external people networks	Constant visibility and accessibility
5. *Assuredness:* Knows what he or she wants	Opportunities for advancement and reward	Career progression process
6. *Penetration:* "Of the people" and builds personal equity; listens with respect; empowers with dignity; confident; good mediator	Flexible organizational structure	Free information exchange, communication, and benchmarking across groups and divisions
7. *Intelligence:* Talent to place right people in right place	Resource commitment to learning	Training and education

Figure 8.1   The Ten Essential Traits: The Larraine Segil Matrix

Even fewer can do it with little or no capital, few assets other than knowledge workers, and an army of people with only the belief, the commitment, and the time to make it happen. I am speaking of D.A.R.E.[1] This remarkable organization now operates in 54 countries. Its community acceptance and local implementation has created a leadership system that would make any Ten Essential Traits advocate proud. The founder, CEO, and chairman of D.A.R.E. is Chief Glenn Levant, former deputy chief of police for the Los Angeles Police Department. He had a dream, and his dream now brings its antidrug/antialcohol message to over 55 million schoolchildren worldwide, more than any other program. It has improved societies all over the globe as generations of young people lead drug- and alcohol-free lives.

The following pages outline the leadership structure of the D.A.R.E. program, known only to a few in its entirety, which offers remarkable insight into a grassroots organization that is more effective than buzz marketing (see Chapter 10) and works in many different cultures and communities.

D.A.R.E. was founded on the belief that government doesn't work. This is the elephant in the room that many refuse to acknowledge (especially those who benefit from government funding). And often, those who do see this elephant in the room would rather be elephant spotters than Ten Essential Traits managers who can make the elephant go away and replace it with something valuable. They feel paralyzed to make a difference.

Additionally, government programs are based on budget cycles and elections and are highly political. Local government controls local law enforcement (often thinly spread police officers or sheriffs). Consequently, if you want to reach children, you must deal with two bureaucracies—the local school systems (of which there are 15,000 in the United States) and local law enforcement (i.e., local politicians). Politicians are often thinking in terms of elections or budgets and are not thinking long term. So the challenge for D.A.R.E. was to come up with a solution that could apply an ounce of prevention to create a pound of cure in a cost-effective and widespread way. What evolved was one of the best models of private-public partnerships ever to be created.

D.A.R.E. established itself in Los Angeles, creating a not-for-profit corporate and tax structure (501c3) and a board of directors consisting of prominent local people. The board included the chief of police, the sheriff, and the superintendent of schools—in other words, all the stakeholders. These influential members of the board of directors were forced to work with each other. Lower-level bureaucrats were not involved, and so could not invent reasons why something could not be done. Creating buy-in by putting all the major stakeholders and decision makers into the same room was brilliant. Any good idea will have lots of followers.

Drug Abuse Resistance Education (D.A.R.E.) is based on the ounce-of-prevention theory from any angle you care to look at it: The business community wants stable employees and a good customer base. School systems want to prevent drug abuse and certainly don't want any of their children overdosing. Law enforcement wants to reduce crime, and 70 to 90 percent of all crime in the United States is related to drug abuse. So prevention is a good idea—and when you have a good idea and make it available at little or no cost to people, the concept will spread.

As stated, the D.A.R.E. pilot project began in Los Angeles with the superintendent of schools, the head of the Los Angeles Police Department, and people from the local business community. People all over the country started hearing about the project and came to Los Angeles to visit the D.A.R.E. operation. Demand was huge for replication of the program. And so D.A.R.E. began to spread. Now, almost two decades later, D.A.R.E. reaches all over the United States and beyond.

The strategy was to set up a *memorandum of understanding* (MOU) that would be the standard for all communities. Every community that wanted a D.A.R.E. program would have to create agreement between the stakeholders (i.e., the local business community, the school district, and the local police). All would have to sign this MOU. This meant that the local school district accepted the concept and the local police agreed to do the training.

The budget cycle in most municipalities takes about 18 months to two years. If an idea is fresh and desirable, it is critical to make it timely, so you want to avoid the budget cycle. Therefore, the approach was taken that once the MOU was signed, instructors would be chosen by the local sheriff or police and sent to a free two-week training course. Only the housing and airfare and related costs would be paid by the city.

Every police department has local resources and a small budget to help children. Generally, that has been used in the past for public relations. D.A.R.E. provided an excellent opportunity to apply these funds for a valuable and lasting effect on the community, so these funds were allocated to the D.A.R.E. training program, after which the instructors returned to their local environments with a one-year supply of educational materials. They could start teaching immediately and did not lose a year.

The implementation was cost effective. The private sector financed the education materials and the costs of training. The city government paid for lodging and transportation. The police department was already paying the local instructor's salary because a department veteran (usually a truant officer) was selected to do the training. This meant that he or she was involved in prevention as opposed to capturing criminals, and research clearly shows that prevention costs are low compared to the huge expense of incarceration.

As more communities learned about this program, enlightened police chiefs promoted D.A.R.E. in their communities as a way to prevent children from choosing a life of crime. Rather than being seen as a force hired to "beat up on bad kids," these police officers were perceived as proactive and enlightened—as helpful partners of their communities, not as negative enforcers of laws. The D.A.R.E. program puts the officers in a situation where a child's first exposure to police shows them as helpers. They are seen as positive role models in their positions as D.A.R.E. instructors and are admired in their uniforms in an elementary school environment.

The good idea has spread by word of mouth. The D.A.R.E. program is one of the first and best examples of the new concept of buzz marketing: simply letting people know that if the MOU between the local police department and the school district was in place, then D.A.R.E. was available to them and their community.

D.A.R.E. started with an idea in 1983. Just four years later, by the end of 1987, over 60 percent of the school districts in the country had implemented D.A.R.E. In 2002, it is over 80 percent!

When leadership is based on a value system that is generally acceptable to most people, when the result is the teaching of intelligence, good judgment, and something that contributes to well-being of individuals and communities, then the idea and its spread is irresistible. The Ten Essential Traits approach has qualities similar to the D.A.R.E. program in that the top-down approach is not needed to make the idea work. People will see the efficacy of the concept and it will spread rapidly throughout the organizational ecosystem.

Other important aspects of the D.A.R.E. program involve the fidelity of its delivery. The curriculum is the same everywhere the program is taught. Police officers, being part of paramilitary organizations, are used to doing things according to the rule book. Officers who become D.A.R.E. teachers are told, "This is the way you are to do things." They are not permitted to skip information they're not comfortable with (which does happen in the school system). D.A.R.E. officers are made to feel comfortable with the material and the fact that they are influencing young people to stay away from bad behaviors.

This is the most important thing that they will do in their careers. The D.A.R.E. program reinforces in officers the very reasons that they went into community service and law enforcement in the first place. For many officers, that idealistic belief becomes tarnished over the years by tough experiences and stress. Generally, police officers tend to be gruff and cynical and when placed in a teaching environment. D.A.R.E. training reminds them of the reason they went into public service and reestablishes their early idealism. They know they are making their community a better place and are credible on the topic they are talking about. Consequently, they teach people how to be credible.

What D.A.R.E. has done for police communities worldwide is to restore their faith in their jobs and their valuable contributions to society. Funding is not an issue because 100 percent of the program's costs are already covered by existing budgets. The instructor earns his salary as a police officer, thus no additional funds are necessary.

As in the corporate world, the real proof is in the implementation. The vast numbers of communities who have adopted the D.A.R.E. program and its success in reaching young people are now well-established facts. The values of the D.A.R.E. program (as with The Ten Essential Traits approach) speak for themselves.

The goal is to teach children to make intelligent decisions. D.A.R.E. understands that people need to know that their work is important—everyone wants to be appreciated, to know their efforts are truly valued, and to see the results of their work. Although communicating this message is very time-consuming, the D.A.R.E. program believes it is essential to let people know their efforts are important and successful. As with The Ten Essential Traits approach in business, the first characteristic, *fearlessness*, requires that the management process include shared learning and shared power. In the D.A.R.E. program, where this aspect of leadership is passed to the very core of our communities (children, parents, education, and law enforcement) sharing learning and insight will perpetuate a culture in which everyone feels valued and is considered a contributor. It also leads to deeper penetration, another of The Ten Essential Traits, being "of the people" and communicating across the silos that develop in organizations. D.A.R.E. understands that nothing is closer to a community's heart than its children. Similarly, in a business environment, no one is too small or too low on the organizational hierarchy to be recognized and involved.

A fundamental belief of the D.A.R.E. program is that there is no such a thing as a child who is not intelligent (unless there is a mental disability). D.A.R.E. believes and espouses that no one should be doomed because of his or her environment or economic situation. Everyone has the ability to achieve their potential—D.A.R.E. calls it "the expanding horizons." Similarly, The Ten Essential Traits matrix is inclusive, not exclusionary. Employees must be given the opportunity to be the best that they can be and must not be typecast because of their environment or history. D.A.R.E. believes, as does The Ten Essential Traits program, that circumstance and opportunity make people terrific leaders. D.A.R.E. does its best to let people, both volunteers and children, know what opportunities are available and how to position themselves to take advantage of them. As with The Ten Essential Traits approach, this program has proven that intelligence and judgment can be taught by example.

The results of D.A.R.E. are impressive—54 nations have adopted the program, and 36 million of the 55 million children worldwide who benefit from the program are in the United States. Drug and alcohol use, as well as smoking and crime statistics, have all declined. There is no question that D.A.R.E. can take some of the credit for that, because the average age of the offenders is getting older. Specifically, those who had the opportunity to go through the program (the oldest are about 16 to 18 years old) are diminishing as a portion of drug- and alcohol-related crime statistics, whereas those who did not are increasing. In addition, those districts that have expanded the D.A.R.E. program to upper and middle schools show better results than those who have not. Another important outcome is that D.A.R.E. has increased parental awareness that their kids could be taking drugs. The program has provided enormous support for parents in coping with their children in the preteen years. Gallup polls indicate that D.A.R.E. has been very helpful in changing attitudes in children because they are taught at an early age that drugs are bad.

What are the challenges? Managing the donated resources of the organization. The instructors are officers employed by the local municipalities and police departments except when they are teaching for D.A.R.E. So D.A.R.E. has created a stakeholder program that develops lots of relationships and liaisons with police chiefs, police organizations, and school associations. In addition, D.A.R.E. has its own cadre of instructors in every country to offer training and motivation. Because D.A.R.E. is a nonprofit organization, all of this is done with money and resources donated by individuals and corporate sponsors. As with The Ten Essential Traits program, a single individual cannot accomplish much. The community of the organization and all the stakeholders who have an interest in the activity must be co-opted. Multiple contributors will increase the environment for buy-in as the results come in.

It is a source of great pride to CEO Glenn Levant that less than 1 percent of the D.A.R.E. budget comes from the federal government. The rest is privately raised. D.A.R.E. develops lots of alliances, with the National Guard, with local law enforcement agencies, with huge groups of volunteers—people who are committed to public service and doing good works.

D.A.R.E. instructors are given 80 hours of training, in which they are taught not only how to teach the curriculum, but also how to be catalysts in the community and how to provide all kinds of support for the children. This has had some remarkable and lifesaving effects. Here are a couple of examples, and scores more happen every day.

On February 14, 2001, in Elmira, New York, a high school student went to school with a satchel in which he had 18 pipe bombs, made from a recipe he found on the Internet. He also had a sawed-off shotgun and two pistols with extra magazines of ammunition. He said he was going to do a Columbine-type massacre. The name of the school was South Side High School, which is in Chemung County, New York, where D.A.R.E. has a program in the elementary schools, but not in middle school or high school.

Some kids in the cafeteria knew what this student had, and they called the police. Deputy Hurley arrived and walked up to the cafeteria. He slowly peered around the corner of the cafeteria wall so that the young man could see his face and head. The young boy said, "Hey, I know you—you were my D.A.R.E. officer in fifth grade." And then he surrendered. He explained that he knew Officer Hurley was a good person who would not hurt him and would talk with him.

Things like this happen thousands of times every day to different degrees. Here's another example.

On the day I interviewed Glenn Levant, he had just received a call from a physician in Florida, who told Levant this story. His daughter is not allowed to ride her bike next to a certain canal in Tallahassee because it is very dangerous. Her girlfriends were pushing her to ride there with them, and she used the D.A.R.E. approach to peer pressure to resist their influence. She came home and told her father, who took the time to call D.A.R.E. to thank them. These are the intangible benefits of a program like D.A.R.E. Similarly, The Ten Essential Traits program will offer many positive results—in improved employee morale, in retention of good people, in increased innovation—that initially are not reflected in monetary value, but prove to be worthwhile over time.

The D.A.R.E. program is voluntary, meaning there are no mandates requiring that communities implement the program. It happens because it works. The proof is there in 80 percent of the school districts throughout the United States and in 56 nations worldwide. Similarly, if The Ten Essential Traits program is initiated only by senior management as a top-down directive, it will fail. It must trickle down, up, sideways, and in all directions as either an organizational or an individual initiative that works, feels right, and gets results.

D.A.R.E. relies on word of mouth to spread its message. The organization has only 31 paid employees worldwide, and its administrative overhead is 0.0003 percent—a remarkable figure.

Here are a few more examples showing how the D.A.R.E. program has changed lives by creating opportunities where none existed before.

In New Haven, Connecticut, right next door to that great beacon of education, Yale University, live children who have no idea what Yale University is. New Haven is an inner-city neighborhood. Even children who did know that Yale was there believed it was for rich people. No one in the school system told them they could go to Yale or made such possibilities believable.

The D.A.R.E. program not only brings officers into the classroom, it also brings in positive role models from all walks of life, including business, government, nonprofits, and more—people from the community who can relate to these kids and tell them how they became successful. These volunteers also tell the children that there are scholarships and financial aid for them if they stay drug free, and they take the children on their first campus tour of Yale. There they meet people just like them who are receiving community scholarships, students who have come from neighborhoods just like theirs. *Then* they believe. No other organization was doing this. D.A.R.E. often rediscovers the tried-and-true ways that forged a successful nation. Levant comments,

> Some things are so basic—teach people to be nice to their coworkers—common courtesy goes a long way. What D.A.R.E. does is try to bring values into the equation—values without religion, although not to say religion doesn't help, but D.A.R.E. is not centric to any thought system. It is based on politeness and respect for the opinions of others, values that are very basic. If opportunities are abundant, why should kids have to seek them out? Why typecast? Everyone should have equal opportunity.

D.A.R.E. also seeks out companies that are enlightened, that have employee programs enabling community outreach. For example, a company called Zenith Insurance resides in a lower-income area of Los Angeles. CEO Stanley Zax gives employees time off for community service. They are helping to mentor D.A.R.E. kids in after-school programs. If there is an employee who likes to make model cars, he is given training to show him how to bring related stories to the children—about the automobile industry, about designing cars, about body shops, about the insurance industry for automobiles, and many other related topics. A lot of children in this community have done well as new employees and eventually as managers at Zenith Insurance due to the company's commitment to offer employees a career path that endures.

Other aspects of the D.A.R.E. program affect not only the children but also improve communities around them. Unfortunately, every town is familiar with graffiti. However, law enforcement studies have revealed that gangs draw symbols because there is no ownership on a wall. So D.A.R.E. takes kids from tough inner-city schools that serve public housing on walks around their schools. The children make up the name for their group, which becomes a kind of club. It's led by volunteers from the community, perhaps local store owners or just good citizens who live in or travel to the area to help the kids. They introduce the children to the shop owners and neighbors.

For example there is a school near Vista Del Mar in Los Angeles, which is a public housing project. In a parking lot of the school stands a kiosk with glass around it. The kiosk is run by a hardworking locksmith, newly arrived from Central America. The children were spray-painting his windows, and it was costing him hundreds of dollars to clean it up and replace the glass over and over again. In response, the D.A.R.E. volunteers took the children to meet the locksmith, thus putting a face on the business. He spoke with the kids, explained that he was a hardworking guy, and said he would rather use the money spent for repairs to buy books for the library and balls for the soccer field. Ever since that time, there has been no graffiti on his business, and each class of children passes on his story to the ones that follow.

Small shop owners, managers of convenience stores, businesses run by immigrants agree that, as a result of these two-way conversations, there has been less shoplifting and graffiti in the neighborhood. In many cases, the shops have become safe havens for the students. The store owners talk about what they do in their businesses and about marketing and commerce. All of this has happened because of the dialogue started by D.A.R.E., its officers and volunteers.

In Chicago, for example, a housing project provides volunteers from all over the area to teach the D.A.R.E. children music, cooking, and other skills, talking all the while about career opportunities beyond just menial jobs.

D.A.R.E. shares stories with children to drive home its values: In the National Basketball Association (NBA) there are only 500 players, whereas the nation needs 5 million teachers. The kids are reminded that the odds of becoming a basketball star are very remote, but becoming a teacher is a realistic option. Similarly, becoming CEO of a business may not be possible for everyone—or even desirable to many. Yet valuable contributions can be made by employees at every level of an organization.

Businesspeople tell D.A.R.E. that not only has their customer base improved by having children with a sense of values (D.A.R.E. has been in place now for 18 years), but their liability insurance rates have decreased as well. In addition, the workforce is more stable. My research established the importance of all ten traits in contributing to a more cohesive organization, as they become part of the culture over time.

In Costa Rica, Honduras, and Guatemala, the D.A.R.E. kids are becoming members of an emerging middle class. Many become entrepreneurial because of exposure to the opportunities opened up by D.A.R.E. Many are seeking higher education, going beyond the eighth grade (which is the highest compulsory grade level in many of these countries). In the Philippine Republic, where the barrios are crime-ridden, the children are overcoming their circumstances and going into jobs that no one else in the family has ever held—the first in their families to break out of the cycle of poverty. Even though many of these economies are fragile, the children are taught by D.A.R.E. that they have alternatives and that they can create their own possibilities. The program is forging a generation of pioneers.

Over the past few years, D.A.R.E. has had its share of naysayers. Often, these detractors are other programs that have sprung up to compete with D.A.R.E. (As always, good ideas attract copycats.) The difference is that these are for-profit programs, and because of D.A.R.E.'s extremely low costs and lack of consulting fees, the copycats cannot compete. Pressure to get government funding has caused some of these competitors to speak disparagingly about D.A.R.E. The facts are clear: D.A.R.E. is an optional program, yet 80 percent of U.S. school districts and 56 countries have chosen this option. The Ten Essential Traits advocates must stand firm and continue to champion a value system that is solid, even though competition may be present.

The Ten Essential Traits are consistent with those qualities espoused in the D.A.R.E. program. D.A.R.E. graduates, who are just now entering the workforce, will have a value system and approach that will complement The Ten Essential Traits program when they meet in the corporate or organizational environment. They draw on the same complementary strengths. Intelligence and good judgment will stand The Ten Essential Traits leaders and D.A.R.E. graduates in good stead as they move through the challenges of the business world.[2]

In an interview in *Red Herring,* Peter Drucker made some startling observations about intelligence and how it factors into the reward systems of organizations.[3]

Those two alumni associations which were the largest—Procter & Gamble and IBM—those alumni love their ex-companies. Microsoft alumni hate Microsoft. Precisely because they feel the one thing it offered them was money and not . . . well, they resent that all the publicity goes to the top people, to one top man, and they don't get recognition. Also they feel the value system is entirely financial, and they see themselves as professionals. Maybe not scientists, but applied scientists. So their value system is different.

The value that these applied scientists placed on themselves had to do with their intelligence and knowledge contribution. Since that is at the top of Abraham Maslow's hierarchy of needs (i.e., self-actualization), shame on Microsoft for not recognizing that. This is not an uncommon problem. Monetary recognition of intelligence is good, but it is not enough. Kudos and credit, exposure and support, recognition in tangible and intangible ways—these things support employees in times of sagging stock prices and are often considered far more valuable than money in both good times and bad.

Having native intelligence is certainly a leverageable asset in an individual. And the concept of emotional intelligence is equally relevant. Can you *teach* an entire organization to be more intelligent? Peter Senge postulated in his work on the Learning Organization that you could. As described by Senge,[4] the undertaking in huge change-oriented reorganizations is monumental and requires an organization-wide and CEO-sponsored effort.

The Ten Essential Traits approach is far more doable and far less costly in time and money. You may not create a learning organization as a result, but you will identify the elephants in the room in every group and activity where The Ten Essential Traits can be found or groomed. Incremental changes accumulate to become integrated into what everyone is doing every day anyway. That does not require an initiative. It requires only a single individual in a small group to identify the elephant in the room, lead it out, and replace it with a valuable solution to the problem that the elephant represented.

Let me give you an example.

The cardinal of Chile was very disturbed by the level of poverty in the country. In 1974 he conceived the idea to create a financial and lending institution that would put money into the community and support the economic development initiatives that were being suggested by the government of Chile. At that time, unemployment was running about 40 percent. The organizing group consisted of civil engineers, none of whom had banking experience. They organized a cooperative of savings and loans and targeted the small single proprietor. Why? Because in reality, this person was the unemployed worker in Chile who had to find a way to survive. And the unskilled, noncompetent "bankers" were really builders of bridges, railroads, and roads. What they all had in common was the goal to make something good happen for the people of Chile. The customer was the uncreditworthy, unemployed worker, who somehow had to make ends meet.

These early bankers in training had the qualities of Ten Essential Traits leaders. They were fearless (not generally a characteristic associated with bankers), but they were also intelligent, not in a book-learning kind of way, but rather in a moral way. They called it *solidarity*, and they worked together to lend small amounts of money to people with no collateral—in a common commitment to make things work. As new employees joined the bank, it became critical to create a way to transfer this cultural intelligence—a way of thinking and behaving that contributed to the mission of the organization. This went beyond having a seminar to teach process and methodology.

So the bank created a theater. A real internal theater with actors and a theme, which would include 100 Ten Essential Traits leaders in the organization (out of a total of 1,500 employees). Vincente Caruso, the CEO of this bank in Santiago, Chile, shared with me this experience as we sat together in his bank's offices in Santiago:

> People may have a technical competence, but it is very difficult to transfer and teach a feeling. So we arranged with the head of the Santiago theater association to engage a very good actor, called Hector Norguerra. His job is to help the managers to engage their employees (each has 10) in a deep, intelligent, and emotional way, to transfer their knowledge, to communicate and express their feelings in a different way. We are helping people in every part of their lives, not just at work, to understand harmony in their environment and to work with others to create an intelligent and feeling way of looking at their lives.

This bank now has over 10,000 customers, most of whom are entrepreneurs or sole proprietors who gross no more than $80,000 annually. The bankers also offer much advice to customers on how to work more intelligently. For example, they may encourage seven or eight people in the construction industry to group together to become more efficient. The bank itself has become a leader in the community, not just a lender of money. They also encourage artisans to guarantee each other's loans, which creates a great deal of social pressure to repay the loans and not default.

Storytelling is a wonderful way to transfer corporate culture. It is also a good way to create an atmosphere of corporate intelligence. It is part of the management process of teaching and education. And storytelling taps into the heart of all of us, evoking the small child within who begs, "Mommy, Daddy, tell me a story!" In all of my education sessions with executives (of any age or at any level), I always include stories. Sometimes I make them up, other times they are stories about executives I have known, and other times I create a story in the form of a game.

Game playing (not normally synonymous with work) is another tool that taps into our childlike alter ego. Acting and game playing are very similar in that they allow people to do things that, in their normal role, they would not dare to do. These tools must be carefully managed, because underlying anger and frustration can boil to the surface and erupt as hostility. For that reason I precede any game playing by interviewing various executives and managers at various levels in the organization. In these sessions, we discuss some of the potential elephants in the room that might come out having to do with interpersonal conflict or managerial style. These are better identified and dealt with in another forum (industrial coaches and psychologists make their livings from these issues), and they get in the way of productive learning.

A Ten Essential Traits game puts executives and managers into a company with a true-to-life situation. Then they have to manage their way through it, identifying the elephants in the room, applying The Ten Essential Traits approach, and making recommendations using the management processes in the matrix and others they may think of.

In Buenos Aires, Argentina, I was fortunate to spend some time with a charming and brilliant lawyer, Juan E. Cambiasso, founding partner of a large law firm that embodied many of The Ten Essential Traits. I asked him if he felt that environment could increase intelligence. His answer was unexpected.

> When I am looking to hire new associates, I go to visit their homes. I see if they read books and, if so, which ones. Or if they listen to music, or if they show a spiritual dimension that might not be readily obvious in the workplace. Or if, in their minds they could fly into other galaxies of imagination.

Juan Cambiasso talked about his experience doing a "dog and pony show," the industry description of doing elaborate presentations to investment bankers, security brokers, or analysts.

> Here were people who were supposed to be very intelligent. Yet they knew nothing of history, didn't even know (some of them) the background of the region, and certainly didn't understand the political or economic situation. All they knew was the money issue. The only decision they focused on was—did they want to buy the securities I wanted to sell—not the context that they were being offered in. These people had MBAs from the best schools . . . and all they were interested in was changing the numbers in the computer, and they were being paid a fortune to do that. They had little time, and no real interest in anything except the numbers. And the past year has shown us that they were not in control. Perhaps no one was in control—just history. So the moral is that what we need are people who are smart in ways other than the degrees they get. We need people who can read books other than finance, know history, enjoy painting and music and understand human behavior and that way predict the future. That will be the leadership of the future.

Juan talked particularly about how intelligence is built by admitting to and learning from mistakes. He connected the two concepts of mistakes and intelligence.

> We do not have consensus decision making that hides mistakes. Here is the rule—if you make a mistake, you go and tell a partner who is senior to you about that mistake. Since I cannot go to another partner because I am the most senior, I must tell all my partners about my mistake. I tell the people who work for me, those below me in the organization. You cannot sit on a mistake to hide it. That is the rule of the house. Do not sit on silly or big mis-

takes. Mistakes can only be righted if another person helps you to do so. When you have made a mistake, it is difficult to find a solution alone. The learning from this mistake must be shared. We have weekly and monthly meetings at which all mistakes as well as good things are shared with the elders of the firm. Each partner has what we call a "welcome group" every fourth night or so, and we share learning there, too, with some grace, about what went right and what went wrong. This teaches people that adaptability and honesty are respected qualities in our firm. It makes people have better judgment.

The quality of *intelligence*—the resource commitment to learning, the training and education that is supported and believed in no matter the economic times—is vital to our growing list of The Ten Essential Traits. Whether it is in the D.A.R.E. environment of public-private commitment to the innate intelligence and potential of each child in our world, or the Kodak commitment to its quality brand and people through its value system and corporate investment in training and education, or a bank in Chile that has reached deep into the community to overcome homelessness and unemployment—these organizations have used their Ten Essential Traits contributions to add to the intelligence and the value of the people they serve.

Each one of The Ten Essential Traits leaders I have featured in this chapter could only have succeeded by combining all The Ten Essential Traits to varying degrees. In Chapter 9, *energy* is the quality that makes it all take flight!

Intelligence: Action Items

- Do you or those around you suffer from a lazy mind? Ask your colleagues to read a book this week on something unrelated to your work—and sponsor lunch with the group to discuss what was read. Stretch the mind a little and, at the same time, learn more about the personal and intellectual preferences of your team.

- How does your organization deal with mistakes? Do you identify them to each other and then discuss how they were handled or how they could be handled? Do that with the next mistake you make as an example, then open it up to others.

Show that people become more intelligent by learning from their own and others' mistakes. The stupidity lies in making the same mistake twice!

• Reexamine the commitment of your organization to learning and training and education. How many hours are required annually from each level of the organization? If senior executives are going to off-site sessions that are considered too costly for entry-level or junior employees, evaluate distance-learning programs (online nondegree programs) such as those offered by Ninth House—The Learning Network.[5]

9

Energy: Opportunistic Optimism

*You've got to be willing to give up what is good
to get what is great. Why settle for good when
greatness is within your grasp?*

—Ron Johnson, vice president and general manager,
Home Décor, Target Stores, Dayton Hudson Group

The ability to mobilize and implement requires energy. *Energy* is defined here as a sense of opportunistic optimism married to a sense of urgency. If we look at the history of some of the world's corporate giants—those who have weathered all types of challenges and adversity—we see a commonality shared by all great managers and leaders: With an eye to economic cycles and market indicators, smart managers seize the moment and act with surety. Consider Royal Dutch Shell, General Motors, Toyota, IBM, ABB, and a score of others. Their leaders navigated through the roughest corporate waters by virtue of their individual energy. These leaders were at every level of the company. No CEO alone can make change happen. It entails creating a "why not" versus a defensive "why" culture. (See Figure 9.1.)

My interview with Ron Johnson, formerly vice president and general manager for Target's Home Décor, took place during his tenure with Target, which he considered to have a why-not culture. When new ideas were suggested under his watch, he answered, "Why not?"

We believe the key merchandise trend for the next decade will be
design. Where the 1980s were about quality, and the 1990s were

Personal Characteristic	Organizational Environment Needed	Example of a Management Process for Implementation
1. *Fearlessness*	Permits failure	Shared learning and shared power
2. *Completion:* Ability to complete; has patience and is flexible	Results-oriented with process freedom	Horizontal, project-oriented management processes with cross-functional and multi-locational teams
3. *Commitment:* Emotionally vested	Encourages individual contributions	Small work groups and flexible work behavior; fun
4. *Inspiration:* Inspires and communicates vision; motivates	Access to internal and external people networks	Constant visibility and accessibility
5. *Assuredness:* Knows what he or she wants	Opportunities for advancement and reward	Career progression process
6. *Penetration:* "Of the people" and builds personal equity; listens with respect; empowers with dignity; confident; good mediator	Flexible organizational structure	Free information exchange, communication, and benchmarking across groups and divisions
7. *Intelligence:* Talent to place right people in right place	Resource commitment to learning	Training and education
8. *Energy:* Opportunistic optimism and sense of urgency	A why-not (not why) culture; open to new ideas and resistant to bureaucracy	Continuous improvement and innovation processes and rewards and quick decision making

Figure 9.1　The Ten Essential Traits: The Larraine Segil Matrix

about price, those are neutral now. The incoming frontier is going to be in design. So my team went and identified a person that we thought was one of the foremost architects and product designers of the twentieth century. He is Michael Grave, who has done all of the Disney headquarters in California, Dolphin Hotel, Vatican exhibits, and is a really great architect who happens to have done high-end design for the home area for companies like Steuben. Michael has a teakettle that sells for $150 and he sold a million of them over the past 13 years—it has been one of the best-selling high-end items for the home. My team said, "We need someone who can provide great design at a value that we can market." So we took that idea and in order to accomplish it, we had to make a major, up-front commitment to him for something that was unproven in our market. Will it work? Will people really want to move into this standard? After all, we know this is Target. This isn't Bloomingdale's. We went forward and signed the agreement. Soon we will be launching over 250 products in the stores (teakettles, coasters, garden furniture, decorative pots, and lighting). It sets an example of our ability to have an idea and go do it. How do you make this happen? Well, internally, you want to get approval and support, but it is not like we go through these series of planning meetings in September, and then have to get all the approvals of what we want to do for next year. It is very entrepreneurial and somewhat informal.

Many times, the elephant in the room is the inertia of the organization. Spotting it is one thing, but moving it out is a monumental task. It would feel like dancing with the elephant—be very careful of your footwork or you will end up a casualty. Many CEOs burn themselves out trying to pour their personal energy into an inert organization.

In an interview with Tom Botts, formerly treasurer of Shell Oil who was put in charge of some of the company's change initiatives, I asked how he had managed to buy into this kind of energetic change, given the fact that most people respond to change with resistance.

Change is always hard, and it's messy and chaotic. It never feels good. But I believe that more people in Shell are beginning to realize that the forces of change in the world are such that this kind of feeling of "almost chaos" will never go away. So it begins to be a feeling that you get used to and anticipate, and then I guess in the later stage you almost begin to leverage that. In that, it becomes what I like to do. This is why I get up in the morning—because I want to be in this more dynamic changing environment. This is not for everyone. And we've lost some people who have chosen to work elsewhere because they just don't like that kind of environment. But I think more people are realizing that this is the way it's going to be. We're not looking down the road for a year or two, saying, well if we can only get to next year, then things will settle down. People are not saying that anymore.

Tom Botts is a Ten Essential Traits kind of manager. He thrives on change and is an architect of change. The excitement and challenge and even the uncertainty of it has become something of an adrenaline rush for him as he attacks issues with energy and optimism.

This energy has to permeate the organization to create change. Jo Pease was the team leader for the customer focus in Shell Exploration and Production as part of the transformation process. She was energized by the openness to change at all levels:

> I see leadership behavior being very engaging, open, and honest, very willing to admit they don't have all the answers even though they are in a leadership position. To me that is just phenomenal. That never would have happened 20 years ago when I joined Shell. At one level, Shell has always been prepared to accept risk. We take risk every day in drilling an offshore well or getting an offshore lease. But what we see today is a very different kind of risk. It's a risk to say what I think, to say I don't have all the answers. I believe that people are moving slowly toward the idea that there are more consequences to not taking risks than there are to taking them.

Jürgen Schrempp, chairman of DaimlerChrysler, met his Waterloo in acquiring his U.S. partner when Chrysler was generating $5.1 billion in profit in 1999. The company may never reach that zenith again, certainly in the short term, but the energy and opportunistic optimism of the new German executive team moved in to turn around the lagging company are generating results. Dieter Zetsche is The Ten Essential Traits leader here, not Jürgen Schrempp. He is energetic and unflappable. Sent in November 2000 to perform a miracle, in 2001 his mission was showing some results. Stepping away from the culture wars that were simmering in the company, he and his deputy, Wolfgang Bernhard, brought in new blood from Ford, Toyota, and GM to improve quality and upgrade the brand.

When the new Zetsche-Bernhard team came in, there were so many elephants in the room that only tremendous discipline, optimism, and energy could identify and attack them.

How do you eat an elephant? One toe at a time. Zetsche and Bernhard began with the details, looking for small wins, incremental savings, which eventually add up to big savings and an improved bottom line.

The Ten Essential Traits leadership of Zetsche is winning the day: His "of the people" approach offers self-deprecating humor rather than attention-getting narcissism, and his enthusiasm for the product (especially the Viper) reflects his energy. He is emotionally vested and has proven his ability to complete, increasing revenue as well as slashing costs by leaning on suppliers and shaving profit margins. Zetsche created 55 teams whose mission is to find more cost-effective ways to manufacture cars. Smart purchasing helps, too. Adding CD players to most cars and trucks instead of buying some radios with cassette players and some with CDs will reduce the company's stereo bill by 15 percent.

Some of the most difficult issues to resolve in this corporate turn-around were deep in the bowels of the cultures of exclusion and elitism. Finally, Mercedes has stopped objecting to sharing various systems with Chrysler (they had considered Chrysler products inferior and resisted integrating Mercedes parts into the Chrysler line). The integration problems that were major issues when Schrempp was CEO have started to settle down, with acceptance of the partnership on both sides of the Atlantic and a deeper understanding of the need to integrate German and U.S. operations in the parent company. Are things all wonderful and cheery? No, but there are improvements, and once again the stalwart Chrysler is in the land of the living.[1]

In an interview I conducted with Goeran Lindahl, then chairman and CEO of ABB, he described his perspective of The Ten Essential Traits.

> I can motivate people to use their brainpower. I am the trigger of the discussion. But the only way that can happen is for me to go down in the ranks of the people at ABB to use my energy as a trigger to increase extended creativity. Clearly, technology facilitates this—the Internet has helped—but the classical aspect of our business is as important as the new. I want a foot in each world for the company. Of course, it is essential to create an organizational structure that cuts out administration and extra layers that block creativity. It is critical to have a "why not" as opposed to a "why" culture in order to be open to new ideas. I have cut out the regional layer of the company so that global businesses are pulling the strings. This way, the IT system supports the global operations and there are global processes. But the goal is to make access more

immediate and to promote local actions. In reality, the customers are owned by the local people, so they should be responsible for collecting the business, seeing someone, and socializing with them. There is no substitute for that. And that takes local energy.

This is a sentiment shared by Michael Hartman, president of TSI Connections (formerly GTE TSI).[2] Huge change has occurred in the telecommunications industry. Energy is a large part of sustaining that change.

"We have lots of younger employees with enormous energy," says Hartman. "They are driven to grow the business at all levels. Leadership shows at many levels of the organization." Since Mike Hartman was fairly new to the company compared to many employees who had long tenures, he viewed the characteristics of The Ten Essential Traits leaders in TSI Connections as the driving force that would support the company's success in a highly competitive and changing field.

As CEO of CommTouch Software, Inc., a globally integrated outsourcer of e-mail messages that is an Israeli company with offices in Silicon Valley, Isabel Maxwell is a Ten Essential Traits manager who has hired and nurtured other Ten Essential Traits leaders in the company. The energy and demands of the customers for we-need-it-now service drives the company, which provides a turnkey operation to firms that need e-mail messaging—sometimes in languages other than English and often within weeks. An installation in Brazil took nine days from start to finish. This takes burnout-level energy. Maxwell commented on the cultural issues that affect the leadership styles in her company.

> The Israeli culture is highly disciplined and cohesive, very loyal but not good in the service area or interpersonal skills. This has changed in high technology to some extent. Since our company is headquartered in the United States, all the contacts are from here and everyone is making an effort. Service is happening—we will get the job done if you say it has to be done. Our employees try very hard to build trust and follow through.

The *completion, commitment, inspiration,* and *assuredness* characteristics are evident at CommTouch Software, as is the *energy* of all involved.

Ray Ozzie, genius inventor and founder of Groove Networks, is a remarkable person. As we sat at lunch at Esther Dyson's annual jamboree of techno-wizards called PC Forum 2001, Ozzie talked about his view of his company. He was one of the programmers at Lotus who worked on Symphony, an integrating spreadsheet, word processor, and data utility software program. He left Lotus at the end of 1984 to found Iris Associates and to work on a secret project, which eventually became Lotus Notes. He kept Iris Associates independent of Lotus as long as he could, but ultimately it was acquired by Lotus and is now owned by IBM, which has helped Notes to sign up over 68 million users. Although Ozzie is now promoting his new company, Groove Networks, he is very interested in the people who use his tools. He is also puzzled by their behavior.

> Left to their own devices, certain people tend to amass power in much the same way that countries used to amass land. But command and control tends to stifle the creativity out at the edges of the empire, leaving it with no outlet, no place to mutate, and no place to grow. Instead, companies these days need to go in the opposite direction. They must shed the notion of vertical integration and adopt strategic or transformational outsourcing. They must continuously mutate, behave more like complex adaptive systems than closed mechanical systems. At the edges, people choose communication tools that match the nature of their behavior. Their tools of choice today are email, the phone, and the fax. Why? Because they gravitate toward tools wholly within their direct control, tools that "just work" when they need them. But the tools the industry has been building over the past few years follow a strictly centralized-server-based highly administered model, great for business processes but sub-optimal for effective direct spontaneous person-to-person work practices.[3]

Ray Ozzie sees the world from a systems perspective, and his genius is in seeing patterns where others do not. This type of epiphany has enabled him to create intuitively appealing software that, once we have it, we cannot do without.

> The question we asked ourselves at Groove was what fundamental underpinnings do we have to build to bring the semantic level of the Net back up to the point where people can treat it as symmetrical rather than have everything flow from a server representing

corporate control? People want to act locally, in small groups [ABB lives and breathes this point of view]. They're most effective locally. Yet they still want—and need—to be connected."

The challenge to the Groove inventors was to make a system of access and communication that enabled people to connect when the situation was not regular, when it was out of the ordinary. The exception had to become the routine and be managed as efficiently as if it were the rule. This would allow for individual preferences. No one wants to feel that he or she is just a number with no special needs or preferences.

Ozzie created Groove to handle the exceptions. His software acknowledges that unexpected things happen and that people need a way to handle them by communicating and then capturing the learning so that others can learn from the exception handling. Then, of course, that exception could become routine, certainly part of the corporate memory, and Groove moves on to solve another exception.

This is another kind of energy. It's that curiosity of entrepreneurs, inventors, and innovators (whether in their own companies or public entities) that makes new stuff happen. This kind of leadership may not be the kind that exhorts others to follow. In fact, Ray Ozzie is soft-spoken, understated, and doesn't see himself as the Iacocca-type leader in any way or form. But his intelligence, fearlessness in technological inquiry, and his completion and commitment characteristics create a kind of magnetic energy. Those who understand what he is doing will follow him to the ends of the earth, in awe of his leadership and perspective into the customer need, anticipated or possibly not even yet identified (see Chapter 11). There is room for such Ten Essential Traits leaders. But their creativity cannot be stifled in large organizations that have no appreciation for The Ten Essential Traits philosophy. Ray Ozzie has his own view about how large organizations can nurture this type of leadership—in innovation and technology: "Lotus was most creative when Mitch Kapor was there. Perhaps because of his naïveté, he let people go off into corners and do things under the radar. Once he left, other people had enough power to squash those creative projects."

"Going off into corners" is exactly the kind of behavior that should and must be permitted by a Ten Essential Traits organization. It could be the creative seed that spawns a whole industry. Astute Ten

Essential Traits managers recognize it for what it is. It is not anti-establishment or revolutionary behavior. It is the desire for the organizational environment described in this book, one that supports the individual characteristics comprising The Ten Essential Traits—the leadership model for the world of today and tomorrow.

Organizational Characteristics

Is this a particularly American point of view? It is not my intention in this book to be U.S.-centric, but Robert Reich, former secretary of labor, said recently, "This [the United States] is an overwhelmingly optimistic culture. We are technophiles at heart." His perception is also mine, and the millions who struggle to come to the United States see it as the land of milk and honey. I myself was an immigrant 28 years ago. This was my impression then, and I believe it is just as true now.

In the year 2000, over 200,000 school-age children were sent by their parents from South Korea to such centers of education as Toronto, Sydney, and London. However, the vast majority—126,000—were sent to the United States (118,000 to Los Angeles and 8,000 to Boston).[4] Their goal: to inspire their children with the American optimism and way of learning and life, taking advantage of a system that thrives on problem solving and encourages creativity. I grew up in South Africa, where *no* was the knee-jerk answer to every question. Arriving on U.S. shores, where you are free to be whatever you want to be and are rewarded for hard work and ambition, was a dream come true for me and my family. What are the implications of all this?

Those from different cultures, belief systems, and experiences can learn The Ten Essential Traits approach. It takes an environment that encourages such qualities—and they are described in detail in this book. This kind of leadership is also supported by what *Business Week* defines as the real "new" economy, which is "about an economy capable of growing more rapidly without inflation than it did during the long slump of 1973–1995, because of technology-driven increases in productivity, the world's best financial system, and the unleashing of entrepreneurial energies through deregulation."[5] This does not necessarily mean stability. It means whipsaw-type booms and busts, because the entire economy is now attached to the technology economy, and cyclic activity has always been the norm there.

For organizations to survive, The Ten Essential Traits managers need the energy and optimism to find opportunities everywhere, in both the good and the bad, and the flexibility and fearlessness to take advantage of the out-of-the-box thoughts of those who may not fit the corporate norm (Ray Ozzie is but one example).

The final factor in the energy piece of the matrix is the management process that relates to rewards. This is where the rubber meets the road. To return to my original analogy, the largest elephant in the room is often this:

What's in it for me (WIIFM)?

We can generally assume that all people will work for the corporate or organizational good, and in some cultures the group is more important than the individual. But the group still wants to be rewarded. The effect of rewards cannot be ignored. A good friend of mine, Bob Nelson, has made an industry out of creating 1,001 ways to reward your employees. In alliance creation and management, an area in which I have specialized for the past 20 years, rewards are where many companies fall down. They are great at creating alliances, but not at making the compensation and reward system appropriate for alliance managers. Rewarding managers for the alliance *process* rather than the actual *success* of the alliance is the appropriate way to approach this issue—otherwise, managers will not want to take on the tough alliances that have a high risk of failure.

How do we solve this problem? This is not rocket science. It does, however, involve getting into the shoes of the receiver of the reward and finding out culturally, individually, communally, and fiscally which rewards that person or group will appreciate and value.

Recently, James Smith, a manager at Departemente de Formadoras, Formax, in Illinois, sent me the following story:

> When it comes to recognition, nonmonetary rewards are quite effective. I currently have 45 highly skilled technicians working directly in my service department. I would consider them to be well paid, earning an average of around $60K+ per year. Their hourly pay is structured so that when they reach the top of their grade level, they receive very little monetary increase annually.

Most increases for our highest-skill-level technicians are generally based on cost of living. Since these technicians are used as direct frontline customer contact people, a considerable amount of monitoring and follow-up is done to assure customer satisfaction. Several years ago, I implemented a customer satisfaction survey, which is sent to the customer following every service visit. The purpose is to evaluate the performance of the technician and measure the satisfaction of the customer.

You can imagine the reaction of these technical people when it was announced we would begin this program. Overall, they did not like the idea that big brother would ask the customer to fill out a survey and return it to us. The decision to proceed, however, was not a democratic one. We proceeded, and for every returned survey that we received back, the results were tabulated and proper scoring was kept in order to monitor satisfaction levels. Every survey that was returned from the customers came across my desk. A personal comment was added and a copy forwarded to the technician. Comments sections allowed the customers to express their views, concerns, or praise. Interestingly, the return rate on the surveys remained quite high at around 60+%. The overwhelming majority of these surveys were being returned with excellent reviews and comments. Occasionally surveys would arrive back with less than favorable results and comments. These were used to fine-tune our technical services and improve. Poor performers were identified and additional training was offered.

As time went on I began to see that a number of surveys were being returned for the technicians that showed perfect scores. A number of technicians received repeated perfect scores. I thought that some form of recognition for these perfect scores was appropriate. In order to recognize these outstanding performers, small quality gift key rings were purchased. Etched into the key ring were the words, "In recognition of outstanding service performance," along with the company logo. Regular monthly meetings with these technicians are held. During one of these meetings, all technicians who received perfect scores on two or more satisfaction surveys over a six-month period were brought up before their peers, thanked for their performance, and handed the gift. In addition, all of the individuals from this group were added to a drawing for a gift certificate to a fine dining local restaurant. I would like to say here that this was a magical moment and that every technician immediately improved his or her performance. However, as is the case with the technical people I have had the pleasure to work with, you always get some complainers saying that those individuals were assigned easy trips to easy customers and that their own surveys were not being returned, etc. In light of all the jabbing and joking around that these technicians received from their peers about receiving the awards, it appeared that perhaps this form of recognition in front of peers may have been the wrong way to go about it and may not be making much of a difference. The general perception was that the technicians viewed this as silly.

The month of May should have been the fifth time that recognition awards would have been handed out. Being unavailable to attend this meeting, one of my supervisors stood in for me. Not considering these recognition award ceremonies as being anything looked forward to, I had not taken the time to prepare the awards and decided to put it off until the June or July meeting. Surprisingly, during the May meeting, a number of technicians inquired where the recognition's awards were. In conclusion, it became apparent that although the appearance is that recognition may be unfruitful, the truth of the matter is that deep inside the rough exterior of most people is the desire to be appreciated and recognized for a job well done. While it may not show up on the outside, the satisfaction felt on the inside can't be achieved totally through only monetary reward. Public recognition in front of one's peers, no matter how embarrassed a person may appear, is an excellent tool to motivate, not demotivate. Those individuals who have received the rewards proudly display them before their peers. I look forward to the day when everyone receives them.

I apologize for such a lengthy dissertation. I had originally intended to make this a brief thank-you, but the impact of these events has had far-reaching, positive effects.

Best wishes,

Jim Smith

Smith is a good example of a Ten Essential Traits manager who was open to feedback. His "of the people" accessibility and willingness to do something different gave each individual on his team the feeling that they, too, were Ten Essential Traits leaders in their own work, performers worthy of recognition.

Even the most sophisticated scientists are pleased by the approval and respect of their peers. I have been privileged to work with the brilliant people at Jet Propulsion Laboratory and other NASA centers on a continuing basis over the years, and as we presently work on a variety of alliances, it is heartening to see The Ten Essential Traits leadership characteristics manifested in those who are taking humankind to Mars, are digging deep into the origins of the universe, and are engaged in interstellar and interplanetary exploration. Recognition can be long in coming—some of these missions take 15 to 20 years, a lifetime of struggle and new technology into the future. Creating rewards for such activities means rubbing shoulders with the most fascinating projects that promise new knowledge of humanity, our planet, our universe, and the things we cannot even imagine. Interjecting mundane initiatives that involve lots of paperwork and little innovation is very difficult in such an environment.

In organizations filled with rocket scientists and in all organizations that are home to intelligent people, few people like to do the detailed, repetitive and noncreative busywork. But someone has to do it. Think for a moment about the *Saturday Night Live* television series and "the copy machine guy." He made a career out of a mundane job. He also made us laugh, being clearly "of the people," and probably knew more about what was going on in that company than anyone else. After all, most people (with the possible exception of senior management), at some time during the day, walk through the copy room. The copy machine guy's reward was being right there in the center of things. A promotion might not have made him happy if it took him away from the hub of what was going on. However, a new title with the same job might do the trick, making him feel appreciated and important while leaving him to enjoy what he liked most about his job.

Mark Hodgdon, formerly general manager at the Ritz Carlton Huntington Hotel and Spa talked to me about the Ritz Carlton belief in the importance of rewards:

> There are many ways to reward. Some are monetary, others are through basic recognition. We have programs internally that reward based on monthly performance, quarterly performance, and an annual performance. We have what we call our five-star employees. And the goal of every employee within the Ritz Carlton Hotel is to be a five-star employee of the year. So there are rewards through benefits and financial rewards to be the best that we can be all the time.

But I find in business, what people really enjoy are the rewards through recognition that are not monetary or otherwise but just a thank-you, knowing that they are important and are appreciated and, most important, that what they do within a business makes a difference. To know that you are valued, to come to work every day in an environment that is constant and stable, where you walk in that door knowing "I make a difference relative to the success of this business each and every moment that I'm here, with every moment of truth, with every guest interaction or, for that matter, with every employee interaction, knowing that I as an employee impact the well-being and experience of every guest and other employee."

The Ritz Carlton Hotel Group has a credo, which is part of the core being of every employee. Hodgdon shared it with me:

Here is our credo. Ritz Carlton Hotel is a place where genuine care and comfort of our guests will always be our highest mission. We pledge to provide the finest in personal services and facilities for our guests, who will always enjoy a warm, relaxed yet refined ambiance. The Ritz Carlton experience enlivens the senses, instills well-being, and fulfills even the unexpressed wishes and needs of our guests. We as employees are committed to our guests; we are committed to each other. We know who we are, we know what we are every moment in the day, and our commitment—that is, our motto "ladies and gentlemen serving ladies and gentlemen"—communicates that message from the very beginning. What we do is important, who we are; two-way business has value, and our contributions every day are never taken for granted and are recognized through many means and many instruments as we continue our career paths with Ritz Carlton Hotels.

This eighth characteristic, energy, is something that can be taught. It's easier if it comes naturally in the person of energy, urgency, and optimism. But when people enjoy what they do, this characteristic tends to thrive. When they don't, even if it is part of their nature, it's difficult to act energetic.

Do what you enjoy and the rewards will follow: "To thine own self be true."

And that, in part, is what the next characteristic, integrity, is about. But first, here are some action items for your consideration.

Energy: Action Items

- Do you have a "why" or a "why not" culture? Are you open to new ideas, different ways of doing things? Identify one existing process in *your* organization that does things differently from the way another organization where you may have worked did things. Is there a better way? Is it comfortable merely because you know how to do it? Was the way you did it at your former job better, or just more (or less) comfortable there?

- Ask your team to do the same exercise. Once a week, examine every corporate habit or process within your area of responsibility to see if another way is more efficient, more effective, easier—better for all the stakeholders, not just yourself.

- Do you consider yourself energetic? Do others? Do you have the late-afternoon draggies (desire for a nap?) Find a way to engage in a physical activity in the afternoon (e.g., take a walk with a colleague to talk about what you would have done in a meeting).

- When things get tough at home or at work, do you see the glass as half empty or half full? If you see it as half empty, try to see the brighter side. Make positive comments instead of the negative ones. Try it out on small things first. Think of the positive spin and say it in your head until it sounds natural. Then say it out loud to someone. It's amazing how you can train your brain to think positively if you want to, just as an athlete can train his or her brain before a race. Avoid detractor phrases ("I suppose this is the way I have to look at it," "I am not sure this will even happen but . . .") and other modifiers that impose a negative spin on an otherwise positive statement. Everyone will hear the negative and miss the positive altogether.

- Do you reward people for innovation and quick decision making? How? Sometimes recognition awards are the best way. Consult some how-to-reward-your-employees books—one CEO recently wrote a letter to employees' parents telling them how wonderful their son or daughter was. He received grateful responses from parents, some of them weeping on the phone with pleasure and gratitude. Money isn't everything!

10

Integrity: Building Trust and Credibility

One person's logic is another's irrationality.

—Anonymous

rmed with the previous eight traits and filled with a sense of energy, the new leader must now look deep within to make sure that energy does not overwhelm and sidestep *integrity*. (See Figure 10.1.) Often, lack of integrity *is* the elephant in the room. This trait is made up of the two components: trust and credibility. Trust is bidirectional: trust of others and trust within yourself. Credibility in regard to The Ten Essential Traits means that trust is well applied. Good evidence of this balance of trust and credibility, which together define integrity, is the concept of 360-degree feedback, which is the management process that can bring integrity to light (or not!).

Defining Corporate Culture

Living through culture change in an organization is a difficult and exciting experience. I asked Tom Botts, former treasurer of Shell Oil and then team member of a corporate transformation project, about the changing nature of Shell's corporate culture. Here's his response:

Personal Characteristic	Organizational Environment Needed	Example of a Management Process for Implementation
1. *Fearlessness*	Permits failure	Shared learning and shared power
2. *Completion:* Ability to complete; has patience and is flexible	Results-oriented with process freedom	Horizontal, project-oriented management processes with cross-functional and multi-locational teams
3. *Commitment:* Emotionally vested	Encourages individual contributions	Small work groups and flexible work behavior; fun
4. *Inspiration:* Inspires and communicates vision; motivates	Access to internal and external people networks	Constant visibility and accessibility
5. *Assuredness:* Knows what he or she wants	Opportunities for advancement and reward	Career progression process
6. *Penetration:* "Of the people" and builds personal equity; listens with respect; empowers with dignity; confident; good mediator	Flexible organizational structure	Free information exchange, communication, and benchmarking across groups and divisions
7. *Intelligence:* Talent to place right people in right place	Resource commitment to learning	Training and education
8. *Energy:* Opportunistic optimism and sense of urgency	A why-not (not why) culture; open to new ideas and resistant to bureaucracy	Continuous improvement and innovation processes and rewards and quick decision making
9. *Integrity:* Trust and credibility	Values honesty	360-degree feedback

Figure 10.1   The Ten Essential Traits: The Larraine Segil Matrix

I think it's more a deeper understanding of what we have been and have always known. The idea of helping people build a better world is our continual and evolving anthem at Shell—we call it "Count on Shell"—those things are core and always have been at the core of people at Shell. It's only recently that we are really beginning to realize how deep and meaningful that purpose and those feelings are in the Shell people.

The very presence of Sixtus Oechsly, executive director of corporate identity for Shell Oil, is an indication of the sincere desire of Shell to be true to itself and its heritage. His job is to discover what Shell stands for to its customers, the general public, and its employees (see Chapter 2, "Fearlessness"). His "differentness" is what made him perfect for that job. It took a fearless Ten Essential Traits company to hire him. It wasn't easy. Oechsly explains:

> I didn't grow up in Shell. I have been here for about eight years. I didn't go to an Ivy League school; I was in the Navy and I went to night school. I was brought in by Michael Grazeley [The Ten Essential Traits manager who took a chance on Oechsly] to do merger and acquisition work in Shell Chemical, and I told Michael that he couldn't even hire me because I was different from everyone else at Shell. He disagreed. He said, "I've got thousands of people who have all sorts of degrees, but they can't do what we need right now. You have a different skill set that you bring." I'd say for the first few years it was really rough going for me. I was counseled by one person who said, "You are very different. So here's my advice. For every degree that you are different, to be accepted you are going to have to be five degrees better than anyone else." And then he said something to me that I have never forgotten. He said, "Based on how different you have chosen to be, I can't imagine that you will ever be that good." Well, there was a point in time when I used to spend lots of energy trying to figure out how I could create the environment in which I could succeed in whatever definition of success that was. And through several defining moments I came to a personal conclusion that I'd be far better off letting go. And the longer I stay true to that—listening to the system and watching for how I am being received and trying to make sure that inconsistencies aren't there in my behavior so that people can understand what is driving my behavior—the more successful I have become. As long as I can keep myself in the role that my decisions are always about what's in the best interest of Shell, not what's in the best interest of Sixtus, then I have found there is a level of acceptability of my "differentness." I live the adage, "To thine self be true," and it works for me.

Very often the very presence of someone like Oechsly is the elephant in the room. No one really understood at first what he was doing. Many people just didn't get it. However, when he started to dig deep into the corporate psyche, it became clear. The real elephant in the room was the fact that everyone knew what Shell stood for, but no one was articulating it. It can be summarized as follows: "We like to do good works, we like it when people count on Shell. We are honest people who tell the truth."

This statement of self-worth has been one of the most delightful aspects of my work with Shell in recent years. This company is one of the most ethical organizations that I have worked with, with high integrity and a surprisingly understated opinion of themselves. As a partner, Shell gives more than added value to their alliances because of their dependable culture.

Mark Hodgdon, general manager of the Ritz Carlton Huntington Hotel and Spa talked to me about Ritz Carlton's belief in the importance of integrity, infused throughout the organization from the beginning by the spiritual business founder of the Ritz Carlton.

> Horst Schulze has had a remarkable career in the hotel business. Prior to coming to work for Ritz Carlton Hotel Company, Horst was successfully working for Hyatt Hotels as a high-end executive. He grew up in the hotel business, starting as an hourly employee and really understanding the business from a grassroots prospective, working in many different hourly capacities, moving into middle management, then becoming a general manager at the property level before working at corporate. Looking at Horst from a leadership perspective, he understands. He can embrace the feelings and the emotions of an hourly employee, understands what happens at a property level, and delivers the level of service that our guests expect from a Ritz Carlton Hotel. From a leadership perspective, his fundamentals are there.
>
> He joined Ritz Carlton Hotel Company as a founding father, originally as executive vice president of the company, and had the opportunity to become president of Ritz Carlton Hotel Company shortly thereafter. He has been clearly the leader in conveying the message of who we are and what we are. He is dynamic, he is charismatic, he communicates well, he shares his heart and soul with each and every employee. He gets involved in every aspect of the business. He goes to every hotel opening. He visits properties on a regular basis. He believes in constant communication and an open-door policy and makes himself available to really do what it takes for us to be successful out in the field. Horst was directly

involved in developing the culture and components of the Ritz Carlton gold standard throughout our quality process. He created how we define value and how we ensure that each employee has value. How we communicate, how we interact, and how we treat one another—be it internally or externally—really comes from him.

Does Your Organization Have a Heart?

In the introduction to this book, I posed certain questions, asking you whether your organization was the preferred place to work in your industry and whether it had a heart. The Ritz Carlton Hotel Company prides itself on exactly that. And it is that kind of integrity that draws employees to work there.

Integrity is also about saying what you will do and doing it. Although many organizations have the best of intentions, and their employees' offer well-meaning promises to each other, to their customers, and to suppliers, often those promises don't eventuate. Huge fiefdoms of quality, TQM, large groups of meetings, quality circles, and other mechanisms have been brought into organizations worldwide, not the least of which are the Six Sigma programs used by George Fisher at Motorola and Kodak and by Jack Welch at General Electric. At the Ritz Carlton, quality is who they are. And they are the proud winner of the Malcolm Baldrige National Quality Award.

Mark Hodgdon continues:

> With the quality process, our intent is to minimize and eliminate defects within the workplace, but this is a real world and we recognize every once in a while there are going to be issues and opportunities in the guest experience even though we make every effort to avoid that situation. There is a real sincere and clear trust in every employee to represent the Ritz Carlton Hotel and the company well when interacting with a guest. They are—*we* are—empowered to make decisions and accept responsibility in every guest interaction relative to this issue. This means you have ownership of guest complaints. This imbues every employee with a sense of ownership to address those issues and see them through to a satisfactory conclusion. We convey that message across the board to every employee within every Ritz Carlton Hotel. We ask

them to look at the issue from the guest's perspective. First apologize, let them understand that we sincerely care. Then communicate. "If we have fallen short, please let us take this opportunity to learn from you." Seeing it through means that we do not pass that guest along from one employee to another. It's a message that says, "You interact with me, I have ownership. I'll see it through, I'll get it resolved, and not only will I get it resolved, but I'll come back to you with a resolution that is satisfying to you." This ensures that we have integrity and credibility in the eyes of our guests and creates the impetus for them to come back many, many times.

Many organizations talk about this issue. Yet I have never seen it handled as well as in the Ritz Carlton family.

Hodgdon went on to explain.

We believe that with a problem, we often have an opportunity to make that a plus rather than a minus, and that is what builds long-term loyalty and commitment of guests to businesses. Obviously, the expectations are that everything goes well and that guests come back, but if there is an opportunity, how do we accept ownership of it, how do we take charge, how to we make the guest feel good about that scenario, how do we resolve it to their satisfaction, and how do we even *strengthen* those relationships through adversity—so that guest returns and knows that he or she made the right choice in staying at a Ritz Carlton Hotel?

When I asked Hodgdon what integrity means in the hospitality context, this was his response:

We educate employees from their very first day, letting them know that there is a personal interest in their success and a level of trust and confidence from the very beginning that gives them the self-confidence to go out and accept ownership of their success. They must go forward, knowing that we are partnering with them toward common goals, a common dream, and a common vision. I honestly believe that any successful business is a grassroots effort. There's not a general manager in business who can be the impetus every day toward success, but you create alignment and partnerships through personal relationships that create teamwork, and that builds momentum in a business, which, over time, carries it toward greater levels of success—be it improved product, quality, or services. I honestly believe that a business that is self-motivated is getting that drive from grassroots employees every day—not from the top down. So I believe—through relationships, commitments, trust, and confidence, through empowerment, through leadership [The Ten Essential Traits]—in allowing employees, over time, after effective training, education, and development, to truly step back and lead and drive a business toward higher levels of performance.

I could not have said it better myself!

Leadership in today's organization has so many different forms that only by integrating The Ten Essential Traits in various combinations can the right fit be found to suit the organization and its industry.

In 2000, a new CEO was appointed for Amgen, a biotechnology company known for its pharmaceuticals in cancer and dialysis treatment, which is headquartered in Thousand Oaks, California. George Rathmann, a charismatic and prescient individual with whom I have had the privilege to spend some time (we were both members of a CEO technology network in California in the late 1980s), founded Amgen. The company has expanded and grown well beyond Rathmann's early dreams.

The new CEO, Kevin Sharer, has no background in biotech. However, his early training as an aeronautical engineer and then chief engineer on a nuclear submarine prepared him for all kinds of situations. Even so, a career at GE and MCI presented far different challenges from the ones he is now facing at Amgen. In a recent interview with *Fast Company* magazine, Sharer clarified his role and his experience, showing that many of the qualities embodied in The Ten Essential Traits are part of his psyche and inherent in the management style he is bringing to the company.

> I made a mistake at MCI that was ultimately important in my success here. At GE there was a presumption that a new general manager would make an impact on the business quickly. That if you run one business, you can run any business. So then I went to MCI. I was 40 years old and reported to the CEO. Within a month or two, I came to him and said, "I think you all have misconceptualized this business and we need to fundamentally reorganize this place." The fact that I was right didn't matter. What I hadn't done was build sufficient internal credibility.

This was the elephant in the room. You needed to build credibility internally at GE at that time before trying to bring about change.

Kevin Sharer had learned his lesson. Particularly at Amgen, since he had no biotech background, it was critical that he make no drastic moves until he cemented his acceptance as an insider. He entered the company and learned as much as he could about its business and culture. When it became clear to him that he had strong expectations of being the next CEO, he did something very unusual.

> I put myself on a half-time sabbatical. I said, I am going to learn everything I can about the science of research and development and its management. For probably a year and a half I was a steady student. . . . I don't presume to be scientifically or medically qualified, but I can participate in any discussion now at the level I think a CEO ought to be able to participate.

Being a person of integrity, building credibility, and valuing honesty were the driving factors that helped Kevin Sharer take his position as CEO with confidence and assuredness. His style is inclusive:

> . . . This business is so darn complicated and the decisions are so important, there is no one person alone who is going to be maximally effective in making those decisions. I want my executive committee—the seven or eight top people—to collectively run the company. I don't shirk the ultimate responsibility as CEO. But I don't want to make the decision as the sole integrator. I want us to debate and really think through the major decisions about the company together.

Turnaround companies are particularly in need of management with integrity. Too often, faith has been lost, trust fractured, and promises broken. A recent example is Lucent.

Lucent was fortunate to attract a shining star from Boeing, Debbie Hopkins. She had been at Boeing for 16 months and was a contender to run the company. She stunned Boeing management by leaving for the position of CFO at Lucent. Her competency as a turnaround star certainly preceded her. Rich McGinn, CEO of Lucent at that time, presented to her the fact that they would work together to turn the company around. Then, without warning, the board ousted McGinn, and Hopkins moved forward to remediate the mess he had left behind. In another surprise move, Hopkins herself was fired by CEO Henry Schacht.

This kind of management musical chairs is exactly what a turn-around company does *not* need. Hopkins had the fearlessness and completion characteristics of The Ten Essential Traits, as well as assuredness. But being "of the people" with its accompanying personal equity would have stood her in good stead in this situation. What does the hiring and firing do for the rest of the people who work at a company where willy-nilly turnover occurs at the most senior management level? Most become fearful of their survival at the company and keep their heads down to avoid being noticed, which creates its own level of paralysis, thus making the whole situation worse.

When George Fisher entered Kodak, the environment was similar to the situation at Lucent—low morale, difficult market conditions, insecure management, and a deficit of confidence in good people with fear of the future of their industry as well as their position in it.

His first job was to listen. This created the ability to build credibility. He also had to demonstrate that Kodak was an organization where there was hope again. Fisher told me how this happened:

> When times get difficult, people are in need of an even more clearly defined plan for the future. Because they want to know there is a future, it becomes so much more important that you communicate with people. Even though you think you may be doing a good job of it, you never have enough time to get around to people, which is one of the frustrations of leadership. It is absolutely essential that in tough times you become even more visible. It's even more important if your organization is transitioning, not only from a life-cycle point of view, but also from a technology standpoint.

George Fisher is retired now, but many of his insights have longevity in the world of The Ten Essential Traits. Integrity has been a large part of his life, and it is an interesting observation that no matter how many pundits may have beaten up Kodak over the years, no one ever said a single disparaging word about Fisher as a leader or as an individual. He characterized his philosophy this way:

> In the business world, I pray that I have not only courage but wisdom to do the right things and to get them done. People understand the right things to do, but it takes courage not to act too fast. Plus, courage to do the right thing now may not be the same as the

right thing to do three years from now or four years ago. Whatever you do, do it with compassion and respect for the values that are part of the organization or that you live by. Most people know that the organization has to change, and as long as we have the dedication of employees like that there is great hope for the future.

Building Trust

Organizational integrity will attract and retain the knowledge workers whom everyone wants. According to the Information Technology Association of America, by the end of 2001, U.S. companies faced a shortage of 425,000 information technology (IT) workers in spite of the economic downturn. What does this mean? It means that IT professionals will be able to leverage their positions, request certain workplace perks—and get them. After all, they are the knowledge workers everyone wants. CFOs are factoring into their budgets the coffee bars and other office amenities that arose in the hot days of the dot-coms rather than terminating them as trifles and luxuries. The first-year cost of a coffee bar is $50,000. Compare that to spending an average of $150,000 to replace an employee whose compensation package is about $100,000. It's small potatoes. In addition, as Steven Hoffman (CEO and founder of The Iris Group) discovered, the soup and salad bar for lunch (his includes free soft drinks, coffee, fruit, and cookies, as well as Net-connected computers for employees to use on their personal time) can be a great productivity enhancer. This is another side of integrity, showing faith in employees, a commitment to their well-being, and support for their hard work.[2]

A recent marketing technique formerly used mainly by the entertainment industry has now become mainstream and can stretch the limits of personal and corporate integrity, especially if it is outsourced. It's known as *buzz marketing*. The Harry Potter books, *The Blair Witch Project* movie, and the craze of Razor Kick scooters are all examples of hugely successful buzz marketing. However, not every buzz campaign will meet with the same success. The technique relies on basically untrained and often short-term subcontractors of a branded organization, generally hired by an agency or outsourced to a firm considered expert in the technique. These so-called experts, surreptitiously and often without identifying their role, build grassroots interest in a brand, product, or concept. Vespa importer Piaggio USA hired a gang of bikers to travel about on snazzy Vespas in highly trafficked areas or cool places (e.g., Los Angeles), striking up seemingly innocent conversations with people to whom being cool is important and telling them where they, too, can buy a Vespa. The bikers were on the Vespa payroll and the technique was highly successful. This kind of marketing is far less expensive than buying national advertising. The carefully identified candidate who receives the marketing message is sure to carry that message to other opinion influencers, who in turn spread the message throughout their own networks. The result is similar to receiving a virus on your computer—widespread exposure of the idea, product, or brand. The metrics of such a campaign are difficult to pin down, although many outsourcing companies who are developing expertise in this area are trying. But the more troubling aspect of buzz marketing is the issue of integrity, The Ten Essential Traits characteristic that tells both the organization and the public whether what you say and do is what you believe and reward.[3]

IBM ran into difficulty for its peace symbol images (among others) on sidewalks in Chicago and San Francisco promoting their "Peace live Linux" campaign and building support for open source software. Although the campaign was hatched by one of its agencies, it was illegal and backfired with negative publicity for IBM. This offends some. *Adbusters* has organized protests against multinational marketers. And Sony attempted to create a buzz about its movies by fabricating quotes from a fictitious film critic and employees of the company. Perhaps the counterargument is that the public is used to being gypped and is tolerant and forgiving—or maybe just forgetful. Nevertheless, beware of these kinds of tactics. They open the door to unscrupulous marketers, who may damage your reputation even if your corporate goals are credible and your buzz campaign is aboveboard. Agencies that use questionable ad campaigns and marketing practices may pull you and your organization into uncharted and unethical situations.

Southwest Airlines is an often-cited success story, perhaps because it is so unique in many ways that its performance and culture are impossible to duplicate. Even Jet Blue, another upstart low-fare airline that is beginning to establish itself, while not emulating the Southwest culture, is the first to really compete with its quality, fares, and profitability (although, at this point, not with its convenience or availability).

In an in-depth interview with *Fortune* magazine, Herb Kelleher, Southwest's chairman of the board (who in 2001 ceded the management spot to two deputies), talked, as he always does, candidly.[4] I was particularly interested to see how he learned through the school of hard knocks to become adept at practicing The Ten Essential Traits. Kelleher's kind of integrity is not everyone's taste. But it works for him, for Southwest, and for his fiercely loyal employees—over 30,000 of them. He is completely intolerant of elephants in the room. And he wants employees who can spot them and move them out, bringing in good stuff instead. Lets examine The Ten Essential Traits in relation to Herb Kelleher.

- *Fearlessness.* No question there. Kelleher single-handedly took on the entire airline establishment, as well as the regulators and all his many critics who said, "It can't be done."

- *Completion.* When sued by competitors, Kelleher took the challenge like a terrier—and never let go until he won, ten years later.

- *Commitment.* Same as above. Committed not just to the concept, but also to the employees. "No one, I mean *no one*, gets terminated when things in the industry are bad." In fact, Kelleher's mantra is, "Not furloughing people breeds loyalty. It breeds a sense of security. It breeds a sense of trust. So in bad times you take care of them and in good times they're thinking, perhaps, 'We've never lost our jobs. That's a pretty good reason to stick around.' " Kelleher's integrity and personal belief system have become so much a part of the culture that he concerns himself about what will happen now that he is gone: "The thing that would disturb me most to see after I'm no longer CEO is layoffs at Southwest. Nothing kills your company's culture like layoffs. . . . It's been a huge strength of ours."

- *Inspiration.* What Herb does best—tales of his high jinks are epic.

- *Assuredness.* No one ever accused Herb Kelleher of being uncertain or lacking in confidence! That mind-set transfers to the people at Southwest.

- *Penetration.* "Of the people"—Kelleher is a master at this tool. "You have to take the time to listen to people's ideas. If you just tell somebody no, that's an act of power and in my opinion an abuse of power. You don't want to constrain people in their thinking." Kelleher loved to hang around with his employees at every level. That's when he had the most fun. For example, everyone gets a budget for Halloween. It is a *big* deal at Southwest. People dress up and decorate and whoop it up, day and night.

- *Intelligence.* Kelleher is smart. But beyond that, he spots and rewards smart people around him. Take the new president of Southwest, Colleen Barrett, who was Kelleher's secretary in the law firm where he used to practice. A master implementer, Barrett now oversees all marketing, advertising, customer service, and human resources. She is the keeper of the culture. Whether Southwest will sustain the great culture created by Herb Kelleher will depend mainly on Barrett and CEO Jim Parker (former general counsel), who keeps his eye on the cost structure to ensure that the low-fare, no-frills airline stays that way.

Southwest Airlines is an organization that values honesty. Kelleher is adamant that a suggestion box is too late. You have to be accessible (at *all* levels of management) to hear what employees are saying and to use their ideas.

Gaining Credibility

For many organizations, the largest elephant in the room is the *value system*. It's one of those elephants that carries a large sign saying,

I AM A GIRAFFE.

Anyone with any sense can see that the elephant with the sign that says I AM A GIRAFFE is an elephant. A long trunk is not a long neck no matter how many times you call it that.

This is similar to the value systems of many organizations. It is beautifully printed out and pasted all over the place. It's in the annual report. Some organizations even have it printed on everyone's business cards.

It's an interesting exercise to open my two-day seminar and executive education programs on this issue with the question:

"Who here can recite their corporate value system?"

After everyone has shuffled their feet and looked sheepish, I ask the next question: "Tell me of one incident in which a member of senior management used the corporate value system to solve a problem?

Sometimes I get some examples. Many times I get cynicism.

Don't waste your corporate resources on value statements unless you are going to live by them. Ritz Carlton lives by theirs. So does Southwest Airlines.

If you don't resolve problems and investigate opportunities by living by your value system, you will not only lose integrity with those who work for your organization, but with those you serve.

The "Count on Shell" campaign showed that the community and the customers were open to the idea and that employees bought into it, too. The resulting awareness, image building, and loyalty that resulted from the company's "Count on Shell" efforts have led to the Shell brand being listed among the world's top global brands.[5]

Valuing honesty means that people are not penalized for saying what they think, for expressing their opinions when they think it's in the best interests of the company, or for revealing problems rather than sweeping them under the carpet.

How different might the Firestone debacle (defective tires) have been had valuing honesty been the organizational and cultural norm (instead of saving face). In many cultures, saving face is critical, but valuing honesty is not necessarily counter to that value. Take the 2001 amazing apology from DBS banking group in Singapore, for example. The company apologized publicly for bad-mouthing competitors, indicating they had received advice from Goldman Sachs to do so. Cultural differences may have accounted for poor communications, but the overriding principle among bankers in the small country of Singapore, where cohabitation in the business community is a must, is valuing honesty. When a mistake was made—no matter whose fault—saving face meant admitting to the mistake and making attempts (monetarily and otherwise) to remediate.

Peter Drucker, the premier management guru, has an opinion on this. I have been privileged to meet him and to speak at various

Drucker Foundation conferences. He never fails to impress, and he has strong views on corporate integrity:

> The worst trend in management is those enormous millions paid out to people at the top at the same time they lay off 12,000 people. You have no idea how contemptuous upper-mid-level managers are of those people. They are the ones who do all the work, the ones who tell the people they are fired. These execs don't mind their bosses getting millions. But just not for dismantling things. There is no bitterness about Michael Eisner [taking a huge salary and bonus] because his success doesn't come out of anybody's hide. That bitterness has a very high price to pay. I once read a book about Marco Polo in which he asked Genghis Kahn what he expects of his officers. And he said, "Of an officer I expect that he takes care of the men before he takes care of himself. Of a general I expect that he takes care of the horse before he takes care of the men." Polo asked why, and he said, "An officer leads by doing, a general leads by example." CEOs should lead by example. But they violate that principle with their exorbitant compensation for eliminating employees. That's a terrible trend.[6]

In other words, it's dishonest and lacks integrity.

The management process of 360-degree feedback (feedback from all sides) is one that has been around a while. It has received varying report cards.

George Fisher used it very effectively at Kodak.

> It was something I found to be very revealing at Kodak. It's not the problems of 80 percent of your people that become evident. Rather, what you do is pick up the extremes, and some of them are very surprising. Some of the people, who are so good at upward management and seem to be living as perfect exemplars of the corporate value system, come off very poorly. And some people who tend to be at the bottom of your expectations come off as absolute stars in their people's eyes and in the eyes of their peers. We are using it to affect people's pay and their progress through the organization. It makes people believe that we are really serious about the corporate value system and the culture we are trying to create.

This is not something done only for lower echelons. The senior management team of an organization has to be part of it as well. Evaluations are anonymous so that people can say what they really think. The results may change depending on what is going on in the organization (e.g., downsizing, growth) and can be compared to what is happening with other companies inside or outside of your industry.

Analysis of results is revealing, but the real payback comes only if action is taken on those results. Attaching the value system to rewards, both tangible (e.g., compensation) and intangible (e.g., recognition), will incentivize everyone to get with the program! In other words, the system is a good mechanism for identifying and dealing with the elephants in the room, but only if the reward system is connected to the results.

Regardless of all the good outcomes of the 360-feedback approach, the real problem lies in getting employees to participate with appropriate seriousness! How do you make that happen?

You give them a good reason. An amorphous "It's good for the organization" is rarely enough to get people's attention. Communicating that this is a critical part of the system on which pay and promotion will be evaluated tends to get people's attention. That's the fear part. A more effective tactic is to wholeheartedly, as a Ten Essential Traits leader, participate in this process. This is a concrete way to demonstrate that Ten Essential Traits leaders value honesty and integrity. Action will go a long way in proving sincerity.

Some of the thousands of people who receive my newsletter have shared horror stories (on the condition of anonymity) about breaches of integrity in their organizations, many having to do with personal trust issues. Employees who are lied to or misled will have that trust destroyed. For an organization to recover from the negative influence caused by a breach of trust in leadership (perhaps not even senior leadership but someone with authority and influence) is time-consuming and fraught with failure. Here is one, not atypical story:

> I work in a large organization where teamwork is supposedly valued. Yet the only people who really get ahead are those who curry favor with politically savvy senior managers. This is our elephant in the room—we talk teamwork, but we reward political and individual self-interest. The result is that most people spend their time looking to see where their efforts will best be spent in order to get political mileage rather than doing something that is actu-

ally good for the company. Then the CEO stands up and makes one statement after another about doing away with administrative stuff and focusing on the customer, and I believe he has no real idea of what is going on just two levels down. The senior management team is competing to see who among them will be the next CEO, so no one is really looking after the business of the company. And there is so much emphasis on being honest, the corporate value system, telling it like it is, and so on. But those who have done so are no longer with the company. The talk may sound good, but whenever someone speaks up—by the next reorganization they are history. The result? Everyone keeps their head down and tries to stay invisible.

If I were free to reveal the name of this company, you would definitely want to short its stock. Of course, this is only one person's opinion, and who knows what grudge they may have and why. But the complaint is not uncommon.

The 360-Degree Feedback Process

The first time I experienced the 360-degree feedback process, I was with a group of executives, all from different companies, at a CEO roundtable. In one off-site session we shared opinions about each other (according to well-defined criteria) with a neutral facilitator, who ensured that the process was constructive. This is important, because verbal feedback after a survey can quickly sink to the level of character destruction. I was amazed to learn of my faults, many of which were unknown to me, and equally amazed to learn of my assets, some of which did not coincide with the way I perceived myself. The opportunity for change and self-knowledge was enlightening. It dramatically changed my self-perception and management behavior to such an extent that I believe I am a better person, and not just a better leader, from the experience.

Can you change your approach to leadership or management midcareer? If I didn't believe you could, I would have wasted neither my time nor yours with this book. You can, and I did, and here is an example of another leader who has.

Andy Pearson is in his midseventies. He changed his approach to leadership and management late in his career. Earlier, his reputation was dependent on his aggressive and often destructive leadership style when, as CEO of PepsiCo in 1980, he was named by *Fortune* as one of the ten toughest bosses in America based on his ability to inflict pain. Now he is founding chairman and former CEO of Tricon Global Restaurants (PepsiCo's spin-off of its three premier brands, Pizza Hut, KFC, and Taco Bell). In recent years, he has learned to be tough in a different way. Perhaps he has mellowed with age. Or maybe he is getting results with his new approach. Now he *guides,* he does not control. Where did he learn to do this? The teacher became the student. David Novak, chairman and CEO of Tricon, has established a culture that brings out the heart of the organization. (See Introduction: Does your organization have a heart?) And Pearson has recognized that the heart *is* the competitive edge. It's there at Southwest, at the Ritz Carlton, and now it is there at Tricon. Says Pearson,

> Great leaders find a balance between getting results and how they get them. A lot of people make the mistake of thinking that getting results is all there is to the job. They go after results without building a team or without building an organization that has the capacity to change. Your real job is to get results *and* to do it in a way that makes your organization a great place to work—a place where people enjoy coming to work, instead of just taking orders and hitting this month's numbers.[7]

He is singing my song! As living proof that learning takes place at any age, Andy Pearson has some wisdom to impart to other CEOs:

> It's all about having more genuine concern for the other person. There's a big difference between being tough and being tough-minded. There's an important aspect that has to do with humility. But I've been modestly disappointed at how hard it is to get leaders to act that way. I think it's going to take a generation of pounding away on this theme.

That's precisely why I created The Ten Essential Traits matrix—as a guidebook to help with the pounding!

The next characteristic of The Ten Essential Traits addresses the issue of genuine concern, explaining how being in the internal and external customer's head will accelerate this process. First, here are a few action steps to help you start pounding away at this theme!

Integrity: Action Items

- On a scale of 1 to 10, have your team members (anonymously) rate the level of integrity of your organization (with 10 being the highest level of integrity). Do the same with your particular working group or division. Then discuss the results. Is your organization more talk than walk? Do opinions vary? If so, why?

- Ask your team (and yourself) to decide whether integrity is one of the elephants in your room. If so, how does it manifest—in reward systems, in the way employees are treated (or customers or suppliers)?

- Is your elephant posing as a giraffe? In other words, does your organization only *talk* about values without acting on them? If you cannot change the whole organization, can you at least implement consistency in the way your group functions? This means setting up goals and rewarding people for achieving them. It also means stopping political game playing the moment you spot it.

Try the following scenario-planning exercise with your next team project: Before you start, state your goals and write them on a white board. Have the group discuss typical political game playing ways that might be used to achieve these goals—write those down, too. Then discuss integrity-based ways of achieving them and write those down. Now you have identified the elephant in the room. Only by letting everyone see it can you move it out. You have also enabled everyone to see what the game playing would look like—which serves to shine light on an elephant that is, frankly, too big to hide. You can apply this technique to customer interfacing (do the scenario planning first, play it through, and decide how to handle the relationship with integrity), to suppliers, and to internal customers.

11

Perception: Being in the Customer's Head

We are "ladies and gentlemen serving ladies and gentlemen." The Ritz Carlton sign outside the hotel means nothing when the heart and soul is not in it. For new staff, we first let them know what we are all about, so they don't just fulfill a function. Each will discuss what he wants to do and we help him set up his goals. We will give him time to set up his mission for himself."
—Horst Schulze, president, Ritz Carlton Hotel Company

There is an old story about four blind men in India who approach an elephant. One holds onto the tail, another the trunk, the third grasps the elephant's leg, and the fourth blind man hugs the elephant's side. Another man, who is observing them, asks each one what they think they have.

The one at the trunk says he has something long and flexible that will raise him up as high as he wants to go. The man at the leg says, "Oh no—what I am holding is grounded and solid and would move very slowly." The third blind man disagrees. "I have something that is like a wall—nothing can budge this thing, nor can it be penetrated." The blind man holding the tail says, "You are all wrong. I have a thin little thing here that is easy to manipulate and move around."

Identifying the Elephant

And so it is with our elephant in the room. The nature of the elephant will be defined by who is looking at it. (See Figure 11.1.) Which means that defining the elephant (or the problem) will be a task in

Personal Characteristic	Organizational Environment Needed	Example of a Management Process for Implementation
1. *Fearlessness*	Permits failure	Shared learning and shared power
2. *Completion:* Ability to complete; has patience and is flexible	Results-oriented with process freedom	Horizontal, project-oriented management processes with cross-functional and multi-locational teams
3. *Commitment:* Emotionally vested	Encourages individual contributions	Small work groups and flexible work behavior; fun
4. *Inspiration:* Inspires and communicates vision; motivates	Access to internal and external people networks	Constant visibility and accessibility
5. *Assuredness:* Knows what he or she wants	Opportunities for advancement and reward	Career progression process
6. *Penetration:* "Of the people" and builds personal equity; listens with respect; empowers with dignity; confident; good mediator	Flexible organizational structure	Free information exchange, communication, and benchmarking across groups and divisions
7. *Intelligence:* Talent to place right people in right place	Resource commitment to learning	Training and education
8. *Energy:* Opportunistic optimism and sense of urgency	A why-not (not why) culture; open to new ideas and resistant to bureaucracy	Continuous improvement and innovation processes and rewards and quick decision making
9. *Integrity:* Trust and credibility	Values honesty	360-degree feedback
10. *Perception:* Being in the customer's head	Customer-focused, both internal/external and domestic/international	Creates and values alliances

Figure 11.1   The Ten Essential Traits: The Larraine Segil Matrix

itself. Rather than getting stuck on defining it, let each person decide what it is, and then develop an approach to move it out of the room. That way the definition, and the different perceptions due to various points of view, will not prevent a major cleanup of difficult issues.

For example, one group sees the elephant as the fact that the organization is not honest with customers. Another sees the elephant as the fact that they don't know who their real customers are. Yet another sees the elephant as an inappropriate customer-relationship management system. And another sees the entire bureaucracy of the organization as the major impediment to real communication with the customer.

Does it matter who is right? Not really. All that matters is that when a problem is spotted The Ten Essential Traits step in to clean it up. Find out what your customers believe. Tell them honestly what you can and will do to satisfy that belief or change it. Keep your promises and deliver on time and in a quality style. Find out who your real customers are by asking the ones you think are good customers—they will tell you. Could it be that they are your *indirect* customers and that *their* customers are the ones you should be worrying about? For the dissatisfaction with the customer relationship management issue, find another way to do the same thing that is equally as efficient or cost effective—if you can't, accept that this system is here to stay and adapt to it. As far as the bureaucracy in your organization, you may not be in a position to affect the whole company. If not, then adapt your own activities and groups to reduce paperwork, busywork, and political work by finding a different way. In other words, build a no-nonsense island of efficiency within a swamp of game players.

Vision and Getting into the Customer's Head

Ron Johnson, who was general manager of Target stores at the time of our interview, shared some of the remarkable ways that Target has become a leader in its retail space, positioning its stores to serve customers of all income and demographic levels—a spectacular example of being in the customer's head. Target contributes substantially to the communities in which it operates. Being a good corporate citizen is a part of its customer orientation and getting into the customer's head. It all comes from refusing to let the elephant in the room be ignorance of their customer. Everything at Target is customer-centric. In his interview with me, Johnson had this to say:

We want everyone to view the business as their own and produce great results. This could be a store team leader who views his store as his own business. Or the merchandising executive, whether a senior buyer or a general merchandise manager. At each level, these people have their own area of responsibility and produce results. World-class performance means always exceeding your best-ever results. I think great leaders produce consistently superior financial performance. It is not a one-time thing. It is doing it all the time.

Johnson, who has a Harvard MBA, was considered a visionary at Target. His experience in the stores and on the front lines of the company led to his appointment as vice president and general manager for the Home Décor area of the business. He continued:

For a long time there was this view that to expand volume you had to do it through lower margin rates. Now I think there is a belief that you can expand your volume and grow your profits simultaneously, and that really ought to be your objective and your reward for creative innovation in the marketplace. One of the great challenges and opportunities of Target is providing higher quality, but with a low price. This is a major driver for everybody at the organization. Target is evolving. We started out as a discount store in 1961, and at that time there were three of us, Kmart, Wal-Mart, and Target—all started at the same time. Target and Wal-Mart were the same size in 1984. We both met our growth plan. Interestingly, Wal-Mart is the largest retailer in the world, and Target is a very successful large-volume retailer, but nowhere near Wal-Mart's size.

Clearly, Wal-Mart and Target are competitors. I asked Johnson how Target was able to get into the customer's head and understand what they need. I also asked how Target educates the customer about the difference between the two companies.

Target differentiates its stores, whereas Wal-Mart does not. We tend to appeal to higher-income guests who have a taste level that tends to be more upscale; they are more trend-oriented; they tend to care about not just the function of an item, but they understand the relative value of the fashion of an item. If you look at Wal-Mart, they tend to always carry products that functionally meet the requirements and that can be sold at the lowest possible price.

On the other hand, we tend to carry items that functionally meet the requirements but also have an esthetic value.

For example, I try to instruct my team that if they carry a $3 cookie sheet, then we ought to carry a $3 cookie sheet. At least 25 percent of our selection must be roughly comparable to Wal-Mart's selection, so if the guest wants to buy inexpensive baking items, inexpensive cookware, inexpensive picture frames, we carry that, too, from a price-point perspective. We will then hopefully offer a higher-quality item at the same price. This way, all guests can find great value at Target. On the balance of the assortment, which can be as high as 75 percent of it, we ought to be probing up to a significantly higher price, significantly more fashionable taste level, and that is where we make our point of difference.

Getting into the customer's head at Target is both an art and a science, as Johnson explained:

We have the current sales of items in our stores. The beauty of retail is that we have technology that enables me to look today at what has sold in every store in the country yesterday and watch the pattern of that selling. Through our own selling of products, we can identify trends—trends in color, trends in features—trends that people are looking at. We are changing all the time, adjusting the amount of inventory we carry every day based on what we sold. At a minimum, we adjust our content annually, meaning that every item in the store goes under annual review to decide whether or not we should keep it. In addition, we are continually bringing new ideas onto the perimeters of our floors—and our end caps [end-of-counter displays] change every six weeks. So, it's a combination of approaches, but we want the guests to feel like every time they shop at Target they see a new idea. It is important that the store appear as if has even more changes than it might actually have.

I asked Johnson how often customers visit Target stores. His answer was astounding:

In our market here in Twin Cities, some incredible number, like 89 percent of the population, is at a Target store every two weeks. I think it has to do with the fact that we intuitively understand how guests respond. Everyone tells about their "Target run" and that its tough to go in there because every time they go to Target they spend $100 when they only planned to buy toothpaste.

A very common statement that you hear people making about Target is "I can't believe how much money I spent." They spend more time in the store than they anticipated they would and they found things that they didn't expect to find. That is really important to our formula, and that is why we try to change the store, the main aisles, as frequently as we can to present new ideas for the guests. A good analogy, I think, is when you walk through a Crate & Barrel store, the front window changes all the time and makes the whole store feel different. Pottery Barn and Williams-Sonoma are also normally focused on their front windows. Those change all the time because that is the entry to their store. It makes you want to come in and shop. The balance of the store doesn't change as much. Similarly at Target, we try to change the really visible parts of the store on a regular basis. The guest feels the environment of the store. Wal-Mart almost always has on their end caps in their main aisle single, low-priced items. Target tends to display decorative, theme, and fashion statements that are seasonally correct or trendy, and that sets us apart. Here's how we get into the customer's head: First we look at the established rate of sales. Second, we spend a lot of time observing culture—walking through retail stores, watching cashiers, and reading magazines. We travel to Europe, walking the streets of London and Paris and Copenhagen—all of the key influencing markets—and we try to see what is becoming popular. As we identify the trends, we present that to our guests in a very fresh, innovative, and appealing way.

Being in the customer's head is not a static activity. Both the customer and the trends change daily, so it is no small undertaking to design and order products in advance that will succeed. Johnson continued his comments:

We have our own approach to scenario planning. We have what is called the *trends curve,* and we have full-time trend people who travel the markets and make presentations to us on fresh style trends, merchandise trends, and color trends. All of our stores are in the United States. But we are very global in that we probably import merchandise from 150 countries.

We try to bring the best of the ideas that we see in the world to our guests. For example, I just returned from shopping through London. If I see something that looks new and fun and seems to fit the spirit of our guests, then I bring that back. I spend my entire

life watching what our guests are buying. We have excellent demographics on the age, income, austerity, and interests of our guests.
We recognize the increasingly significant growth in the Hispanic
and African-American segment, especially in California, and
respond to that knowledge.

Target has an interesting mechanism for contacting its customers, or "guests," as the company prefers to call them. Johnson
explained:

> The guest relationship is really nurtured through the circular,
> which every Sunday is the second most read part of every newspa-
> per, after the comic strips. The Target circular is part of the rela-
> tionship. The attributes of the store are the clean, bright fun of the
> store, and this is also part of the relationship. It is the merchan-
> dise and the friendly helpers in the store that create the fun at Tar-
> get. It is a positive feeling. You walk into the store and people feel
> happy. The merchandise of the store is bright. It illustrates the
> concept of fun, newness; it's young and it has an attitude of being
> "with it."

During our interview, I asked Johnson how a store like Target
rises above all the noisy sales offers of local stores or catalog companies. His answer was interesting.

> I personally find it very distracting when I get a bunch of catalogs
> at my home that I never asked for—like someone is kind of intrud-
> ing in my life. We believe that the Target stores are readily acces-
> sible, and guests can wander around in them however they choose.
> That doesn't mean we don't analyze our customers and try to fig-
> ure how to market directly to them, but we really want to be their
> choice because of what we offer.

Target is but one of a family of companies in the fold of Dayton
Hudson. However, it is a very important family member. I asked
Johnson how that internal relationship worked.

> We have an excellent transfer of internal information. We have a
> very clear vision of what we value, what we want to accomplish.
> The company moves with great speed. Yes, we want to achieve
> superior financial performance. We want to have a fun, friendly
> culture—both internally and with our guests. We want to be a
> trend leader in everything we do, whether that is product or sourc-

ing, and we want to be an industry leader as well. We want to be different from a merchandising perspective and from a service perspective. We want to reward and retain high-quality people. We want to support family life for our employees and for our guests. We are by far the largest donor of profits to the communities in which our guests live. For 50 years we have given back over 5 percent of pretax profits to our communities. (We give something like $1 million a day to all the communities we serve through this source.) These are some of the values, I think, that attract customers.

Whereas many retailers live and die by their focus groups and researchers, Target is different, according to Johnson:

We don't do focus group studies or a lot of that sort of activity. The reality is that we get merchandise into our stores quickly and the guests respond to it quickly. . . . We can get into real customer response quicker than all the focus groups and pilot programs could do for us. We will know within a day what is working or not. At our store, our inventory turns 7 times, which means the average item, from the time it hits our warehouse until it goes out to the guests, would be about 7 weeks on the shelf. Therefore, if I can put product into the store and sell it, I can respond to that quicker than I can do all this studying and surveying. We benchmark different retail stores for different categories of merchandise. For instance, for food preparation products we look to Williams-Sonoma as leader. For decorative home products we look to Pottery Barn or Crate & Barrel. The senior buyers who are responsible for the merchandise assortment would spend time paying attention to what these other stores are doing. Then we benchmark them for product. We benchmark them for pricing. We benchmark how they promote. We benchmark how they present their merchandise. The objective is never to copy what they do, but to understand their core strengths and try to develop relative strengths for ourselves. We don't intend or want to copy anyone's style of approach. There are other retailers that do that, but that is not our objective.

Because Target is a leader in customer knowledge, I was interested to know whether any mistakes had been made in this area. I asked Johnson whether the company had ever misjudged what customers might want. He was very candid in his answer.

We do it all the time. There is merchandise that doesn't sell. You mark it down. You bring in something else. Fortunately, our misjudgments have been small. We haven't had any major errors. Many retailers have gone through identity crises. The Limited is a perfect example. The Limited stores have their Limited Divisions and their Limited Express stores, and every season they are targeting a different guest. They haven't developed what I call a "reliable, consistent brand character." Their performance reflects that. Talbot's did that a couple of years ago. Ann Taylor has gone through that, too, where they change the merchandise so much that they lose their existing guests. The company that is probably the best at managing the brand thing is The Gap. They stand for what they stand for. They market to their guests. They never change. Their basics do not change—their T-shirts. For young, with-it people, they have a great brand character. But several retailers have struggled because they have confused their identity to their guests.

Ron Johnson is a good example of a Ten Essential Traits leader. He has many of the characteristics in large doses.

I am responsible for most of the home area of Target. I don't have to get approval from my boss or anybody for any style that we carry or merchandise strategy . . . I am empowered to just go and do that. Similarly, I don't review every style my senior buyers bring in. They know what the mission is. They have the vision. They are empowered to move with speed to accomplish that. I think this is a big part of why we have been successful. I do think that having a clear vision of what we want our content to be [the merchandise content] is truly empowering buyers. With the power to create your own thing, it is exciting, it's fun, and there is a prize. When you have to work through committees and get approvals from a lot of people, (1) it is not as motivating for an individual, and (2) the idea gets lost in what I call "the compromise" (a case of too many inputs into the decision). What you need in retail is a distinctive style.

Whereas in many organizations, mistakes are the death knell of organizational freedom, at Target mistakes are considered an opportunity to learn. Johnson shared the philosophy of the company:

We share the learning from failure with a lot of very candid discussion, open communication in a nonthreatening environment, where failure is allowed. We don't talk about sharing success, but we talk about sharing learning. So learning comes from success *or* failure. The primary reward comes from promotion. The financial incentives are really geared to the senior buyer level and above, and lower down our rewards are more intangible, like recognition. But 80 percent of the overall reviews are based on financial performance of the area for which people are responsible. We take opinion surveys. People love working for Target—80 percent feel good about their career path and understand where it will lead. People are pretty comfortable with that. We operate with a small-team approach. From headquarters, you have about 12 merchandising divisions. Within that, you might have a total of 60 senior buyers. A division consists of about 50 people. A department consists of about eight. This means that the primary work group is probably eight or ten people. It is my job to put together teams that really work well together. I look for the symphony. There are certain characters whom you want on the team. There are team players—performance-minded, bright, inquisitive—who have a good balance of intuitive and analytical skills. Those are characteristics you want in common, but then you want diversity, too. It is always a plus if your team can reflect somewhat your guests. You want each team to have someone highly organized, good at planning, and then you might want someone who is exceptionally creative. You also might want someone who has really good number skills. Ideally, I think that creating a symphony is the best approach, but the core values of teamwork, cooperation, and high performance are values everyone ought to share. We have had pretty good luck at Target. People who come to Target tend to come here for their first job out of college. They are not from Stanford or Harvard, but they tend to be top-of-their-class A students. All of the large Midwest schools and others—like Indiana, University of Minnesota—have first-rate graduates. We have done a very good job of recruiting people who have the characteristics that I have described.

Target is a good employer of Ten Essential Traits leaders, who go through extensive training during their first few years and again with every assignment, both in the functional aspects of their job and in the systems they use to do it.

Getting into the customer's head is at the baseline of being in business. If you don't know how to do it, your chances for success are limited. In the days of the Internet madness, many companies were created (and died) without a clear understanding of who their customers were, how to get to them, and the cost of acquiring and keeping them. Free stuff was used for customer acquisition, and it worked for a while. But such customers are fickle, as many companies found out when they tried to charge for services that had been free. Also, the cost of acquiring customers became a black box for many companies that were unable to define this number. This resulted in a murky, ill-defined value proposition for both customers and shareholders, and many of those start-ups died.

Defining the Customer

Customer can be defined in many ways: internal (within your own organization), external (the end user of your service or product), or as stakeholders (government regulators, strategic alliance partners, and others). The broadest definition of customer reduces to this simple, biblical truth:

Treat others as you would like to be treated in the same circumstances.

It becomes a matter of perception. For example, human resources departments tend to be underappreciated. The rest of the organization is their customer. Although they want to be seen as a strategic supplier, they are often seen as a necessary (or worse, unnecessary) cost center.

Shell USA has handled this elephant in the room by identifying that services are treated differently inside the organization than outside. Hiring an outside supplier generally receives more consideration and higher levels of respect, quality control, and appreciation. In return, outside suppliers, who are not assured of getting the business, treat the customer with greater care, responsiveness, and service. Consequently, Shell Oil USA decided to spin off its service groups into a separate company (Shell Services), which would have to compete with outside suppliers for Shell's business. The internal customer became the external customer. Daurdie Banister, when he was president and CEO of Shell Services International and global vice president of North, South, and Central America Professional Services International, explained:

What we have been trying to do is to move the Shell USA organization from a perception that the services group is a cost center to being a profit center, which means becoming a stand-alone business. The next natural step is to find out whether you are satisfying your customers. There are some particular issues with this. We have been in a familial relationship with the people in Shell. So now we have to remember, every time we have a conversation with someone, that is a customer. He may have been your best friend yesterday and may still be your best friend tomorrow, but remember, that best friend is now a customer. So think about how you treat them. Think about how you talk to them. Think about how you present yourself when you talk to them and how you represent our business and our company.

Getting into the customer's head for Shell Services has meant becoming a global company from inception. Banister continues:

Some of our customers are global, some are not. As a service provider, when I go to talk to global customers my focus is satisfying their needs globally. I need to show that I have the intelligence, the resources, and the local country knowledge to do that. It's more about how I engage my customers than how I am set up inside my own organization. Perception is key. Having a networked environment is also key. It means being able to access lots of people and information while continually refining our services to meet their ever changing needs. We have brought people in from all over Shell as well as from outside the company.

Culture change is never easy. Shell Oil recognized that its elephant in the room was underutilizing its services people. In addition, its services employees were overlooking opportunities to serve internal customers more efficiently and effectively than outside suppliers. A healthy dose of competition tends to get people focused; in a Darwinian sense, the weak fall and the strong survive. With a series of major reorganizations by Royal Dutch over the past few years, all the Shell companies worldwide have had to rethink their structure, goals, and customer orientation.

What is involved is creating a customer relationship that is a continuum. Figure 11.2 illustrates this concept. It shows that all the goals are interconnected, which brings expected and ongoing added benefits to customers. When you place this in the context of a single orga-

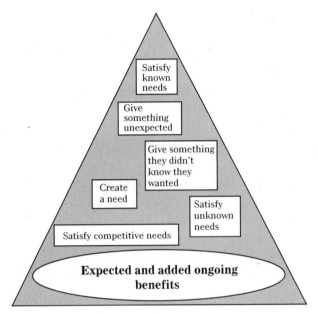

Figure 11.2   The Ten Essential Traits Customer Continuum

nization, it becomes clear that The Ten Essential Traits managers have their work cut out for them. Why? Because few *internal* groups or functions see themselves as suppliers who have the mandate of providing more than is expected to their internal customers. And the customers of those services rarely appreciate or value them as much as the services group would like. Rather, the attitude is one of "That's their job, what's the big deal?" or "It's what they are supposed to do, so why should I see them as a partner?" Only by outsourcing these services, as Shell has (primarily with IT), can you allocate costs appropriately across the company, increase the awareness by the customer of the supplier as a valued vendor, and monitor the quality of the services performed.

Ten Essential Traits Leadership as Supplier of Services

Let's for a moment think of The Ten Essential Traits leadership as the supplier of services. After all, leadership is a kind of service that is offered to a company. It shouldn't be outsourced (although sometimes that happens inadvertently when the tail wags the dog, the tail being Wall Street and the dog being a senior management team driven by stock price, not business fundamentals). What services can a Ten Essential Traits leader offer an organization? All the matrix characteristics. The Ten Essential Traits leader is the supplier of the customer connection, whether directly or indirectly, since every single employee at an organization must be customer-centric for the organization to succeed. This centricity is not the purview only of sales, customer service, or senior management. It means everyone. After all, if there are no customers for the organizational products or services (for-profits or not-for-profits, government or private sector), there is no reason for the organization.

If you accept for a moment that there are two kinds of customers, internal and external, then a schematic can show the kinds of connections that The Ten Essential Traits service would supply. Figure 11.3 visually explains this idea.

How do you do this?

Who Does Jeff Bezos Admire?

Jeff Bezos, founder and CEO of Amazon.com, is an example of a Ten Essential Traits leader who is involved in a critical path between external and internal partners. He connects with the customer, the company and its employees, the analysts and investor community, and his competitors.

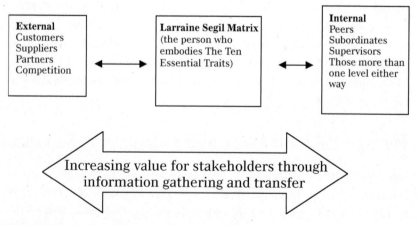

Figure 11.3 Customers and The Ten Essential Traits

I had the pleasure of meeting Bezos at Esther Dyson's gathering of the movers and shakers of the technology world from all over the globe. His presentation to this techno-savvy audience was mind-bending. The first revelation was finding out who Jeff Bezos admires—really admires—to the extent that he quoted him, praised him, and tracked his accomplishments. Who might that be? He is one of the greatest creators of business value of our time—someone you probably never heard of. His name is Joseph Vardi[1] (known to most as Yossi), and one of his most famous accomplishments (along with his son and other young genius inventors) was the creation of ICQ (the instant messaging technology). His company, Mirabilis Ltd., was completely in tune with what the customers wanted before they knew they wanted it, creating a product that customers could not do without once they had it. ICQ is one of the all-time most successful products in Internet technology. And the company spent practically nothing on marketing, attracting 50 million registered users before selling out to AOL for $407 million.

Vardi came up with the Vardi Paradox:

"The value of a dot-com company is in inverse relation to the amount of per-user money invested in it."

In other words, the more an idea sells itself without spending money, the greater its value. This means that people will repeatedly buy your product or service (or visit your web site) not because you spent a fortune on advertising and incentives, but simply because they want to!

Now let us return to Jeff Bezos. He referred to a concept that Yossi Vardi created called the "economic value of dreams." It is essentially a boom-bust way of looking at markets. People, through both greed and dreams, create ideas that they attempt to leverage by grabbing market share (*land grab*)—becoming a key (if not the only) supplier. As that happens, valuation increases to the point of excess, as does deployment of the concept. At this point, complacency sets in. The idea gathers momentum and grows exponentially, but so does the competition, and soon the bubble bursts and the cycle goes into a downturn. At some point, disenchantment sets in and value gets squeezed out. This is followed by panic and what the market calls *capitulation*, when sensible people reevaluate what was done and what could be done, and so value begins to be built again. Jeff Bezos comments:

> Why do I think that value will continue to increase [in our company and our market]? The reason is so obvious that it is easy to forget. Fundamentally, e-commerce is trading real estate for technology. Real estate gets more expensive every year, while technology gets cheap fast. The famous Silicon Valley doubling rate of Moore's Law[2] [which addresses the diminishing cost and increasing power of chips] states that circuit density doubles every 18 months. But data storage is getting twice as cheap every 12 months, and bandwidth is now getting twice as cheap every nine months. If Amazon holds bandwidth costs constant for the next five years, we'll be using 60 times as much bandwidth per customer. It'll completely change the customer experience. If we were to do that at today's bandwidth cost, not only would our customers not be able to handle the bandwidth, but we would more than triple our operating losses. That's how expensive bandwidth is. But we can hold that cost constant for five years and move to interactive video and all the things that haven't even been invented yet. What feeds the [growth] line is continuous improvement in customer experience. The reason that customer experience can get better in this business is because it relies on technology, which gets cheap fast. We have to continuously and relentlessly improve the customer experience. That is what Moore's Law is going to drive. Why do we have broad adoption of cell phones? Because they are no longer the size of cinder blocks. They got smaller and more useful. And now cell phones are so good that I can have an uninterrupted conversation for two or three minutes.

Ah yes, we know what you mean!

In 2001, Amazon.com sold 1 out of every 20 books purchased in the United States. In 2000, over 20 million people shopped there, which represents 8 percent of U.S. households (probably the best-educated and wealthiest demographic in the world). That is an incredible number. Amazon.com's original business plan called for $70 million in sales by 2000. The company did $2.7 *billion*. But no profits until the fourth quarter of 2001. Bezos, however, remains undaunted:

> We cannot charge more for books. We may have to actually charge less. But what [the cheaper technology and more expensive real

estate phenomenon] allows you to do is to compete more effectively with the physical bookstore environment. And the customer
experience will change. You can do personalization better. You can
have more advanced community features. You can let customers
talk to customers in real time, see each other and help each other
make purchase decisions . . . and you can make the full-motion
video online experience as interactive as hypertext. Cheap technology allows for innovation. People don't know that we have thousands of books in our catalog that are printed on demand. That's
the great thing about print on demand—the quantity on hand is
infinite. Our inventory works really well for us, and the reason is
that we can carry so much less inventory and still service a nation-
wide audience.

Jeff Bezos has made an art of being a Ten Essential Traits leader,
with his particular focus on the customer experience. Creating perception and getting into the customer's head has been a mission of
his company.

Our business model was not that different. It wasn't the markets
that told us to grow. It was the adoption of customers. The reason
we planned to grow slowly is that we thought it would take years
for customers to adopt this crazy new way of doing things. But in
July of 1995 we opened our doors, sent out 300 e-mail messages to
our beta testers telling them to tell their friends, and within a few
days everybody in the company was on their hands and knees
packing in the distribution center, which was the size of a one-car
garage. We were caught completely by surprise by the demand.
When something is working that well, it's the right business decision to invest much more heavily than originally planned. The
most important thing to remember is that when we talk about
technology benefiting our business, it's not to reduce our cost. It is
to improve the customer experience.

When Esther Dyson asked Jeff Bezos to state his greatest
achievement, here's what he said:

More than any company that I know of, most of our intrinsic value
has been built through having a culture focused on customer experience. We got very lucky in the early days of the culture of the
company. Because we were so woefully unprepared for the early
volume, every single person in the company had to drop what they

were doing and service customers. Think of a company of 30 people where every software engineer, every marketing person, every person in the company is working until 2:00 A.M. serving customers, wrapping things, driving them to the post office, getting the postal meter refilled. You get a culture that really cares about the customer, and cultures are notoriously stable for good or for bad. The culture of customer obsession is the thing that has built most of our intrinsic value.

Jeff Bezos is a good example of the perception (getting into the customer's head) characteristic of The Ten Essential Traits. There may be other characteristics among those Ten Essential Traits that he and his organization could do better. No one is perfect.

But customer generation can be a mixed blessing in a business where customers come in different sizes. Some are profitable and others are not. This means that the cost of doing business with certain customers exceeds the profits they generate for the company. It is relatively easy for a company to identify its customers. It is, however, quite difficult to identify the unprofitable ones. The high costs of software and data storage, as well as all sorts of technical difficulties prevent many companies from precisely identifying which customers are unprofitable for them. Many companies are now looking to build a profit and loss statement for each customer. Federal Express (FedEx) customers who spend a lot and are easy to service receive different treatment from those who cost more to keep. Customers who spend a lot but are expensive to the company can expect to be charged higher shipping prices. And customers who show few signs of spending more in the future are relegated to the TV ads (rather than company-specific marketing campaigns), which brings down the cost per customer. Using data warehousing and sophisticated analytical techniques can help you to get into the customer's head more effectively to custom-design marketing that fits a specific financial and profit profile.

Innovation and Getting into the Customer's Head

The overwhelming majority of the innovations recorded at the U.S. Patent Office have never been introduced on a commercial basis. Of 1,800 successful innovations tabulated,[3] almost three-quarters were reported to have been the result of perceived market needs and only one-quarter as the result of perceived technical opportunity. This means that there were more market-driven than technology-driven innovations. Customer-centricity creates market-driven opportunities. And this was before the golden age of mass customization (the 1990s) or the Internet boom and bust (the 2000s) and boom again (stay tuned). As Jeff Bezos intimated, who knows what the customer experience will include a decade from now, as market needs and technology work together to create an entirely new customer experience? Then there is the risk of timing. Kline and Rosenberg state it well: "Success means not only selecting the right cost and performance combination but also judging when the timing is just right for the product or service introduction."[4] This means that there are hazards and pitfalls in invoking the wrong criteria for success when judging the significance of an innovation. Potential consumers may not attach a sufficiently great value to the superior performance of a highly sophisticated new technology. Even that innovator par excellence Thomas Edison failed this test with his first invention. He created a machine that would tally votes in the Congress instantaneously, only to be told by several congressmen that it was the last thing they wanted. As a result, Edison wrote in his journal a resolution never to spend time on an invention until he was sure that a sound market existed for it. If he were here today, he might well rephrase that resolution this way: "Without being in the customer's head, and being perceived of value, there is no point to doing something that I think is a good idea but no one else does." I would add a caveat to this statement. It is also true that we may not know what we want and, even more, what we need until someone shows us what it is and how to use it. ICQ is an example of that. It is intuitive to use it, but who would have thought we needed it? And now, we can't do without it! Leadership means taking risks to get into the customer's head, placing a need there, and educating the customer to satisfy that need with your product and service. This is a large part of being an innovative Ten Essential Traits leader.

The personal and organizational characteristic of being in your internal and external customer's heads has been a mantra of The Ritz Carlton Hotel Company, now part of The Marriott Hotel Group. The mission started with Horst Schulze (quoted at the beginning of this chapter) and continued as the group grew and became almost cultlike in its devotion to service. The family characteristics of the employee group were in evidence when I took my satellite television crew[5] into the Ritz Carlton headquarters in Buckhead, Atlanta, and filmed their legendary morning lineup. During this ritual, each employee in every group has a chance to go over the value of the day. It is a time to refresh their minds regarding the purpose of their work—to serve customers. They review the value system of superb customer service ("ladies and gentlemen serving ladies and gentlemen") as it relates to both internal and external customers, which are equally important. Only by serving both will the quality of the whole be improved. My interviews with bellhops, front-desk personnel, general managers, parking valets, and housekeepers at multiple Ritz Carlton locations (in Georgia and California) produced the same comments over and over again: "The hotel company is like our family." "It has taught me how to behave not only here at work but at home and in the community."

Mark Timothy Hodgdon, formerly general manager of the Ritz Carlton Huntington Hotel and Spa, said it best:

> There's a very special mystique about Ritz Carlton as a company and about what Ritz Carlton stands for in the marketplace. There's a clear understanding that Ritz Carlton stands for excellence—from the perspective of the guest, the employee, and, ideally, in our business practices. There's a very strong commitment to a culture that focuses on some fundamentals that we refer to as our gold standards, which basically consist of four elements: The Ritz Carlton credo, our motto "ladies and gentlemen serving ladies and gentlemen," our three steps to service, and our hotel basics. The intent of this mystique is to create total alignment throughout the company on the image of Ritz Carlton, delivering consistently excellent service and product quality from one hotel to another, from one employee to another, with a full commitment to who we are and what we are. Ritz Carlton believes in the importance of the employee. We commit to put our hearts and souls into our businesses to ensure success. Clearly, any investor can choose to build a grand facility, a grand product, a wonderful physical plant. But what makes those products unique in the marketplace are employees who are committed to and aligned with a culture of excellence, delivering value to those guests who choose to purchase either the product or the service. From a culture perspective, complete align-

ment to those gold standards, complete alignment to what the company is and its commitment to excellence, a relationship between employees on the property level and the corporate office to ensure integrity and credibility in brand image and in the marketplace—that's how we do business.

Hodgdon went on to explain the lineup.

We believe constant communication and reinforcement of culture is absolutely essential to total alignment each and every day and for long-term success. Within Ritz Carlton Hotels we have what we call *lineups*. Those lineups take place with a standard format. It's when we talk about credo, components of credo. We not only recite it, we talk about what it means to every one of us. We talk about the motto "ladies and gentlemen serving ladies and gentlemen." We talk about what that means to us, how we need to interact, how we view it internally, and how we perceive that motto relative to our guest experience. We talk about the three steps of service. We talk about that warm and friendly greeting, that initial interaction, that first impression. We talk about gracious compliance to guests' wishes, and we talk about second and third steps of service from the perspective of fulfilling even those wishes that are unexpressed. We talk about how we listen to our guests, how we interpret their needs, how we posture and look at the guest experience, not from an employee perspective but from a guest perspective, and deliver on those unexpressed wishes, and then, of course, the fond farewell and the hotel basics. The lineup is a mechanism every day for us to touch base with our employees, to make sure we're totally aligned, to make sure that we have a focus every day, that we know what's happening in our business, but that we know who we are and that we appreciate each other and show genuine care and respect for each other every day. The lineup happens uniformly, shift by shift, in every department in the hotel. It takes place at all levels—hourly employees to senior management. We believe the lineups are the mechanism to keep the culture alive and well throughout every Ritz Carlton Hotel every day. It has been well received in each culture in which we operate globally. To be truly a part of a business, you need to understand what that business is and what's happening within that business every day. So not only do we reinforce the culture, which I believe has real value to every employee, but we also explain to them where our business is and where it's going. And we cover the basic essentials of arrival and departure, groups that are in our hotels, VIPs. Of course, all our guests are VIPs, but we talk about, from a recognition perspective, what our guests are expecting from us based on who's arriving that particular day. We recognize our internal customer employees by highlighting birthdays, and then we talk about certain basics each day relative to what may be property-specific. You can take this lineup, embrace the culture, understand it, reinforce it, talk about basic business practices and what's happening within each business unit globally, and highlight needs and specifics that will help us deliver and execute—whether you're in New York, catering to the needs of that corporate business client who has a fast-moving day, or whether you're in a resort on Kapalua, Hawaii, looking for a more relaxed setting while still doing some business, or whether you are in Dubai or elsewhere. Wherever you go, the lineup has real value.

Many businesses may try to update their employees. The Internet certainly allows for the speedy transfer of information (some authorized by management and some not!) The Ritz Carlton lineup provides a unique opportunity for that information to be transferred worldwide, as Hodgdon points out:

> There is a downloading of information from the corporate office that ensures that we are discussing the same cultural basics and fundamentals on a daily basis at every Ritz Carlton property. There is also information being shared from the corporate level through the lineup relative to bigger and better new practices. There's also the sharing by corporate of information that comes from the property level back up to corporate regarding those best practices and examples of best practices throughout the company. Really, the lineup is a two-way mechanism. It's corporate sharing information keeping us totally aligned with our culture. It's keeping us updated relative to best practices companywide. It's examples of those best practices being shared by employees. It's also those at the property level updating corporate on what we feel is working on a property level that can be shared globally and companywide as well.

Ritz Carlton is growing. As with many companies, when growth occurs the feeling of family can dissipate. The lineup helps.

"I think that a lineup really helps us stay in touch," Mark Hodgdon added. "As companies grow, I think there is a sense of detachment. The lineup keeps us in touch, aligned with a real sense of value, and it keeps us updated with what's happening in our company so that we don't feel alone."

It's easy enough to put mottos and mission statements together. Many companies do so at great (and wasted) expense. The only reason to do it is if your organization is going to live and breathe that vision. Hodgdon had some good insights to share about the Ritz Carlton mission of "ladies and gentlemen serving ladies and gentlemen."

> It is positioning on a high level, a degree of respect for one another within the workplace, how we do business, how we interact, how we communicate, how we support one another. It parlays into a fundamental in our business and within the Ritz Carlton called *lateral service*, which means whatever it takes to serve each other toward our common goals and our common mission. This starts internally with how we interact as ladies and gentlemen, how we perceive ourselves, and how we project to our guests. And it also sends a very clear message. We recognize our guests have choices. They can choose to stay elsewhere. Hopefully, what we do in providing excellence in service and product quality is motivating them [to stay with us]. We put our hearts and souls into our businesses and represent ourselves as ladies and gentlemen to ensure that we exhibit a level of respect to our guests for their choice to stay with us. The intent is to motivate that guest to stay with us many times in the future. It's based on the fundamentals of respect and understanding the importance of relationships and the fact that, as employees, we have choices about where we work. Ritz Carlton always tends to be the employer of choice in every location where there's a Ritz Carlton, based on its culture and its commitment to employees and to those who work within our businesses.
>
> Hopefully, our guests choose to stay at Ritz Carlton Hotels based on our efforts to make them feel at home and to make them feel valued and to let them know we don't take their business for granted.

Much of this relates to how the Ritz Carlton chooses its employees and trains them.

> For every opening at a Ritz Carlton Hotel, there are numerous candidates. It's all about effective selection. There's a process and a system for us to take the time to spend with prospective candidates to ensure that their skill set and their desires in life fit into

the positions that they are selected for. And we have a responsibility once we've gone through an effective selective process to take them through a complete orientation.

An orientation at the Ritz Carlton Hotels is a full two to three days that really give employees on the very front end of their experience a total understanding of who we are and what we are. We do not take them from their initial selection and filling out of paperwork and then ingrain them directly into the operation and expect them to sink or swim. We embrace our employees. We get them orientated into the big picture through a two- to three-day orientation, let them know clearly how important they are, how critical they are to our success, how a win for them is a win for our business, clearly get them orientated to our culture, get them orientated to the place in which they work, get them aligned with one another before they go into a rather significant departmental orientation relative to their specific tasks and responsibilities. And this all happens before they are certified over time to be fully competent to deliver the high levels of service that our guests expect. When someone is selected, it is as important to us as an employer as it is to them as an employee that we're making a decision that's going to work for them and work for us long term. That's the beginning and the foundation of a relationship that carries us from selection through orientation, through training certification to ongoing educational development. It is the maintenance of that relationship that ensures their success, which inevitably ensures our success as a company.

The Ten Essential Traits philosophy is all about the qualities of leadership, and according to the Ritz Carlton belief system, every employee has to have many of those qualities, so I asked Mark about some of the qualities the company looks for in its people.

We look for people who are charismatic, who communicate effectively; we look for those with positive attitudes, open minds, and an understanding and willingness and need to serve. The hospitality business requires of us an oft-repeated expression:

Be prepared to be on stage at all times.

On stage at a Ritz Carlton Hotel doesn't mean only in front of our external guests who are our customers, but also on stage in the heart of the house, where we're interacting with one another as fellow professionals, supporting each other to make that magical guest experience everything it needs to be. We look for dynamic, charismatic candidates to fill critical positions in our business— those who are open-minded and prepared to constantly learn and to develop their abilities to reach higher levels of performance. This means hiring "natural smilers," people who have a tendency to fulfill those criteria. It's irrelevant whether you're joining us for a housekeeping position or room service or a wait staff position or front desk, whether it's an hourly position or salaried is irrelevant. We take you through a rather regimented orientation process that ensures that everyone is totally aligned with culture, our mission, our commitments to each other, and our commitments to our guests. We send a message to you that you're important to us as a business. You make the essential difference. As an employee, you have determined and will continue to determine our success—yesterday, today, and into the future. We let employees know, regardless of task or function, they are part of a process that allows us to deliver a level of excellence and service to our guests. Each individual within our business makes an immeasurable contribution. Through orientation, we let them know right up front that they are going to determine our success: "We're committed to you. We're obligated to you who ensure that we create a level of well-being in the workplace. We provide you with a level of support from the very beginning that's continuous and ongoing to ensure your success into the future." Through that commitment, we are there for them as they grow professionally and personally.

Hodgdon gave me a concrete example within his hotel at Pasadena.

Several examples have occurred of employees who walked in with their limited expectations, possibly even looked at the opportunity at the hotel as being for the moment. These people have turned around and made careers of our business. We have a gentleman who is a concierge for us in the lobby. He is continuing his education, is going to get a master's in business administration, but through his experience here the last few years and his embracing of the culture and his enjoyment of hospitality, from starting in an hourly position, he has moved up into a supervisory capacity and is now a salaried management employee with a sincere interest in having a long-term career with Ritz Carlton. He was focused more toward finance and marketing with his bachelor's degree, going on to get a master's in business administration, but is now taking another look at a career direction that would enable him to stay with Ritz Carlton and hospitality for a lifetime, simply because of his experience within a Ritz Carlton Hotel, his love and appreciation for the culture, which makes sense not only personally, but from a business perspective. There are many examples like this. At the same time, we have employees who have made multiple moves throughout the industry from one hotel to another, never really having found a home, not looking for upward mobility but looking for lifelong stability. Ritz Carlton Hotels and its culture provides for ongoing support regardless of your interest to be promoted internally. Our employees find a level of enjoyment and well-being in growth and constant development with stability and a real sense of love and appreciation for what they represent and who they are within the significant business.

Alliances

The management process critical to making the personal and organizational characteristics work in a perceptive and customer-centric organization is all about alliances. This means both internal and external alliances, domestic and international. I have spent the past 20 years immersed in the concept of alliances, so I could wax poetic here. However, it would be more efficient to refer you to two books I have written on the subject.[6] What I will say is this: Alliances are *the* management tool that will integrate employees internally and give competitive advantage to an organization by applying The Ten Essential Traits approach throughout the organization and its internal ecosystem. This means creating internal networks of relationships that are nurtured and managed over time, with continual care to add value and treat the relationship partners as valued customers.

External alliances are the tools to create competitive advantage in the marketplace and to ensure preemptive positioning for future success, technological, geographic, and service knowledge capture, as well as the spreading of risk and capital investment that can be amortized through the risk taking and investment of others.

In applying The Ten Essential Traits, it is necessary to see alliances in the broadest possible way. Don't look at alliances only as strategic relationships with other companies that are the purview of senior management. Regarding all relationships as alliances that can add value within the corporate and personal networks operating around us will enable you to reach a level of competency and excellence that would not be achievable without such alliances.

Perception: Action Items

- Are you "ladies and gentlemen serving ladies and gentlemen"? Examine the belief system of your organization as well as your own to see how well they match. Where could you improve the work environment by making it a more personal environment in which you are happy?

- Are customers the center of your organizational universe? If not, why not? What can you do to change this?

- Do your customers perceive you to be as terrific as you think you are? If not, find out where they think your competencies and deficiencies lie. Spending weeks on core competency analysis is futile if all you do is talk to yourself. Find out what the real world thinks by meeting with customers, both internal and external. Make sure that everyone in the company at some stage has the opportunity to meet a customer (remember Amazon in its early days?). Then learn from his or her customer perception. You may be surprised!

- Do you consider your internal service providers (IT, finance, HR, manufacturing, sales, marketing, etc.) to be alliance partners or just commodity suppliers? Are some of them strategic so that you are made more or less competitive by their involvement? Can you improve on these relationships? Set up metrics to define a baseline for "respect" and "customer service" for your internal alliances and measure it over time. Is it improving or getting worse? Tracking it as a metric will give you something to work with—and toward.

The summary in Chapter 12 ties all the matrix characteristics together.

12

Summary

hanging behavior is one of the most difficult challenges, personally and professionally, that face us in a lifetime—whether that span is measured in human years or organizational life cycles.

Subscribing to The Ten Essential Traits demands a change of habit. The good news is that the change is being stimulated by many different sources. Employees no longer expect lifetime employment in a patriarchal organization that will protect them. Similarly, the organization doesn't expect undying loyalty and longevity of tenure from even their best and smartest. Benefits must be realized in the short term. Obligations are seen as mutually beneficial—helping both employee and employer—and are subject to change. Competition for talent means that change must accelerate. Individuals as family members expect different kinds of support from their employers— more flextime, paternity leave, recognition of the burdens of aging or ailing family members, and many other adaptations to the demands and pleasures of living in the twenty-first century.

Assuming you prefer eating to herding, The Ten Essential Traits matrix is the way to spot and consume elephants—one toe at a time.

If you attempt to swallow an elephant whole, the task is overwhelming. Approach it one nibble at a time and tangible success will emerge early in the game. Because the matrix is interconnected, nurturing or changing one quality will naturally lead to developing others. Here is an example of how the characteristics of the matrix work together.

Fearlessness (Chapter 2) is a quality that is desirable only when combined with the ability to complete. Why? Because deciding to take risk is seen as foolhardy unless it is accompanied by the discipline and patience required to complete the task (Chapter 3). Being fearless as an employee means being willing to take risk and fail. Being a fearless employer means allowing those who work for you to fail, as well as sharing power with them. The management processes for making all this happen include changing compensation systems to reward results-oriented risks (rather than process rigidity). This may mean addressing some activities from a venture capital type of perspective (i.e., many deals fail, some represent the living dead, and a few are winners). This may require selecting employees who feel comfortable with uncertainty. It means mandating continuing education, not only for those in senior ranks, but also for those in the middle part of the organization. Other processes include encouraging cross-functional teams and using online working methodologies to extend multilocational and multinational interaction.

In order to achieve these changes, the most desirable employees are those who are emotionally vested and committed to the goals of the project and the organization (Chapter 4). Why would they want to participate? Well, good feelings go only so far. An organization that encourages individual contributions and rewards them (with appropriate salaries, bonus, recognition, promotion, and opportunities for new challenges) will attract people who know what they want from their work life (Chapter 6). "Feeling appreciated" may sound like soft, touchy-feely, 1960s-style stuff. In truth, it is exactly what small work groups, flexible work behavior, and appropriate reward systems create. Combine this with a career progression plan, and you will have people who can see the future—theirs and the organization's (Chapters 2, 3, and 6).

Inspiring, motivating, and communicating vision (Chapter 5) are the responsibilities of all managers, yet many middle managers in the organizations I work with are clueless about the vision and direction of the company—which makes it difficult to lead others. Being accessible ("of the people") is not easy for senior managers in organizations with hundreds of thousands of employees. But it is the continuing responsibility of all managers to be visible, with sufficient flexibility in the organizational structure so that the *real* information trickles upward (Chapter 7). Being out with the troops, penetrating the organization from the front lines outward and inward, with the customers and sales force, in the warehouses, data centers, and factories, in the company cafeteria (rather than in an executive dining room)—these are the activities that make for folklore and community (e.g., Southwest, DaimlerChrysler, George Fisher). The consequence is the building of personal equity—interconnected networks of people who respect you, relate to you, and contribute to your education, knowledge, and excellence. The management processes that make it easier to communicate across divisions and groups and to get rid of the not-invented-here syndrome ("if *we* didn't think of it, it isn't any good") are reward systems that compensate for information sharing, cross-divisional or group collaboration, and benchmarking.

One of the most exciting gifts of the dot-com era is the unveiling of vast wells of intelligence (Chapter 8)—new ideas, new technology, new ways of doing old things. This spawns adrenaline-pumping energy (Chapter 9), a 24/7 mentality, and hyperkinetic excitement in companies globally, in both developed and emerging economies. The past five years has seen an explosion of innovation and entrepreneurship—much of which has survived regardless of stock market gyrations. Organizations are realizing that placing the right people in the right jobs is a key talent in itself—as time-to-market shortens and competition appears unexpectedly from those not previously on one's competitive radar—for example, third-generation (3G) convergence of computers, telephony, wireless, and other kinds of communication). Combining fearlessness, the ability to complete, commitment, inspiration, and assuredness with a reality-based view of the world and its opportunities builds intelligence. This translates into knowledge and contributes to innovative, energetic, urgent implementation of the tasks at hand. Those who procrastinate will die. The qualities comprising The Ten Essential Traits will weed out employees and organizations that cannot change fast enough to meet the opportunities of the present and future (especially the needs of customers) by forming alliances[1] (Chapters 2 through 10).

Finally, the whole package is wrapped in the mantle of integrity and trust. You cannot hide a lack of ethics in a wireless and connected world. It is naive to imagine that people will not discover activities that are under the bar of what's acceptable. Whether via whistle-blowers or chat rooms, all information ends up very quickly in the public domain, and organizational (brand) and individual reputation is more important than ever before (Chapter 11).

If The Ten Essential Traits matrix is seen as a series of complementary and integrated characteristics, you will be able to effect change while using it as your guide, moving forward one step at a time.

If the enormity of the task seems daunting, remember the words of my grandmother—a smart, witty, and elegant lady from the East End of London—who always had the ability to cut to the chase lest I (or anyone else around her) might be feeling rather self-important:

> *If things seem to be too overwhelming and you want to forget your problems, here is what you do—wear tight shoes.*
>
> —Charlotta (Lottie) Cohen, first said in 1920

APPENDIX A

The Ten Essential Traits

Assessment Tools

Personal Characteristics

Instructions: On a scale of 1 to 10, rate yourself on how closely you match the characteristic as described.

Fearful									Fearless
1	2	3	4	5	6	7	8	9	10

Inability to complete									Ability to complete
1	2	3	4	5	6	7	8	9	10

Not emotionally vested									Emotionally vested
1	2	3	4	5	6	7	8	9	10

Unsure of goals									Know exactly what you want
1	2	3	4	5	6	7	8	9	10

Does not relate to others in lower positions									"Of the people"
1	2	3	4	5	6	7	8	9	10

Does not collaborate									Builds personal equity and networks
1	2	3	4	5	6	7	8	9	10

Lethargic									Energetic
1	2	3	4	5	6	7	8	9	10

Does not value integrity									Highly values integrity
1	2	3	4	5	6	7	8	9	10

Opportunistically pessimistic									Optimistic
1	2	3	4	5	6	7	8	9	10

Unaware of customer needs									Gets into the customer's head
1	2	3	4	5	6	7	8	9	10

Lack of common sense								Raw intelligence	
1	2	3	4	5	6	7	8	9	10

No sense of urgency								High sense of urgency	
1	2	3	4	5	6	7	8	9	10

Analysis

Evaluate each personal characteristic individually.

Ratings from 6 to 10 in each category indicate a propensity toward becoming a Ten Essential Traits manager. Of course, unless you can honestly rate yourself a 10 in every characteristic, there remains a learning and growth opportunity!

Ratings within the 1 to 5 range isolate areas in need of significant improvement. Refer to appropriate chapters in the book for strategies to develop your Ten Essential Traits skills.

Organizational Characteristics

Instructions: On a scale of 1 to 10, rate yourself on how closely the organizational environment matches the characteristic as described.

Failure is unacceptable					Failure is permitted				
1	2	3	4	5	6	7	8	9	10

Results-oriented with process freedom					Not results-oriented and/or no process freedom				
1	2	3	4	5	6	7	8	9	10

Does not encourage individual contributions					Encourages individual contributions				
1	2	3	4	5	6	7	8	9	10

No opportunities for advancement or reward					Unlimited opportunities for advancement and reward				
1	2	3	4	5	6	7	8	9	10

Rigid, hierarchical organizational structure					Flexible organizational structure				
1	2	3	4	5	6	7	8	9	10

Work groups are isolated from others					Openness to internal and external networks				
1	2	3	4	5	6	7	8	9	10

A "no" culture					A "yes" culture				
1	2	3	4	5	6	7	8	9	10

Does not value honesty					Values honesty				
1	2	3	4	5	6	7	8	9	10

Not open to new ideas					Open to new ideas				
1	2	3	4	5	6	7	8	9	10

No understanding of customer needs					Internally and externally customer-focused				
1	2	3	4	5	6	7	8	9	10

No resources committed to learning					Resources committed to learning				
1	2	3	4	5	6	7	8	9	10

High level of bureaucracy					Resistant to bureaucracy				
1	2	3	4	5	6	7	8	9	10

Analysis

Evaluate each environmental characteristic individually.

Ratings from 6 to 10 in each category indicate an environment conducive to The Ten Essential Traits. Of course, unless your organization rates a 10 in every characteristic, there remains a learning and growth opportunity!

Ratings within the 1 to 5 range isolate areas in need of significant improvement. Refer to appropriate chapters in this book for strategies to improve your organization as a breeding ground for Ten Essential Traits managers.

APPENDIX B

The Ten Essential Traits for Managers' Matrix Top-Line Results

Research Data Collected from 1999–2001

Response Rate

- 138/900 paper and pencil = 15%
- 105/2550 Web = 3.4%
- Overall response rate = 6%

Respondents' Profile

- 74% male
- 9.7 years in their organization
- 4.2 years in their current position
- 87% in the United States, with 17 other countries represented (Europe, Latin America, Asia, Africa, Canada)
- 55% upper management (CEO, CFO, COO, and other executives); 45% middle management or employees (supervisor, hourly, alliance manager)
- Industries: 34% computers and technology
  16% manufacturing
  5% telecommunications
  5% service
  40% other (electronic commerce, government, utility, retail, aerospace, consumer products, healthcare financial services, education, transportation, food, energy, other)

- Alliance status: Average return on alliance = 5.3 on a 10-point scale, where 1 = less than expected and 10 = more than expected.

- Ranking order of causes for disappointing alliances (on a scale of 1–7):

  1. Misaligned expectations/goals (2.49)

  2. Inadequate alliance process accepted by organization (3.10)

  3. Alliance management expertise not good enough in partner (3.37)

  4. Mismatch in corporate culture (3.38)

  5. Market factors (4.17)

  6. Lack of senior management buy-in (4.23)

  7. Other (4.44)

48% of respondents had less-than-expected value from their alliances

- Note: Executives surveyed had been educated in alliance competency by Larraine Segil of The Lared Group, which may account for the higher than normal positive results in alliance outcomes; earlier research by Segil (*Intelligent Business Alliances*, 1996, Times Books, Random House) found that close to 60% of alliances returned less-than-expected results.

- Business stage: 31% start-up/high growth
                   43% professional
                   26% mature/declining

- 84% reported themselves to be among the top 20 leaders in their industry

  17% small

  15% medium

  68% large

The average survey respondent was a male upper manager in a large professional-stage U.S. computer/technology company (among the top 20 leaders in its industry) who has been with the company for ten years and in his current position for four years and who has received average return on alliances formed.

Domain Importance

Eight leadership domains from each of two perspectives (*individual* and *organization*) were derived from the pilot survey. (See Table B.1.) Respondents rated the importance of each domain in contributing to their organization's success on a scale of 1 (not at all important) to 5 (critically important). The higher the score, the more important the domain. No domain was rated lower than 3.0 on this scale. Certain domains were combined (3 and 4, 6 and 10). *All domains are important.*

Differences in perceived importance are shown in Tables B.2 through B.9. The initials in each cell of the matrix denote a high-importance score (4 or 5).

Table B.1 Perceived Importance of Each Domain

Domains (16 total)	Individual characteristics (8)	Organizational characteristics (8)
1. Fearlessness	3.6	4.0
2. Completion	4.3	4.1
3./4. Commitment/inspiration	4.2	3.9
5. Assuredness	3.8	4.2
6./10. Penetration/perception	4.1	4.2
7. Intelligence	3.4	4.1
8. Energy	4.0	4.2
9. Integrity	3.4	4.1

Table B.2 Profile of Importance by Industry

	Personal characteristics	Organizational characteristics
Fearlessness		S, Tele
Completion	M, S, C/T, Tele	M, S, C/T, Tele
Commit/inspire	S, C/T	
Assuredness		M, S, C/T Tele
Penetration/perception	S, C/T, Tele	M, S, C/T, Tele
Intelligence		S, C/T
Energy	S, C/T, Tele	M, S, C/T, Tele
Integrity		M, S, C/T, Tele

M = manufacturing; S = service; C/T = computers/technology; Tele = telecommunications. C/T is significantly more important than Tele.

Table B.3 Profile of Importance by Stage in Life Cycle

	Personal characteristics*	Organizational characteristics*
Fearlessness	S/H	S/H, M/D
Completion	S/H, P, M/D	P, M/D
Commit/inspire	S/H, P, M/D	
Assuredness		S/H, P, M/D
Penetration/perception	S/H, P	S/H, P, M/D
Intelligence		S/H, P, M/D
Energy	S/H, P	S/H, P, M/D
Integrity		S/H, P, M/D

S/H = start-up/high growth; P = professional; M/D = mature/declining. S/H is significantly more important than P or M/D.

In the telecommunications industry, having committed individuals and providing staff development opportunities is less important to success than in the other three industries. In the computer, technology, and manufacturing industries, permitting failure is less important to success than in the other two industries. Computer/technology perceives individual integrity as being more important than does telecommunications.

Table B.4 Profile of Importance by Position

	Personal characteristics*	Organizational characteristics*
Fearlessness		U
Completion	U, M/E	U, M/E
Commit/inspire	U, M/E	
Assuredness		U, M/E
Penetration/perception	U, M/E	U, M/E
Intelligence		U, M/E
Energy	U	U, M/E
Integrity		U, M/E

*U = upper management; M/E = middle management/employees. U is significantly more important than M/E.

Table B.5 Profile of Importance by Top 20

	Personal characteristics*	Organizational characteristics*
Fearlessness		N
Completion	Y, N	N
Commit/inspire	Y, N	
Assuredness		Y, N
Penetration/perception	Y, N	Y, N
Intelligence		N
Energy	Y	N
Integrity		N

*Y = Yes; N = No. N is significantly more important than Y.

Start-up/high-growth organizations find individual fearlessness and assuredness to be more important—and results orientation with process freedom to be less important—than do organizations in other life cycles. Mature and declining organizations place less importance on fearlessness, penetration/perception, assuredness, and energy than organizations in other life cycles. Professional organizations find fearlessness and permission to fail less important than organizations in other life cycles.

Upper management finds energetic individuals with integrity, and permission to fail to be more important in success than do middle managers and employees.

Organizations in the top 20 find energetic individuals to be more important than those companies not in the top 20. Those not in the top 20 find permission to fail, results orientation, commitment to learning, a why-not culture, and valuing honesty to be more important to success than do organizations in the top 20.

Large organizations do not find commitment, energy, or permitting failure to be as important as small and medium companies do. For small companies, individual contributions are more important than for medium and large companies.

Table B.6 Profile of Importance by Organizational Size

	Personal characteristics	Organizational characteristics
Fearlessness		S, M
Completion	S, M, L	S, M, L
Commit/inspire	S, M, L	S
Assuredness	S, M	S, M, L
Penetration/perception	S, M, L	S, M, L
Intelligence		S, M, L
Energy	S, M	S, M, L
Integrity		S, M, L

S = small; M = medium; L = large. S is significantly more important than L.

U.S. companies believe that completion, commitment, penetration/perception, assuredness, energy, permission to fail, results orientation, opportunities for advancement, and a why-not culture to be more important to success than do foreign organizations.

Table B.7 Profile of Importance by Geographic Location

	Personal characteristics	Organizational characteristics
Fearlessness		US
Completion	US	US
Commit/inspire	US	
Assuredness		US
Penetration/perception	US	US, O
Intelligence		US, O
Energy	US	US
Integrity		US, O

US = United States; O = other. US is significantly more important than O.

Table B.8 Profile of Importance by Alliance Success

	Personal characteristics	Organizational characteristics
Fearlessness		E, L
Completion	E, L	E, L
Commit/inspire	E, L	
Assuredness		E, L
Penetration/perception	E, L	E, L
Intelligence		E, L
Energy	E	E, L
Integrity		E, L

E = expected; L = less than expected.

Organizations that achieved expected results from alliances find that individual energy is more important to success than organizations that achieved less-than-expected results.

Females found that individual energy and permission to fail were more important to success than did males.

Table B.9 Profile of Importance by Gender

	Personal characteristics	Organizational characteristics
Fearlessness		F
Completion	M, F	M, F
Commit/inspire	M, F	
Assuredness		M, F
Penetration/perception	M, F	M, F
Intelligence		M, F
Energy	F	M, F
Integrity		M, F

M = male; F = female.

Domain Performance

- Computer/technology and manufacturing subjects rate themselves significantly higher on individual integrity than do telecommunications subjects. Otherwise, there are no significant differences in ratings of domain performance across the four industries that could be compared: manufacturing, service, computer/technology, and telecommunications.

- One individual domain and seven organizational domain scores were significantly different for organizations in different life cycles. Mature and declining organizations performed at a lower level than other life cycles in the following areas: commitment, permission to fail, results-oriented, encouraging individual contributions, opportunity for advancement, flexible/customer-focused, commitment to learning, values honesty, as shown in Figure B.1.

- Three individual domains and seven organizational domain scores were significantly different for upper management than for middle management and employees. Middle managers and employees rated themselves or their organizations as performing significantly worse in the following areas: fearless, commitment, assuredness, permission to fail, encouraging individual contributions, opportunity for advancement, flexible/customer-focused, commitment to learning, a why-not culture, and values honesty. (See Figure B.2.)

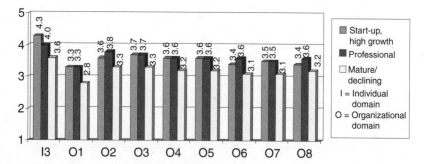

Figure B.1   Domain Performance by Life Cycle

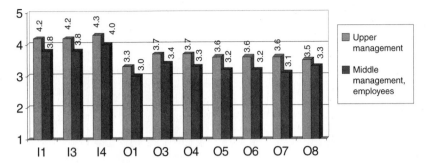

Figure B.2 Domain Performance by Position

- Two individual and one organizational domain were significantly different for males versus females. Males rated themselves as more fearless and more focused and their organizations as more committed to learning than did females. (See Figure B.3.)

- There were no significant differences in domain performance between organizations in and not in the top 20. However, for four individual and all organizational domains there were significant differences between small, medium, and large organizations. Large and medium organizations performed significantly worse than did small organizations in the following domains: fearlessness, commitment, penetration/perception, intelligence, energy, permission to fail, encouraging

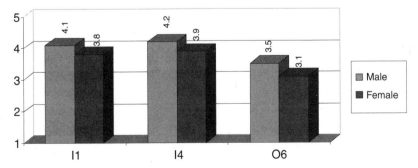

Figure B.3 Domain Performance by Gender

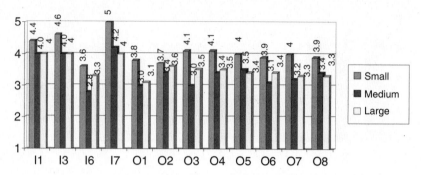

Figure B.4 Domain Performance by Organizational Size

individual contributions, opportunity for advancement, flexible/consumer-oriented, committed to learning, why-not culture, and values honesty. (See Figure B.4.)

• Organizations in the United States performed significantly better on two individual and two organizational domains: assuredness, penetration/perception, encourages individual contributions, and a why-not culture. (See Figure B.5.)

• Organizations whose alliances performed at or above expectation performed significantly better on three organizational domains: opportunities for advancement, flexible/consumer-focused, and commitment to learning. (See Figure B.6.)

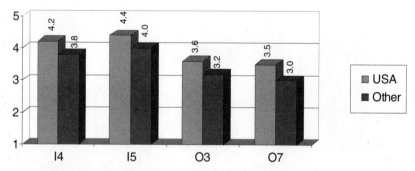

Figure B.5 Domain Performance by Geographic Location

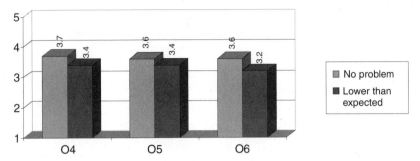

Figure B.6 Domain Performance by Alliance Success

Discrepancy Scores

- By and large, the discrepancy scores are positive, meaning that the subject is rating his or her individual characteristics at a higher performance level than that of his or her organization.

- There were no significant discrepancies between individual and organizational performance by industry.

- There was a significantly larger discrepancy for fearlessness and permission to fail in mature/declining organizations than in professional organizations (individual more fearless than his or her company permits failure). (See Figure B.7.)

- There was a significantly larger discrepancy score for the penetration/perception domain and the energy domain among

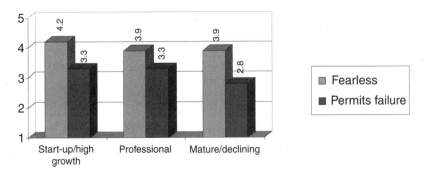

Figure B.7 Discrepancy Scores by Life Cycle

middle managers/employees than in upper management (individual more penetration/perception and more energetic than his or her company was flexible/consumer-oriented or why not culture). The discrepancy for the raw intelligence/ resource commitment domain was significantly larger in upper management than in middle management/employees (individual's raw intelligence rated lower than company's commitment of resources to learning). (See Figures B.8 to B.10.)

• Males had a significantly higher discrepancy than females on the raw intelligence and resource commitment domain. Males rated their raw intelligence lower than their organization's resource commitment to learning. (See Figure B.11.)

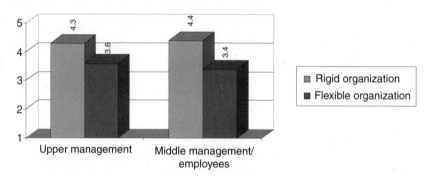

Figure B.8   Discrepancy Scores by Position

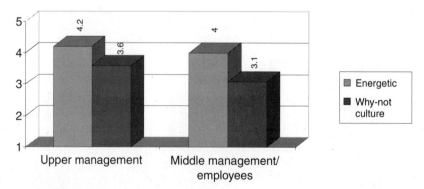

Figure B.9   Discrepancy Scores by Position

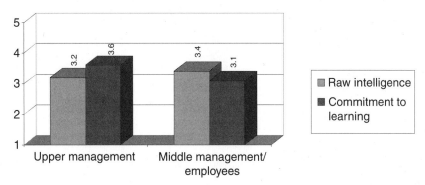

Figure B.10   Discrepancy Scores by Position

- There were no significant differences in discrepancy for top 20 organizations versus those not in the top 20. Large organizations had significantly greater discrepancy than did small organizations on penetration/perception focus, with individuals rating themselves as better performers than their organizations. With such a low showing, it is possible that discrepancy between individuals and their organizations does not predict success. (See Figure B.12.)

- There were no significant differences in discrepancy by geographic location (U.S. versus non-U.S. organizations).

- There was a significantly greater discrepancy in focus/opportunities for advancement domain among organizations whose alliances did not perform as well as expected. These subjects rated their own focus as exceeding their organization's opportunities. (See Figure B.13.)

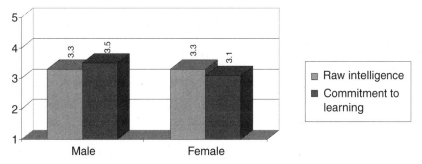

Figure B.11   Discrepancy Scores by Gender

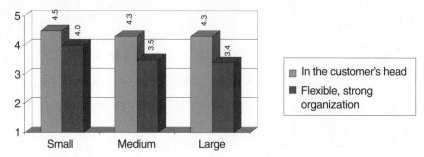

Figure B.12   Discrepancy Scores by Organizational Size

Relationship between Domains

The 16 domain scores significantly discriminate between large organizations and those that are medium/small. The discriminant function is dominated by three organizational domains and two individual: unimportance of raw intelligence, energetic, process-oriented, encourages individual contribution, and flexible organizational structure. Organizations with high scores on this function tend to be small to medium in size. Thus, the smaller organizations are characterized by high-energy individuals who do not believe raw intelligence is essential; they encourage individual contributions, focus on process rather than result, and provide a flexible structure. Conversely, large organizations are characterized by low-energy individuals who believe in raw intelligence, discourage individual contributions, are results-focused, and have a rigid structure. The interaction of the domains is demonstrated in Figure B.14.

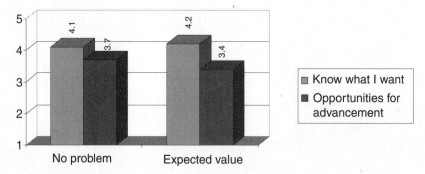

Figure B.13   Discrepancy Scores by Alliance Success

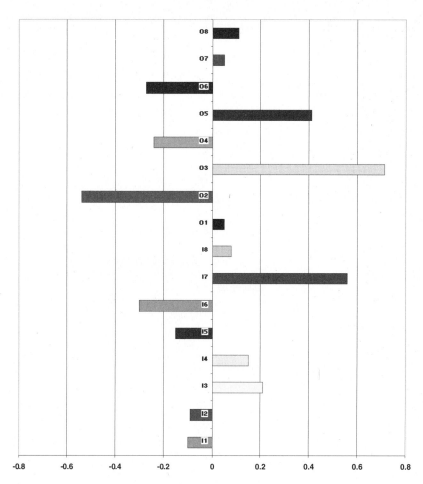

Figure B.14 Standardized Discriminant Functions

The domain numbers 08–18 represent the 16 domains (8 for individual characteristics and 8 for organizational characteristics) shown in Table B.1. For research purposes, the domains have been consolidated from the 10 domains (i.e., 20 for both individual and organizational characteristics) comprising the Larraine Segil Matrix of Ten Essential Traits.

Classification of Organizational Size by Domain Scores

Domains also differentiate upper management from others in organizations. Upper managers score higher on a function characterized by fearlessness, lack of belief in raw intelligence, not building personal equity/penetration or being customer-focused/perception, commitment of resources to continuous learning, and process orientation.

Classification of Position by Domain Score

It is expected that increased performance on any or all of the domains would improve success. There is also much unexplained that is probably accounted for outside of The Ten Essential Traits (i.e., the ten traits alone may not result in success because of market factors, capitalization, etc.). (See Figure B.15.)

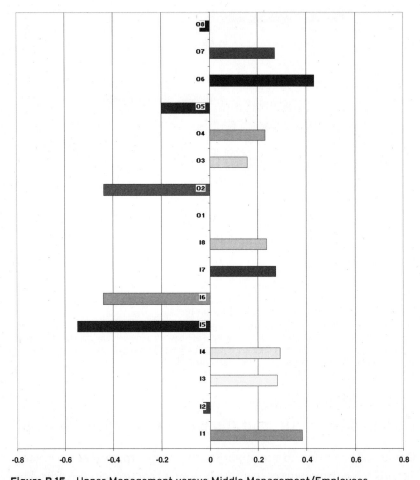

Figure B.15 Upper Management versus Middle Management/Employees

The domain numbers O8–18 represent the 16 domains (8 for individual characteristics and 8 for organizational characteristics) shown in Table B.1. For research purposes, the domains have been consolidated from the 10 domains (i.e., 20 for both individual and organizational characteristics) comprising the Larraine Segil Matrix of Ten Essential Traits.

Classification of Gender by Domain Score

The domains discriminate between males and females in organizations. Men score higher on a function that is dominated by inability to complete, assuredness, encouragement of individual contributions, commitment of resources to learning, and honesty. (See Figure B.16.)

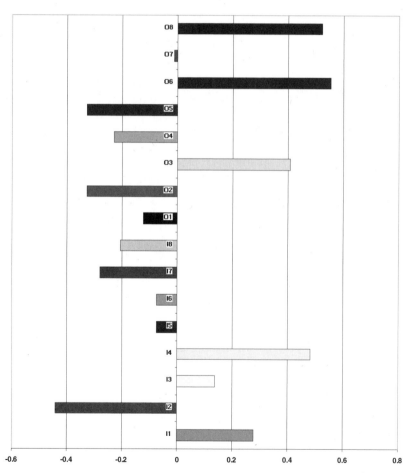

Figure B.16   Males versus Female

The domain numbers O8–I8 represent the 16 domains (8 for individual characteristics and 8 for organizational characteristics) shown in Table B.1. For research purposes, the domains have been consolidated from the 10 domains (i.e., 20 for both individual and organizational characteristics) comprising the Larraine Segil Matrix of Ten Essential Traits.

APPENDIX C

Seminars

Seminars offered by The Lared Group and Larraine Segil Productions Inc. and by Larraine Segil/The Lared Group for the California Institute of Technology (Caltech) are as follows:

Alliances. Domestic and global. Keynotes, one- and two-day programs.

FastAlliances. Using the Net and online alliances for customers, suppliers, and more.

Leadership in Turbulent Times. The Ten Essential Traits for managers. Keynote, one- and two-day programs.

Customized in-company programs are also offered, tailored to your organizational needs on these and related subjects.

Consultation, coaching, and advisory services on all the preceding topics are available in person, through videoconferencing, or online.

Visit: www.lsegil.com for more information, or phone (310) 556-1778; e-mail lsegil@lsegil.com.

APPENDIX D

Interview Questions

The following interview questions served as the basis for the in-person, telephone, and television interviews conducted by Larraine Segil with the principals in this book.

Ericsson

This document is copyrighted and is the intellectual property of Larraine Segil and Larraine Segil Productions Inc. It includes confidential information meant for the reader's eyes only and is intended as an introduction to the interview that Larraine Segil conducted in Richardson, Texas, with Ericsson executives. The concepts herein may not be communicated or used by the reader in any applications. They remain the intellectual property of Larraine Segil.

Introduction

The Larraine Segil Matrix encourages The Ten Essential Traits managers to set a vision, create an environment for achieving it by providing the necessary tools, and then get out of the way. The Ten Essential Traits managers are those with the ability to create this system and execute within it. The Ten Essential Traits are as follows: the ability of individuals and organizations to fearlessly complete tasks, to know what they want, to work with others in a variety of roles, and to combine intelligence, integrity, energy, optimism, and creativity to serve the present and anticipate the future. Creating an organization for the future means attracting, retaining, and rewarding employees who fit this model today. The following questions address how these qualities manifest at Ericsson.

Leadership

- What is your reaction to that definition?
- How does Ericsson enable The Ten Essential Traits kind of leadership?
- What kind of leadership qualities are important at Ericsson?
- What qualities in general are rewarded within your culture?
- What do you have to do at Ericsson to get promoted?
- What type of reward systems does Ericsson have?

Getting into the Customer's Head

- How does Ericsson define *customer?*
- Describe who your customer(s) is (are).
- How are customers analyzed (e.g., demographically, geographically, by product)?
- If you could see Ericsson from your customer's eyes, what would you see?
- Why do your customers buy from you?
- Describe the relationship between Ericsson and its customers. What role does the customer play in your business?
- How do internal customers fit into the external customer relationship?
- How do you balance internal and external customer needs and issues?
- How, exactly, does Ericsson get into the customer's head?
- What are the subconscious decisions of customers in your business?
- Let's talk about meeting customer needs. I'm going to describe three scenarios in which a company can satisfy customer needs. Please tell me how you do each, and give an example of a product/service:

1. Satisfying known needs and expectations
2. Satisfying needs the customer didn't expect from you
3. Satisfying needs the customer didn't know they wanted

- How does Ericsson obtain, analyze, and implement customer feedback?
- How do you differentiate yourselves from your competitors in terms of getting into the customer's head?
- Who does Ericsson benchmark against?
- Describe an example in the industry (doesn't have to be Ericsson) of how a company missed the mark with the customer.
- What is the relationship between services and products at Ericsson?
- How do you measure success for your products and services? (Is it sales only?)
- How do you understand your global customers?
- Do you tailor products and services to individual cultures?

Processes

- Does Ericsson operate in large-scale procedures or small-group activities?
- Do you work across divisions? Within divisions?
- What are Ericsson's processes for finding and commercializing innovation?
- What continuous improvement processes are in existence?

Culture

- Would you characterize Ericsson as a why-not culture or a why culture? Give an example.
- How are decisions made here at Ericsson?
- Does the corporate culture at Ericsson allow/encourage internal colleagues to get into each other's heads? Does this carry over to the external customer? (Example: Ritz Carlton's "ladies and gentlemen serving ladies and gentlemen.")
- Is there internal information sharing at Ericsson?

- How do people build internal networks here at Ericsson? How does Ericsson leverage those internal networks to create buy-in?
- What is Ericsson's commitment to continuous learning for its employees?

Target

This document is copyrighted and is the intellectual property of Larraine Segil and Larraine Segil Productions Inc. It includes confidential information meant for the reader's eyes only and is intended as an introduction to the interview that Larraine Segil conducted by phone with Target executives. The concepts herein may not be communicated or used by the reader in any applications. They remain the intellectual property of Larraine Segil.

Introduction

The Larraine Segil Matrix encourages The Ten Essential Traits managers to set a vision, create an environment for achieving it by providing the necessary tools, and then get out of the way. The Ten Essential Traits managers are those with the ability to create this system and execute within it. The Ten Essential Traits are as follows: the ability of individuals and organizations to fearlessly complete tasks, to know what they want, to work with others in a variety of roles, and to combine intelligence, integrity, energy, optimism, and creativity to serve the present and anticipate the future. Creating an organization for the future means attracting, retaining, and rewarding employees who fit this model today. The following questions address how these qualities manifest at Target.

Leadership

- What is your reaction to that definition?
- How does Target enable The Ten Essential Traits kind of leadership?
- What kind of leadership qualities are important at Target?

- What qualities in general are rewarded within your culture?
- What do you have to do at Target to get promoted?
- What type of reward systems does Target have?

Getting into the Customer's Head

- How does Target define *customer*?
- Describe who your customer(s) is (are).
- How are customers analyzed (e.g., demographically, geographically, by product)?
- If you could see Target from your customer's eyes, what would you see?
- Why do your customers buy from you?
- Describe the relationship between Target and its customers. What role does the customer play in your business?
- How do you develop a relationship with your customer when Target is a self-help store (contrast to Nordstrom's service reputation)?
- How do internal customers fit into the external customer relationship?
- How do you balance internal and external customer needs and issues?
- How, exactly, does Target get into the customer's head?
- What are the subconscious decisions of customers in your business?
- Let's talk about meeting customer needs. I'm going to describe three scenarios in which a company can satisfy customer needs. Please tell me how you do each, and give an example of a product/service:

  1. Satisfying known needs and expectations
  2. Satisfying needs the customer didn't expect from you
  3. Satisfying needs the customer didn't know they wanted

- How does Target obtain, analyze, and implement customer feedback?

- How do you differentiate yourselves from your competitors in terms of getting into the customer's head?

- Who does Target benchmark against?

- Describe an example in the industry (doesn't have to be Target) of how a company missed the mark with the customer.

- What is the relationship between services and products at Target?

- How do store placement, demographics, and product selection interrelate?

- How do you measure success for your products and services? (Is it sales only?)

- Describe your merchant policy and how it relates to your customer strategy.

Processes

- Does Target operate in large-scale procedures or small-group activities?

- Do you work across divisions? Within divisions?

- What are Target's processes for finding and commercializing innovation?

- What continuous improvement processes are in existence?

Culture

- Would you characterize Target as a why-not culture or a why culture? Give an example.

- How are decisions made here at Target?

- Does the corporate culture at Target allow/encourage internal colleagues to get into each other's heads? Does this carry over to the external customer? (Example: Ritz Carlton's "ladies and gentlemen serving ladies and gentlemen.")

- Is there internal information sharing at Target?

- How do people build internal networks here at Target? How does Target leverage those internal networks to create buy-in?
- What is Target's commitment to continuous learning for its employees?

The Permanente Company

This document is copyrighted and is the intellectual property of Larraine Segil and Larraine Segil Productions Inc. It includes confidential information meant for the reader's eyes only and is intended as an introduction to the interview that Larraine Segil conducted by phone with Cal James, a Permanente executive. The concepts herein may not be communicated or used by the reader in any applications. They remain the intellectual property of Larraine Segil.

Introduction

The Larraine Segil Matrix encourages The Ten Essential Traits managers to set a vision, create an environment for achieving it by providing the necessary tools, and then get out of the way. The Ten Essential Traits managers are those with the ability to create this system and execute within it. The Ten Essential Traits are as follows: the ability of individuals and organizations to fearlessly complete tasks, to know what they want, to work with others in a variety of roles, and to combine intelligence, integrity, energy, optimism, and creativity to serve the present and anticipate the future. Creating an organization for the future means attracting, retaining, and rewarding employees who fit this model today. The following questions address how these qualities manifest at Permanente.

Leadership

- What is your reaction to that definition?
- How does Permanente enable The Ten Essential Traits kind of leadership?
- What kind of leadership qualities are important at Permanente?
- What qualities in general are rewarded within your culture?

- What do you have to do at Permanente to get promoted?
- What type of reward systems does Permanente have?

Getting into the Customer's Head

- How does Permanente define *customer?*
- Describe who your customer(s) is (are).
- How are customers analyzed (e.g., demographically, geographically, by product)?
- If you could see Permanente from your customer's eyes, what would you see?
- Why do your customers buy from you?
- Describe the relationship between Permanente and its customers. What role does the customer play in your business?
- How do internal customers fit into the external customer relationship?
- How do you balance internal and external customer needs and issues?
- How, exactly, does Permanente get into the customer's head?
- What are the subconscious decisions of customers in your business?
- Let's talk about meeting customer needs. I'm going to describe three scenarios in which a company can satisfy customer needs. Please tell me how you do each, and give an example of a product/service:
  1. Satisfying known needs and expectations
  2. Satisfying needs the customer didn't expect from you
  3. Satisfying needs the customer didn't know they wanted
- How does Permanente obtain, analyze, and implement customer feedback?
- How do you differentiate yourselves from your competitors in terms of getting into the customer's head?
- Who does Permanente benchmark against?

- Describe an example in the industry (doesn't have to be Permanente) of how a company missed the mark with the customer.

- What is the relationship between services and products at Permanente?

- How do you measure success for your products and services? (Is it sales only?)

- How do you understand your multicultural customers?

- Do you tailor products and services to individual cultures?

Processes

- Does Permanente (and Federation) operate in large-scale procedures or small-group activities?

- Do you work across divisions? Within divisions?

- What are Permanente's processes for finding and commercializing innovation?

- What continuous improvement processes are in existence?

Culture

- Would you characterize Permanente as a why-not culture or a why culture? Give an example.

- How are decisions made here at Permanente?

- Does the corporate culture at Permanente allow/encourage internal colleagues to get into each other's heads? Does this carry over to the external customer? (Example: Ritz Carlton's "ladies and gentlemen serving ladies and gentlemen.")

- Is there internal information sharing at Permanente?

- How do people build internal networks here at Permanente? How does Permanente leverage those internal networks to create buy-in?

- What is Permanente's commitment to continuous learning for its employees?

APPENDIX E

The Ten Essential Traits Indicator

If you would like to receive information on the application and outcomes of The Larraine Segil Matrix, which is used by a variety of companies, we ask that you participate in an online survey for that purpose. Please go to www.lsegil.com and follow the instructions for accessing the survey page. Your name and your company name will be kept confidential. Data will be entered into a database, and when sufficient information has been gathered for analysis, you will receive a copy of the report at no charge (our thanks for your participation).

There are no right or wrong answers to these questions. Your answers are only indications of your way of doing things, your preferences, style strengths, and challenges.

Read each question carefully and mark your answer in the online space provided. Do not spend too long on any one question. There are no trick questions. If you cannot decide on an answer, skip the question, but be sure to leave that number blank so that your answers are all in sync with the appropriate questions. Then simply submit your online answers to the author. Should you have questions, please e-mail lsegil@lsegil.com. If you encounter access or site problems, phone Larraine Segil at (310) 556-1778.

You may also download the questionnaire from the web site www.lsegil.com, answer the questions, and fax your completed survey to 310-556-8085.

Thank you in advance for participating in our ongoing research.

NOTES

Chapter 1. The Elephant in the Room

1. According to the 1999 California Work and Health Survey by Professor Ed Yelin, University of California, San Francisco, *Los Angeles Times*, September 6, 1999, 40 percent of Californians have been at their jobs less than three years, and two-thirds of the workforce do not work outside the home, full-time, year-round as daytime employees. The mode is part-time, multiple jobs, home-based jobs, churning and changing jobs.

2. Now part of my video series on leadership available from www.lsegil.com.

3. See Larraine Segil, *Intelligent Business Alliances*, Times Books Random House, New York, 1996; Larraine Segil, *FastAlliances: Power Your E-Business*, Wiley, New York, 2001; and *Larraine Segil, One on One* biweekly e-mail newsletter (www.lsegil.com).

4. Report #1190-98-RR, "Bridging the Leadership Gap," Executive Summary, p. 5.

5. Alvin Toffler, *The Third Wave*, William Morrow, New York, 1980.

6. Larraine Segil, *Intelligent Business Alliances*, Times Business, New York, 1996.

7. Thomas L. Friedman, *The Lexus and the Olive Tree*, FSG, New York, 1999, p. 48.

8. "Shell" in this case connotes a company created to conceal illegal activities or one that has no ongoing operations.

9. Ikujior Nonaka and Hiroshi Yamagata, *The Knowledge Creating Company in Japan*, The Institute of Business Research at Hitotsubashi University, 1998.

10. "Commercializing Technology Resources for Competitive Advantage," IC2 Institute, The University of Texas at Austin, 1986, p. 4.

11. From the Academy of Management Symposium on *Knowledge Capitalism: Competitiveness Reevaluated*, August 1997.

12. Peter Drucker, "Management's New Paradigms," *Forbes*, October 5, 1998, p. 166.

13. Ibid.

14. From the Malcolm Baldrige National Quality Award 1998 scoring worksheet, description of criteria for participants in the leadership category.

Chapter 2. Fearlessness

1. Ann Marsh, "The Man Who Listens to Horses," *Forbes*, May 4, 1998, pp. 123 ff.

Chapter 3. Completion

1. Larraine Segil, *FastAlliances*, Wiley, New York, 2001.
2. Nevens, Summe, and Uttal, "Commercializing Technology: What the Best Companies Do," *Harvard Business Review*, 1990.
3. See research results in Appendix B.
4. *The Process Edge*, Peter G. W. Keen, Harvard Business School Press, 1997, pp. 2, 3, 5, 16
5. Nevens, Summe, Uttal, "Commercializing Technology: What the Best Companies Do," *Harvard Business Review*, 1990.
6. Bob Nelson's *1001 Ways to Reward Employees* is an excellent resource for creative rewards.

Chapter 4. Commitment

1. Elmer Nordstrom, *A Winning Team: The Story of Everett, Elmer and Lloyd Nordstrom*, published by Elmer Nordstrom, 1985, p. 59. An earlier book, *The Immigrant in 1887* (Dogwood Press, 1950, reprinted in 1992), was written by John W. Nordstrom to chronicle the Nordstrom immigration to the United States from Sweden. Elmer Nordstrom's book traces the development of the business.
2. Ibid., p. 33.
3. Kevin and Jackie Freiberg, *Nuts! Southwest Airlines' Crazy Recipe for Business and Personal Success*, Bard Press, 1996, p. 102.
4. Ikujior Nonaka and Hiroshi Yamagata, *The Knowledge-Creating Company in Japan*, from The Institute of Business Research at Hitotsubashi University, 1998.
5. David Packard, *The HP Way*, HarperBusiness, 1996.
6. Rosabeth Kanter, John Kao, and Fred Wiersma (eds.), *Innovation: Breakthrough Thinking at 3M, DuPont, GE, Pfizer, and Rubbermaid*, HarperBusiness; New York, 1997, p. 70.
7. Peter Schwartz, *The Art of the Long View*, Doubleday, 1991, p. 223.
8. Leigh Gallagher, "Death to the Cubicle," *Forbes*, September 7, 1998, p. 54.
9. John Naisbitt, *The Global Paradox*, Morrow, 1994.
10. APQC Benchmarking Study on Sales and Marketing Alliances, Houston, Texas, President Carla O'Dell, phone (713)685-4661.
11. Keith Bradsher, "A New Route for General Motors," *The New York Times*, Sunday August 9, 1998.
12. Larraine Segil, *Intelligent Business Alliances*, Random House, Times Business, 1996.
13. David Packard, *The HP Way*, HarperBusiness, 1996.
14. Larraine Segil, "Daddy Where Are You? The Biblical Struggle of HP and Compaq," *Larraine Segil One on One*, e-mail commentary and newsletter (www.lsegil.com), January 2002.
15. T. S. Kuhn, *The Structure of Scientific Revolutions*, Chicago University Press, 1993.

16. R. Katz and T. J. Allen, "Investigating the Not Invented Here (NIH) Syndrome: A look at the Performance, Tenure and Communication Patterns of 50 R & D Project Groups," *R&D Management,* vol. 12, no. 1, 1982.

17. Jeremy Kahn, "The 100 Best Companies to Work For in America," *Fortune,* January 12, 1998.

18. For further details, see "Managing Across Cultures," an executive briefing course offered by Larraine Segil (www.lsegil.com), phone (310)556-1778.

Chapter 5.   Inspiration

1. Ian Wylie, "Harry Potter's Corporate Parent," *Fast Company Magazine,* September 2001, pp. 54–58.

2. Aaron Bernstein, "America's Future," *Business Week,* August 2001, pp. 118–123.

3. Larraine Segil PRM system. For more information, contact lsegil@lsegil .com.

4. John P. Kotter, *Matsushita Leadership,* Free Press, 1997, pp. 239–241.

Chapter 6.   Assuredness

1. *Business Week,* June 8, 1998, p. 104

2. Adapted from a story told by Daniel Burrus, author of *Technotrends.*

3. Peter Schwartz, *The Art of the Long View,* Doubleday, 1991, pp. 27ff.

4. William H. Calvin, *The Cerebral Symphony,* Bantam Books, New York, 1989, p. 29.

5. Ikujior Nonaka and Hiroshi Yamagata, *The Knowledge Creating Company in Japan,* 1998, from The Institute of Business Research at Hitotsubashi University.

6. David Packard, *The HP Way,* Harper Business, 1995, p. 138.

7. David Packard, *The HP Way,* Harper Business, 1995, pp. 80–82.

Chapter 7.   Penetration

1. "The Jack and Herb Show," *Fortune,* January 11, 1999, p. 164.

2. My first book, a novel called *Belonging,* traced the friendship of two women from different worlds who grew up in South Africa, the country of my birth (available from www.lsegil.com). Larraine Segil, *Belonging,* Penguin, 1994. Republished 2001, I-Universe Publishing available online.

3. Larraine Segil, *FastAlliances: Power Your E-Business,* Wiley, 2001.

4. Hans Selye, *The Stress of Life,* McGraw-Hill, New York, 1975.

5. Fred Wiersma, John Kao, and Tom Peters, *Innovation: Breakthrough Thinking at 3M, DuPont, GE, Pfizer, and Rubbermaid,* Rosabeth Moss Kanter (ed.), Harper Business, New York, 1997.

6. Ibid.

7. Kevin Freiberg and Jackie Freiberg, *Nuts: Southwest Airlines' Crazy Recipe for Business and Personal Success,* Bard Press, NY, 1996, p. 71.

8. Ibid., p. 83.

9. In 1993, John Guare wrote a play called *Six Degrees of Separation,* which went on to become a movie by the same name.

10. Nellie Andreeva, "Do the Math—It Is a Small World," *Business Week,* August 17, 1998, Nellie Andreeva, pp. 54 ff.

Chapter 8.   Intelligence

1. I am proud to sit on the worldwide board of directors of D.A.R.E. and so have a somewhat biased opinion of the worth of the organization. However, my comments on the leadership structure are observational, and I have made an effort to present the organization with a fair evaluation of both positive and negative elements.
2. To contact Chief Glenn Levant at D.A.R.E., go to www.dare.com.
3. Mark Williams, "LEAD—Prophet Sharing," *Red Herring*, January 30, 2001, pp. 100–108.
4. Peter M. Senge, *The Fifth Discipline: The Art and Practice of the Learning Organization*, Doubleday, Currency, NY, 1990.
5. Ninth House creates markets and distributes my online Partnering for Profit Program. Visit www.ninthhouse.com for further information on my programs and the programs of Tom Peters, Ken Blanchard, Peter Senge, and others.

Chapter 9.   Energy

1. Robyn Meredith, "The Anti-Iacocca," *Forbes*, August 20, 2001, pp. 50–54.
2. A client of The Lared Group.
3. Excerpted from *Esther Dyson's Monthly Report*, Release 1.0, March 26, 2001, www.edventure.com, p. 41.
4. Moon Ihlwan, "A Long Trip to School," *Business Week*, August 27, 2001, pp. 62–63.
5. Peter Coy, "The New Economy—How Real Is It?" *Business Week*, August 27, 2001, p. 80.

Chapter 10.   Integrity

1. Excerpted from Charles Fishman, "A Dose of Change," *Fast Company*, August 2001, pp. 50–51.
2. Joan Urdang, "The Workplace—Perk Up," *CFO*, July 2001, p. 17.
3. Gerry Khermouch and Jeff Green, "Buzz Marketing," *Business Week*, July 30, 2001, pp. 52–56.
4. Katrina Brooker, "The Chairman of the Board Looks Back," *Fortune*, May 28, 2001, pp. 63–76.
5. *Business Week*, August 6, 2001, p. 50.
6. Interview by Brent Schendler, "Peter Drucker Takes the Long View, *Fortune*, September 28, 1998, p. 168.
7. David Dorsey, "Andy Pearson Finds Love," *Fast Company*, August 2001, pp. 78–80.

Chapter 11.   Perception

1. Principal of International Technologies Ventures, founding investor and former chairman of Mirabilis Ltd. There are so many accomplishments in Yossi Vardi's career that I recommend you do a search on Google.com to find articles that have been written about him.
2. Gordon Moore was the founder of Intel and a visionary in chip technology as well as a pioneer in Silicon Valley. His perspectives have driven the semiconductor industry for decades.

3. Michael L. Tushman and William M. Moore, *Readings in the Management of Innovation,* Marshfield, Mass. Pitman, 1982.

4. White paper article by Stephen J. Kline and Nathan Rosenberg.

5. See www.lsegil.com for copies of the videos relating to those interviews.

6. *Intelligent Business Alliances* (Times Books, Random House 1996); *Fast-Alliances: Power Your E-Business* (Wiley, 2001); and my web site www.lsegil.com, which has a number of articles, videos, newsletters, biweekly and online programs, and live seminars to immerse you in the wondrous world of alliances.

Chapter 12. Summary

1. See Larraine Segil, *Intelligent Business Alliances,* Times Books, Random House, 1996; Larraine Segil, *FastAlliances: Power Your E-Business,* Wiley, 2001.

ACKNOWLEDGMENTS

The main thanks for this book goes to Shana Tehrani—a remarkable human being of great talent and insight. She researched, edited, brainstormed, and contributed not only intelligence and hard work, but also true friendship. We hiked, we walked, we spoke by phone, by e-mail, and by fax. It took five years—and never-ending commitment. Shana, thank you again and again.

And to Nancy Ellis—one of a kind—her whiz-bang energy and editorial brilliance made this book a reality. Without you, Nancy, none of this would have happened.

To Gwen Uman Ph.D., CEO of Vital Research in Los Angeles, a superb resource for statistical research, survey design, and data analysis—thank you for your continued competency.

And then to Airié Dekidjiev and the team at John Wiley & Sons— you are the best—great ideas, good advice, and total support throughout! Thank you all.

Of course, to James, my son, whose enthusiasm and style embody the ultimate Ten Essential Traits manager. You are my most honest critic. Thanks for being the best son any mom could wish for.

Finally, to my executive assistant Raquel Galindo, for keeping the world at bay and for helping me find the time to finish this book—and move to the next one! Thank you for your professionalism and listening to me spout new ideas for your feedback!

INDEX